The Ci
of Preston Sturges

The Cinema
of Preston Sturges
A Critical Study

ALESSANDRO PIROLINI

McFarland & Company, Inc., Publishers
Jefferson, North Carolina, and London

LIBRARY OF CONGRESS CATALOGUING-IN-PUBLICATION DATA

Pirolini, Alessandro.
   The cinema of Preston Sturges : a critical study /
Alessandro Pirolini.
      p.   cm.
   Includes bibliographical references and index.
   Includes filmography

   ISBN 978-0-7864-4358-1
   softcover : 50# alkaline paper ∞

   1. Sturges, Preston — Criticism and interpretation.
I. Title.
PN1998.3.S78P57   2010
791.4302'33092 — dc22   2010016093

British Library cataloguing data are available

Cover image: Screenwriter and director Preston Sturges,
circa 1942 (Photofest)

Manufactured in the United States of America

McFarland & Company, Inc., Publishers
   Box 611, Jefferson, North Carolina 28640
   www.mcfarlandpub.com

To Mrs. Sandy Sturges

Acknowledgments

I would like to thank Tom Sturges for giving me permission to publish my interview with Sandy Sturges and the rare notes and documents written by Preston Sturges. I also thank Todd Wiener, motion picture archivist at UCLA Film & Television Archive, for helping me locate and view rare prints, and the Special Collection Department of the UCLA Library, where the Preston Sturges papers donated by Sandy Sturges are currently stored.

I am especially grateful to John D'Amico, Prof. Thomas Harrison (UCLA), Brian Leitch, Dr. Alessandro Pamini (Metacultura Institute), Daren Salter, and Dr. Melvyn Stokes (University of London) for their constructive criticism and insightful revisions of my work. This book would not be possible without their precious suggestions and contributions.

Table of Contents

Introduction

More than fifteen full-length studies, among them critical books, biographies and doctoral dissertations, have so far been written about Preston Sturges, not to mention the many articles and essays published in film magazines all over the world. Works such as *Between Flops* by James Curtis,[1] *Madcap* by Donald Spoto,[2] and *Christmas in July* by Diane Jacobs[3] have analyzed with scrupulous attention the most minuscule events in Sturges's life, while critical studies such as Andrew Dickos's *Preston Sturges and the Movies*,[4] James Ursini's *Preston Sturges*,[5] and — above all — Jay Rozgonyi's *Preston Sturges's Vision of America*[6] have offered in-depth analyses of Sturges's movies and screenplays.

Different generations of scholars have investigated Sturges's fascinating past, emphasizing his adventurous career as a self-made-man, and capturing his private life as a personality. "The fact that he was a colorful dresser with an interesting office and a popular restaurant," observes James Curtis, "merely served to strengthen the association between Preston Sturges and the films of Preston Sturges, much as the late Alfred Hitchcock capitalized on the exposure he gained from his weekly television series."[7] A 1940s article in *Vogue* observed: "Lubitsch and Hitchcock, each with the stamp of a great personality on his work, are names not half as familiar to the general public [as Preston Sturges]."[8]

Sturges was an author according to the system, and too much a journeyman for the *auteurists*[9] (the *Cahiers du cinéma* editors never dedicated to him the same attention they reserved for Fritz Lang, John Ford or Howard Hawks, and Andrew Sarris' *Cahiers*-inspired taxonomy of American directors placed him in the "Third Line"[10]); Sturges was soon forgotten. His Hollywood career was as spectacular as it was brief. His popularity as a writer-director-producer lasted not more than six years (between 1940 and 1946), and it was followed by a rapid decline that forced him to go back to France in order to avoid tax problems. His critical fortune did not meet a better fate: not sufficiently provocative to "engender the enthusiasm and controversy that Welles's films did,"[11] but also not stereotypical enough to be assimilated to that "fairly coherent aesthetic tradition"[12] that allowed film semiologists to do with Hollywood what Propp had done with Russian fairy tales, Sturges became neither a case study of Classical Hollywood *auteur*, nor the occasion for more recent postmodern rediscoveries, and he was mainly confined to the territory of the Hollywood personality, whose life (more than his movies) deserves to be told.

Some of the above-mentioned studies, however, often mention a generic "modern" aspect that lies beneath Sturges's cinema. Already in 1948, for example, while observing that "American comedy weakened and died like an uprooted tree," as the war had "disturbed the naïveté and unclouded optimism of [the American] myths," André Bazin was defining Preston Sturges as a genius who had "made the most of this aging process"; a modernizer who had based "his humor and the comic principle of his gags on the sociological displacement of the classical comedy."[13]

Likewise, other scholars have acknowledged, but seldom investigated, the characteristics of such modernity, and instead of focusing on the narrative and stylistic differences between Sturges's work and the Classical Hollywood Cinema (as defined by David Bordwell, Janet Staiger, and Kristin Thompson), or on its similarities with modernist cinema, they simplified the issue by ascribing Sturges's pioneering style to the sensibility of a "slapstick artist, cynic, wit, satirist, sentimentalist."[14] As a consequence, Sturges's films have been left lingering in the limbo of "timeless classics," in a no man's land as vague and imprecise as the so-called "Lubitsch Touch."

Without a doubt, movies such as *Christmas in July* (1940) and *The Lady Eve* (1941) contributed to shaping modes and forms of the classical screwball comedy, and Sturges's vast amount of work for the big studios in the 1930s, as a screenwriter, allowed him to master the consolidated rules that the Hollywood system was applying to all its products. From swashbuckling to period movies, melodrama to comedy, biopics to farce, Sturges's screenplays touched almost every popular genre of the era, and they have often been considered as typical representatives.

However, many of these movies and screenplays reveal a restless and impatient attempt to escape codified rules and narrative schemata, and to push the mechanisms and conventions of their genre to the extent of unveiling them to the spectator. To take just a few examples, the disruption of standardized timelines in films such as *The Power and the Glory* (1933) and *The Great McGinty* (1940) reveals an effort to move away from classical patterns, as well as an unconscious anticipation of postmodern non-chronological narratives. The way an apparently classical comedy such as *Unfaithfully Yours* (1948) shifts into the realm of multiple and hypothetical narratives suggests comparisons with Akira Kurosawa's *Rashômon* (1950) and with such anti-classical literary experiments as Raymond Queneau's *Exercices de style* (1947) or Alain Robbe-Grillet's deconstruction of conventional narrative models in *La jalousie* (1957) or *DJINN* (1981).[15]

Part of the reason why Sturges has never gained any recognition for these postmodern characteristics can be traced to the theoretical difficulty in defining the boundaries between classicism, modernism, and postmodernism in cinema. Of the three terms, in fact, only classical cinema can be identified as "a distinct mode [...] with its own cinematic style and industrial conditions of existence."[16] Such characteristics translate into: a standardized system of production based on a broad market segmentation[17]; a series of aesthetic norms aimed at creating Aristotelian realism; and psychologically motivated narratives in which the characters are the reason for the chain of events, and the storytelling process has to remain concealed.[18]

The concept of modernist cinema, instead, appears more difficult to grasp, as it seems to comprise all kinds of aesthetic, cultural and production alternatives to the Hollywood paradigm — from the loose, open-ended Neorealist narratives to the provocative violations of editing rules operated by the *nouvelle vague*, from the non-psychologically motivated narratives of Yasujiro Ozu to the hyper-realistic tales of John Cassavetes.

Things get even more complicated when we move to postmodernism, as its application to cinema is usually exemplified by a rather amorphous corpus of films, including all sorts of periods, genres, cultural sensibilities and production systems. In his essay on "Postmodernism and Consumer Society," for example, Fredric Jameson generically identifies "everything that comes out of Godard" as postmodern cinema, but then he extends the concept of postmodern cinema to what "is generally known as 'nostalgia film,'" enlisting movies such as *American Graffiti* (1973), *Chinatown* (1974), *Il conformista* (*The Conformist,* 1970), and *Star Wars* (1977) as examples of this type.[19] Even the most consolidated theories that define postmodernism in traditional arts as a reaction to — or, better, a "rejection" of— modernism, find it difficult to establish when the latter gave way to its postmodern successor, and sometimes they even venture to propose postmodernism as part of a larger modern framework. Besides, in the post-modern debate, cinema has always emerged as a postmodern form of art *tout court*. "Film was always, from its beginnings, postmodernist," writes Maureen Turim, "in the sense that it conjoined citation of the traditional with a newness of form and inscription."[20]

The controversy attached to the term "postmodern cinema" and its lack of a commonly accepted definition are reinforced by the aesthetic paradox connected to the history of the Seventh Art: born and developed right on the threshold of the modern, mechanical age, cinema immediately became (together with the car and the airplane) a symbol of modernism, while early film-makers and producers were looking to provide the medium with a cultural dignity, by borrowing stories and narrative styles from classical literary and theatrical texts,[21] and by adopting consolidated representational and lighting techniques drawn from painting and theater.

Even later, with the expansion of film theaters, and the birth of an audience that crossed over opposite categories (elite and mass, high "art" and "vulgar" entertainment), cinema kept looking for an "artistic" elevation by returning to the practice of literary adaptations or to the composition of romantic symphonic scores, and by establishing a system of conventions (including the Aristotelian unity of place, time, and action, a visual composition based on classical rules of balance, proportion and frontality) adopted by other consolidated art forms, such as painting and theater. Such search for a classical dignity found its more easily recognizable paradigm in the Classical Hollywood Cinema.

Soon, however, as in a Hegelian dialectic, came the reaction: the "modernist" antithetical answer to the classic *thesis*: the groundbreaking work of Godard, Resnais, Cassavetes, and other directors who rejected Hollywood's cinematic laws of continuity editing, narrative coherency, cause-effect motivation, and psychological causality. The European anti–Hollywood reaction of the 1950s and 1960s, in consequence, could be regarded as a phase in film history that corresponds to the definition of modernism in art: something that "functioned against its society, in ways which are variously described as critical, negative, contestatory, subversive, oppositional and the like."[22]

The traits of "postmodern cinema" are more difficult to identify. The lack of an exact definition, in fact, leaves us with generic attributes such as "pastiche," "citation," "fragmentation," "textuality,"[23] which simply point at a practice of deconstruction of previous texts — some sort of cinema

about cinema, that applies to different directors from different periods —
from François Truffaut, Jean-Luc Godard and Alain Resnais to Robert
Zemeckis, Tim Burton and the Coen Brothers.

If for the modern directors of the 1960s such practice was a reaction
against the mechanisms of Classical cinema, for the Hollywood film-makers of the 1980s and 1990s, the act of quoting and deconstructing classical texts was essentially a deferential homage to a narrative, stylistic, and
production model which was regarded as an ideal.

Movies such as *What's Up Doc* (1972), *Young Frankenstein* (1974),
Blazing Saddles (1974), *Silent Movie* (1976), *Star Wars* (1977), *High Anxiety* (1978), *Stardust Memories* (1980), *Raiders of the Lost Ark* (1981), *Dead
Men Don't Wear Plaid* (1982), *The Purple Rose of Cairo* (1985), *The Color
Purple* (1985), *Always* (1989), *Who Framed Roger Rabbit* (1988), *Ed Wood*
(1994), *Mars Attacks!* (1996), and *Artificial Intelligence: A.I.* (2001), in fact,
do not expose — in a critical way — rules and mechanisms of the classical
Hollywood model, but they rely on the same entertaining values, in a nostalgic and indulgent glorification of the classical model itself.

In this sense, the key factor in the definition of postmodern cinema
seems to be the goal behind the practice: a self-reflexive attitude towards
the film medium and its history that recuperates, instead of rejecting, the
original model (the *thesis*), through the same deconstructive tools developed by the modernist reaction (the *antithesis*), in a Hegelian *synthesis* of
opposite aesthetics.

In this difficult system of categories, Sturges's work belongs only in
part to the realm of the classical *thesis*. Like Frank Capra, Ernst Lubitsch
or Howard Hawks, Preston Sturges is a classical comedy director who put
his talent at the disposal of the Hollywood system, contributing to the creation and reinforcement of its genres.

On the other hand, the self-reflexivity, and the deconstructive
approach his movies support, indicate similarities with movies and directors from the 1980s and 1990s often quoted in books and articles about
postmodern cinema. Sturges's work, for example, requires the same "active
participation," and the same knowledge of cinematic referents that is necessary to decipher, and fully enjoy, a Mel Brooks or a Coen Brothers movie.
With these and other postmodern directors, Sturges shares the same awareness that Kenneth Von Gunden attributes to postmodern film-makers,
who "are not only the creators-authors of their films; they comprise those
texts' ideal readers as well."[24]

This book investigates the relationships of Preston Sturges's work to classical and postmodern cinema by looking at the cinematic practice of text deconstruction, rather than through focusing on the recurrence of themes and motifs. Sturges's life and work, after all, refute the *auteurist* myth of the director-artist struggling to establish his vision against the blind, insensitive, money-driven studio. His understanding and appreciation of the "genius of the system"[25] (and of its necessity for his own survival) goes along with his lucid awareness of the classical mechanisms of storytelling. Such consciousness leaves no room for the romantic conception of the individualistic genius in quixotic conflict with the system, and makes of Sturges a pragmatic director who fully comprehends the mechanisms of text composition and of the system that generates them.

Analyzing Sturges's movies, screenplays and projects in the light of these considerations encourages the emergence of a new and unusual possibility: that of contemplating his work as a pragmatic work of textual deconstruction of the classical paradigm.

1

Career

The life and career of Preston Sturges have exerted a powerful fascination over several generations of writers, providing material for authoritative biographies as well as frivolous articles. Suggestive titles referring to the *intrepid*[1] personality behind Sturges's *fabulous life*[2] perfectly illustrate the allure of his personal history.

Many biographers and scholars have interpreted Sturges's unbeatable optimism and his adventurous life as a sign of pragmatism and strong will typical of the American dreamer, and they have tried to look for similar traits in the personalities of Preston's fictional characters. In the context of this book, however, it is more important to underline the differences between Sturges and other self-made American men who pursued the same career. Sturges's approach to screenwriting, for example, was vastly different from that of the many Leftist playwrights of the 1930s and 1940s, who felt the urge to fight for social changes and to denounce the danger of foreign dictatorships. Solidly convinced of the ethical and cultural relativism of his era, Sturges avoided all political movements as assiduously as he avoided all discourse on religion. As Sturges's wife Sandy recalls:

> [H]e was brought up in a way, for instance, with his mother embracing one religion, and then another, and then another ... and different husbands and lovers.... So he was quite accustomed to know nothing being steady. You know, people who have strong opinions on political situations usually don't have the history that he had, where he realized that it doesn't really mean that much, because you've seen how it changes.[3]

If postmodernism has often been said to embrace "multiple perspectives, typically refusing to privilege any one truth claim over another,"[4] Sturges certainly predated such behavior with an attitude towards all ide-

7

ologies and their systems of values that postmodern philosophers such as Gianni Vattimo would define, several years later, with the term "weak thought."[5]

In his mid-thirties, with things taking a turn for the worse — his mother dead, his second wife about to leave him, having failed as an inventor, a businessman, and a playwright — Sturges was offered a $1,000 contract with Universal Studios to go to California and write dialogue and adaptations for the big screen. In less than three years Preston became a sensation in Hollywood: His original screenplay for *The Power and the Glory* was treated by the studio and the critics as an innovative work of art, and Sturges became the first screenwriter to be acclaimed and marketed by the film industry as an author. The movie not only paved the way to Sturges's directorial career, but it also opened up the possibility of more Hollywood screenwriters directing their own screenplays.

Sturges later wrote:

> I worked out a rather deep-dish theory defining the theater as a form of architecture rather than a form of literature. From this, I deduced that the motion picture was theater in its modern form, being handy and cheap and necessary and used constantly by hundreds of millions of people worldwide, instead of being something one sees once on a wedding trip, like Niagara Falls or Grant's Tomb.
>
> I compared the theater to transportation, which evolved from sledges to the helicopter, but remained transportation. And I compared pooh-poohers of the movies to the myopics who used to holler, "Get a horse!" when an early automobile exploded by.
>
> I did not claim that moving out of the legitimate into an illegitimate house was the best thing that could have happened to the theater. I did not think that a good movie was the equivalent of a good stage play, any more that I thought an automobile ride was as exhilarating as a drive behind a spirited horse, nor a trip by steam as soul-satisfying as a voyage by sail. I merely claimed that the move had taken place.[6]

In less than fifteen years, Sturges wrote forty screenplays, directed twelve movies, worked on dozens of projects, founded an engineering company to produce his own inventions (from vertical rising planes to yachts and boat accessories), and married for the fourth time. His prolific output made an impression on Hollywood, but it cut both ways: "Preston is like a man from the Italian Renaissance," noted René Clair. "He wants to do everything at once. If he could slow down, he would be great; he has an enormous gift and he should be one of our leading creators. I wish he would be a little more selfish and worry about his reputation."[7]

Sturges was perfectly conversant, even comfortable, with studio practices. His understanding of genre requirements and text specificity was so much a matter of course that, when he reluctantly agreed in 1949 to shoot *The Beautiful Blonde from Bashful Bend*, clearly a star vehicle, he fought to have it filmed in Technicolor, not for aesthetic reasons: when producer Darryl Zanuck announced that Fox could not afford to shoot the movie in color, Sturges wrote back: "You can make a so-called Sturges picture in black-and-white and it might even have Miss Grable in it, but you can't make a Grable picture in black and white without losing your shirt, your drawer and your long winter underwear with the flap in the back ... Miss Grable is the child of color."[8]

When his contract with Paramount ran out at the end of 1943, Sturges returned home and began writing spec scripts. He also reverted to his own innate nature as inventor and, in some ways, dreamer. He conceived the idea of a restaurant that converted to dancing, stage, and film-showing through a complex mechanism of shifting platforms.[9] "The orchestra pit," recalls Sandy Sturges, "was under the stage, and the musicians would sit there, waiting for the end of the play. When the play was over, the orchestra pit would rise."[10]

Sturges's restaurant mixed the most modern ideas of functionalist architecture with an ancient conception of entertainment: "Theater in which you eat," he commented, "is the oldest form of theater."[11]

The restaurant opened in 1940, and was named the Players. It quickly became one of Hollywood's most fashionable places. "During a period of time, in the Forties" recalls Sandy Sturges,

> the Players had been the greatest place in the world to eat: You could see everybody there, get great food, all during the war ... and then of course it fell out of favor, as everything does in Hollywood (you know, then there's a new Greek restaurant you've got to go to...), so the idea of a theater was to build it to bring in customers. And the original idea was to open it with five one-act plays.[12]

Differently to its architecture, the Players' entertainment was to be kept, in Sturges's intentions, as classical as possible: "The *novelty* of all this is that it will not be an experimental theater or group, groping for some new form of expression or new talent, literary or dramatic."[13]

Part of the reasons behind such "novelty" can be explained by Sturges's cultural upbringing, and his reaction to it. As Sandy Sturges recounts:

> When he was a kid, his mother dragged him to every concert, every opera, and then she would put him to bed in the afternoon, to have a nap, so he

could be up late and see these shows. So, while the other kids were going out and play, he had to lie down and take naps, which already set him against it. And that stayed with him for the rest of his life. For example, during the time that I was with him in Paris, José Yturbi came over. He was a classical pianist who also made a few films as an actor (and therefore he was taken less seriously by his contemporaries). He went to Paris to do a concert, and he invited Preston and me to it. It was an evening of *études*, and Preston just couldn't ... I mean, he was very polite, he sat through tapping his fingers — you know when you want to get out of there. He had that look that says: "When is this going to be over?"[14]

In 1945, Sturges founded his own production company, in collaboration with famous tycoon and fellow inventor Howard Hughes, and named it California Pictures. It is not a coincidence that the first film it released was to be the story of "a beleaguered small-town inventor who after much bungling finally devises a useful machine. His 'electrical, high frequency bat sound' succeeds in terrifying mosquitoes. Unfortunately, however, the sound it gives off is the mating call of the bats, and it attracts all the bats in the Western Hemisphere."[15] A note at the end of the treatment was essentially a polemic concerning the ingratitude that the U.S. routinely shows its inventors.

Despite all his enthusiasm, by the end of the 1940s, Sturges's film career appeared to be in decline. Sturges himself— a few years earlier, the third best-paid man in America — was poor, and remembered only by devoted filmmakers. Sturges attributed his fall to Hughes's failure to release the movies he had made for California Pictures, but also the last two pictures he subsequently directed for Twentieth Century–Fox (*Unfaithfully Yours* and *The Beautiful Blonde from Bashful Bend*) were not very profitable or critically acclaimed.

Looking for a way to bolster his restaurant and his artistic career, Sturges began drafting a series of television projects, some of which to be shot at the Players, where he could make the most of elevators, overhead tracks and other back stage devices he had built for the restaurant. But when the Players "sank under the weight of the four mortgages," Sturges wrote, the Internal Revenue Service froze all his assets, and he had to sell not only the restaurant but all his other properties. "It looked as if fate," he later recalled, "were intent on eradicating every trace of my existence in Hollywood."[16]

Sturges continued working on spec scripts, trying to recycle old material for projects that never saw the light. "So many things would be on the verge of happening," recalls Sandy Sturges, even going so far where they would put money in escrow, sign contracts, and all that stuff, and then change their minds. Of course, he had the basis for several lawsuits with that kind of thing happening, but he was not going to waste his time messing around in court. And it wasn't that he didn't find work. People, in Europe, would come to him, and several times you'd be right there: "We got it, it's done." But it wasn't. It was very heartbreaking, actually.[17]

In 1953, independent producer Lester Cowan asked Sturges to adapt and direct George Bernard Shaw's *The Millionairess*, a project that took him to London with his fourth wife Sandy, whom he had married two years before. When the picture was taken off the production schedule, Sturges took the occasion to show Sandy the places where he had lived in Paris as a boy. Sturges's arrival in the French capital was welcomed with considerable publicity and was soon followed by an offer from Gaumont Studios to adapt and direct a movie called *Les Carnets du Major Thompson*. It was the last movie he ever completed.

In 1954, when a producer showed interest in an old story called *Matrix* that Preston had written in the United States, Sandy flew back to California to find it and mail it back. "By the time it got to Paris," recalls Mrs. Sturges, "the guy had no more interest in it than feathers on a fish."[18] The production fell behind, and Sturges flew to New York at the expense of a producer who wanted him to doctor *The Golden Fleecing*, a play already in rehearsal.

By the end of 1958, Sturges was living alone and in poor health, in a New York hotel, looking for projects that would get him enough money to pay for a new home and to fly Sandy and his sons to New York. It never happened. He died in 1959, probably of a heart attack, in his room, having just written a melancholic, yet optimistic, page for his autobiography:

> More than once over the years I had told Sandy that if worse came to worst, that if we lost everything and found ourselves without a roof over our heads sitting on the curbstone at Franklin and Vista, we would not be without resources. From a car passing to the east, I would borrow a pad of paper; from a car passing west, I would borrow a pencil. By evening I would have written a story and we would be back in business. I always believed this.[19]

2

Sturges's "Weak Thought"

Economics

Many recent theorists and intellectuals, including Jean-François Lyotard, Michel Foucault, Fredric Jameson, and Gianni Vattimo, have pointed out that postmodernism is characterized by skepticism in relation to all sorts of ideological beliefs, and by a generic relativism towards all values. As one source suggests:

> Postmodernism attacks the notions of monolithic universals and encourages fractured, multiple perspectives. Utopian ideals of universally applicable truths give way to provisional, decentered, local *petit recits* which, rather than referencing an underlying universal truth or aesthetic, point only to other ideas and cultural artefact, themselves subject to interpretation and re-interpretation.[1]

Sturges's work reflects in many different ways this attitude, by presenting reservations towards most of the moral, sociological and economic values effectively portrayed in Classical Hollywood Cinema, and by underlining the contradictions of that all–American way of life that many other directors were sanctifying.

His cynicism towards the myths and beliefs of Western culture gave birth to explicit parodies of the American West (*The Beautiful Blonde from Bashful Bend*), as well as of the British and French cultures (*Les Carnets du Major Thompson*), and his satirical approach emphasized the contradictions of the capitalist system (*Diamond Jim* [1935], *The Power and the Glory*, *Christmas in July*, *The Palm Beach Story* [1942]), wartime propaganda (*The Miracle of Morgan's Creek* and *Hail the Conquering Hero*), the institution of marriage (*The Miracle of Morgan's Creek*, *The Palm Beach*

Story— originally titled *Is Marriage Necessary?*), and even the tales of the Bible (*The Lady Eve* and *The Miracle of Morgan's Creek*).

Far from singing the praises of the American common man, Sturges's characters strive for survival in a world that forces them to embrace values such as the pursuit of money, success, career and self-esteem. When they are not mistaken for heroes (*The Miracle of Morgan's Creek, Hail the Conquering Hero*), they either end up miserably defeated (*The Power and the Glory, The Great McGinty*), or they are left with the bitter taste of a highly questionable "happy" ending (*Christmas in July, Sullivan's Travels* [1941], *The Palm Beach Story*). Sturges, however, does not propose solid alternatives, let alone "universal truths." He simply exposes the contradictions and the absurdity that lie beneath the cultural, social and economic values commonly accepted by most people.

The first part of *The Sin of Harold Diddlebock,* for example, consists of a long and depressing account of the failure of Mr. Harold Diddlebock, the water boy whom Harold Lloyd had interpreted twenty years earlier in *The Freshman* (1925). *The Sin* begins where *The Freshman* ends, during the final minutes of a football game in the course of which Harold miraculously scores a winning touchdown. Sturges recycles the original sequence where Harold wins and is brought to triumph by the crowd, and continues the narrative in order to show the consequences of this typical case of the American dream: Enchanted by Harold's extraordinary performance, successful businessman Mr. Waggleberry hires him as an entry-level employee. Fastforward twenty years, however, Harold is still sitting at the same desk, wearing the same clothes, reduced to a shabby, worn-out shell of a man who eventually gets fired only because he was unable to take the "great" opportunity that capitalism had given him, and has therefore become a bad example for the company.

As Jay Rozgonyi points out, "Harold is a bad example for the younger workers because he has been at the company long enough to realize that the carrot dangled in front of him for more than two decades will always be out of reach."[2]

Sturges represents Diddlebock's sinking career in a series of sequences that range from a long humiliating talk with his boss to a pathetic love scene where Harold gives his colleague Miss Otis an engagement ring, and asks her to use it when she will meet a man worthy of her love. Lonely and penniless, Harold finds asylum in a bar where, energized by a drink, he begins gambling, winning money, and embarks on the most peculiar enterprises, such as the purchase of a circus.

Sturges not only underlines the chance factor behind Harold's success, but he also presents his entrepreneurialism as an exceptional escape from the rigid mechanics of the capitalistic system. Harold succeeds not "because the system worked or because [he] played by the rules. Sheer luck, the foolishness of others, even dishonesty was more likely responsible."[3] In other terms, it seems as, for Sturges, "in love, just as in his career, a few days of wild abandon yield better results than a whole lifetime of working hard and paying one's dues."[4]

We can find the same unenthusiastic attitude in another light-hearted comedy such as *Christmas in July*. Based on Sturges's unproduced play *A Cup of Coffee* (written in 1931), the screenplay is primarily focused on the miserable social-economic context of the Great Depression, where lower-class characters struggle with financial difficulties and unemployment, while they are constantly reminded by their superiors that every single working individual should believe they are a success. Once again, Sturges shows how values such as money, success, and self-esteem are mere pretexts that capitalism waves in front of the workers' eyes. If, in *The Sin of Harold Diddlebock,* Harold's boss makes clear that capitalism does not "start people at the top" as "That would be too easy. We do it the American way ... from the bottom,"[5] in *Christmas in July,* Jimmy's supervisor theorizes: "No system could be right where only half of one percent were successes and all the rest were failures. That wouldn't be right." As a consequence: "I'm not a failure — I'm a success."[6]

In a Frank Capra movie, the logic of this character would find its counterpart in the common sense of the poor, hard-working character, who is able to break through the layers of mystification created by the individuals who hold the power. Sturges, instead, shows how individuals belonging to opposite social classes end up sharing the same illusory beliefs. When Betty and Jimmy discuss their future, the girl tries to convince her fiancé that they could live happily together in a hyper-functional one-room apartment where the corner turns around and transforms into a bathroom, a kitchenette or a living room. The young man first opposes these foolish ideas with grounded skepticism, pointing out that the requirements for any successful marriage are work and money. His alternative solution, however, is not less improbable than the one devised by the girl: to invent a good advertising slogan and win the first prize in a coffee contest.

Here, as in the rest of the movie, the characters do not have the lucidity to question the system, or to produce alternatives — whether in a Socialist sense or in terms of a Capra-esque restoration of good old American values. They simply look for alternative ways to achieve the same goals imposed by the system through its spokesmen. Every character, in fact, seems to be motivated "by an overriding devotion to materialism"[7] — from Jimmy, who becomes absent-minded and unproductive at work as he gets obsessed with winning the contest, to his supervisor, whose philosophy of success relies on earning money and paying bills; from the poor neighborhood populated by disillusioned immigrants dreaming of improbable lottery wins, to the CEO and the businessmen of the Maxford company, constantly worried about losing or wasting money.

When Jimmy receives a phony telegram forged by his colleagues, notifying him that he has won the contest, the news quickly spreads and it gains him a promotion, a raise, and the admiration of colleagues and neighbors. The orgy of shopping, consumerism and gift-giving that follows will be as brief as Harold's triumphal day, and it will soon bring everyone back to their miserable reality, and to a quick re-evaluation of Jimmy's skills as an advertiser. As soon as the truth comes out, Jimmy, his boss, his girlfriend, his family, and the whole neighborhood will have to recognize not only the uncommonness of success and its illusory aspect, but also their own lack of good judgment in having conferred special talents on someone who did not actually possess any.

Sturges does not provide the characters (and the viewer) with any form of consolation. Instead, he leaves them to face their own naiveté and superficiality, and to reflect on the vacuity and relativity of those values that society creates and believes in. In this way, the misunderstanding does not become the pretext for a moral lecture on money and real values, but is used as an occasion for a complex reflection of the effects of capitalism on every member of society.

It is in this ambivalent representation of a world not based on any binary opposition of values and social classes, and in a general relativism that subscribes to no particular moral position, that we can trace an attitude extremely different from that of other movies of the same period. Postmodern philosopher Gianni Vattimo labeled this kind of cynicism, that does not provide alternative solutions, with the term "weak thought," a concept that invokes

> an end to all categorical pronouncements about the nature of the real and new respect for the finite foundations of human projects, where judgments of value are outcrops of care, and the differences among them are most sensibly to be negotiated by discursive, democratic interaction.[8]

It is interesting that those critics, such as James Agee or Manny Farber, who intuitively perceived this characteristic in Sturges's work, interpreted it as a contradiction, a dangerous ambiguity which made of Sturges a "humanist who resisted fleshing out his characters, an artist whose view of the world as well as his style was fragmented, who couldn't or wouldn't express a cohesive vision."[9]

Rather than lacking a cohesive vision, Sturges did not adopt the simplistic black-and-white approach to which Classical cinema had made its audience accustomed. That is why, in contrast to other classical fables of poverty rewarded by a benign fate, *Christmas in July* does not provide us with any sort of illusory relief. In the end, Jimmy is still granted the chance of a lifetime (Dr. Maxford, after all, decides not to pull back his promotion — only the raise), but he is deprived of that enthusiasm and confidence in the system and his own self that his boss wanted to instill in him. Jimmy not only learns that chance and opportunities seldom turn dreams into reality, but he also faces the contradictions of a system based on the power of self-deception. Betty's final plead to Mr. Baxter clearly reflects this disillusionment:

> [Jimmy] belongs in here because he thinks he has ideas. He belongs in here until he proves himself or fails, and then somebody else belongs in here until *he* proves himself or fails and then somebody else after him and then somebody else after him, and then so on and so on for always. I don't know how to put it in words like Jimmy could, but all he wants ... all any of them want ... is a chance to show ... to find out ... what they've got while they're still young ... and ... and ... burning ... like a short-cut ... or a ... or a ... stepping stone.
>
> (Now she changes her tone entirely)
>
> Oh, I know they're not going to succeed ... at least most of them aren't. They'll all be like Mr. MacKenzie soon enough ... most of them, anyway ... but they won't mind it ... they'll find something else, and they'll be happy because they had their chance ... because it's one thing to muff a chance when you get it ... but it's another thing never to have had a chance.[10]

Such a deterministic interpretation of the socio-economical American mechanisms clearly leaves little hope to any possibility for social changes.

This message, that Sturges coherently carried across many of his movies, is perfectly allegorized in the ending of *Sullivan's Travels*. The movie tells the story of John Sullivan, a Hollywood director who decides to draw inspiration for his sociologically relevant movies, by traveling among the poor people across the country, only to discover that he should instead alleviate the world's suffering by making light comedies. As Jay Rozgonyi points out, Sullivan's recognition of cinema's escapist function is a sad commentary on a society that "can offer only amusement to its downtrodden members." In this way, Sullivan's epiphany is the logical conclusion of Jimmy and Betty's realization: "In some cases it is best not to know what life can be like in America," and "while that realization may justify Hollywood's role in making lightweight comedies even in troubled times, it also implies that there is little hope for changing the living conditions of society's poor."[11]

Sturges's Politics

If Harold and Jimmy have almost nothing to share with the average all–American heroes portrayed by Hollywood, likewise governor Dan McGinty (*The Great McGinty*) is neither the Mr. Smith nor the Mr. Deeds whom Frank Capra sends to town to fight against the greed and the ongoing corruption of American values. He is just a hobo who starts his political career by voting thirty-seven times in the same election, and is then packaged, first as mayor and then as governor, by a group of corrupt politicians to whose dishonest practices he easily conforms.

Likewise, Norval Jones and Woodrow Truesmith, the characters interpreted by Eddie Bracken, respectively in *The Miracle of Morgan's Creek* and *Hail the Conquering Hero*, represent neither the heroes that a country at war was trying to forge, nor the von Stroheimian characters "you love to hate" that Hollywood had typified since its silent days.

Sturges, in other terms, deconstructs that opposition of dualisms and hierarchies that a postmodern philosopher such as Jacques Derrida saw as the core of the Western thought and its texts.[12] Sturges opens up the narration to a universe of doubt, ambivalence, and "weak thought" that has no place for easily identifiable conflicts — such as poor versus rich, or honest versus corrupt.

If, for instance, we take *The Great McGinty* (a movie produced in 1940, but already written in 1933, right in the midst of the Great Depression), and compare it to similar political melodramas of the early 1930s, the difference is astonishing. Movies such as *Politics* (1931), *The Phantom President* (1932), *The Dark Horse* (1932), *Washington Masquerade* (1932), *Gabriel Over the White House* (1933) and *The President Vanishes* (1934) are all based on the political rise of a candid, outspoken man, called to cleanse a corrupted political system, fight crime, reduce unemployment, and bring peace and prosperity to the country. The narrative structure is pretty much the same as that of any other classical comedy or drama, based on a conflict of binary oppositions between political laxness and integrity, public interest and private profit, and on the clearly antagonistic views on politics held by male and female characters.

The Great McGinty, instead, tells the story of a homeless man packaged as a politician, whose weak attempts to fight the corrupted political machine to which he had previously belonged lead to catastrophic results. McGinty is neither Jud Hammond (the corrupted politician who becomes an honest, strong and authoritarian U.S. president after experiencing a vision of the angel Gabriel, in *Gabriel Over the White House*), nor the idealist senator Jefferson Smith, who resists corruption and manages to triumph over (and even redeem) his manipulators in *Mr. Smith Goes to Washington* (1939).[13] Compared to these characters, McGinty is just "someone who prefers to survive as a bum rather than perish as an idealist,"[14] someone with no conscience nor remorse for what he is doing, until his wife Catherine mentions that he could use some of his influence to defend the interests of the poor people.

Contrasted with Jefferson Keane (the truthful senator who is framed by a group of lobbyists and by a scheming seductress in *Washington Masquerade*), McGinty does not turn into an honest and courageous individual who stands for high moral values. He rather ends up being caught somewhere between self-interest and a vague form of altruism, frustrated by the fact that his last-minute attempt to redeem himself triggers a chain of events that will cost him his career, and ultimately his freedom.

Catherine, as well, is not the one-dimensional vamp who in *Washington Masquerade* tricks Keane into following the interests of the lobbyists. If she initially agrees to become an accomplice of the astute political plot that will help McGinty to win the election, later she convinces him to use his power for a good cause. But, as Rozgonyi points out, her "glimpse of morality [...] is soon offset by her proposal that she and McGinty marry to further his political career [and] while there is an undercurrent of genuine affection on her part [...] there is also a clear sense of expediency."[15]

The lack of a happy ending (whether in the form of final redemption or a Capra-esque miracle) emphasizes further this unusual representation of characters and their ambiguous values. Punished for his previous mistakes, McGinty will end up in prison and, instead of accepting his defeat with dignity, he will decide to escape with the same gang of crooked politicians who made his brief fortune. As Rozgonyi writes:

> By the movie's end the protagonist has been stripped of his wealth and position and driven out of the country; a couple who truly loved each other are permanently separated; two children who came to love their stepfather will never see him again; and the corrupt politicians, if they ultimately have not profited from their crimes, at least have not been punished for them.[16]

In other words, the film fails to satisfy the requirements of both its genres, comedy and political melodrama (that is, reunion of a temporarily separated couple and victory of the honest individual over corrupted institutions), in favor of an apolitical and amoral perspective which is well underlined by the title card that Sturges had originally written for the opening:

> This story has no moral.
> This story has no end
> This story only goes to show
> There is no good in men.[17]

War

Sturges's disillusionment with all–American values became even clearer during the war — that is, right at a moment when the studios were requiring a stricter compliance to both government directives and the Hays Office.[18] In 1942 and 1943, Sturges wrote three Paramount movies about weak, non-heroic individuals whose only fault was their incapacity to meet the requirements endorsed by public opinion for making wartime champions. In *The Great Moment, The Miracle of Morgan's Creek,* and *Hail the Conquering Hero,* Sturges reversed the political perspective dictated by the new Office of War Information (to which the studios were supposed to submit scripts for approval), and replaced the patriotic cries of support for the troops with toned-down praise of non-heroic civilians.

Sturges's "war movies" tell stories of outcasts, whose unhappiness is the result of a conflict between themselves and the values commonly accepted by their community, now amplified by the war. In *The Great Moment,* for example, Dr. Morton is the misrecognized inventor of anesthesia who gives up his career to spare other people's sufferings, while being attacked and vilified by both the scientific community and the public opinion. *The Miracle of Morgan's Creek* is the tale of a truthful countryman who is rejected by the army and decides to marry a girl who is already married and even pregnant with the kids of an unknown soldier. *Hail the Conquering Hero* is the ironic drama of the proud son of a much-decorated Marine, who is discharged for chronic hay fever.

It is not a coincidence that all three stories were initially rejected not only by the studio executives (who used to inundate Sturges with long production notes and censorious memos for almost every movie), but also by the Office of War Information (OWI). In Sandy Sturges's words: "What Preston said he did was: 'Obey strictly the letter of the law ... and totally ignore the spirit.'"[19]

In both *The Miracle of Morgan's Creek* and *Hail the Conquering Hero*, the simple-hearted characters played by Eddie Bracken are discarded by the military and become impostors as a result of the pressure that town pride, heroism and other community values exert on them. In underlining the chronic condition of the American system, Sturges points out the absurdity and stupidity of public opinion, which is too blind and self-centered to recognize Dr. Morton's noble act of renouncing his patent to spare a little girl the pains of surgery (*The Great Moment*), and too narrow-minded to appreciate Norval's decision to marry his already-married, already-pregnant friend Trudy (*The Miracle of Morgan's Creek*), or to discern between real and fake heroes, good and phony politicians, as happens in *Hail the Conquering Hero*.

In both *Hail the Conquering Hero* and *The Miracle of Morgan's Creek*, the portrayal of the military is far from heroic. The soldiers are never shown in military action, but are depicted romping about the city day and night, blocking the traffic, begging waiters for a beer after losing all their money gambling, harassing girls, getting them pregnant, and "leaving the hard part of fathering to a draft reject."[20] And even if Sturges still finds the time to abide by the rules imposed by the OWI (for example, by reminding his audience that women should go easy on butter on their pancakes, and youngsters forget about sugar in their lemonade), his attitude towards the war is far from celebratory.

In these movies, military heroism seems to belong to the past, and it is something soldiers do not talk about. A civilian like Woodrow is the only one who, at the beginning of *Hail the Conquering Hero*, remembers and lists one by one the glorious battles of the Marines. Contrasted with Capra's heroic activism (a colonel of the U.S. Army, he had an important role in war propaganda with his documentary series *Why We Fight* [1942–1945]), Sturges had — as he later confessed:

absolutely no desire to get in. Either this war was not as well advertised as the last one, or there is a great difference between the thinking of an eighteen-year-old boy and a man in his early forties. Or maybe one doesn't fall for the same guff twice or something.... Maybe if people got to be old enough, there wouldn't be any wars. Maybe war is just youthful exuberance, a recurring form of exercise in the spring.[21]

In a scene from the original script of *The Miracle of Morgan's Creek* (later removed by the studio), the speech of the rector of the church reinforces this perspective:

The uniforms, the brass buttons, the bright colors, the helmets with plumes and horses' tails, the music ... all of these have so captured the imaginations ... electrified the emotions ... of all young women from the beginning until now, that more little children, little boys especially, are born in wartime than at any other time ... which is excellent in itself, but attended, as are so many excellent things, with dangers.... Let me be the first to remind you that all is not gold that glitters, that the young are impetuous, that wartime is a thoughtless time, and that in any large group of good men, there are of necessity some fools and scoundrels ... and against these I warn you. Beware of the spell cast by jingling spurs ... of the hasty act repented at leisure.[22]

Sturges, however, as Andrew Dickos notes, "hardly derides the possibility for true heroism; he only laughs at our creation of golden lambs which we delude ourselves into accepting as heroic gods."[23] In other words, his lack of interest in the glorification of the world and its heroes, does not translate into a call for anti-militarism, but it takes the form of a much more complex approach that, instead of diminishing the value of the concept of the war hero, questions its social exploitation.

At the same time, instead of victimizing his weak, non-heroic civilians, Sturges shows how they become accomplices in this collective behavior. Both Woodrow, in *Hail the Conquering Hero,* and Norval, in *The Miracle of Morgan's Creek,* salute patriotism and heroism, and their own existential drama is born out of the impossibility of carrying out such values as active performers. In this way, as Dickos points out: "Sturges reveals the dilemma of our culture: the phenomenal capacity we have for excitement or, at least, for becoming excited, and how the by-products of our excitations are confusion, misapprobation, heroic celebration, excessive patriotism, and mother love."[24]

War and Amnesia

Sturges's war movies not only share the same attention to civilians and their conflict with a hero-obsessed society, but also the same narrative motifs and themes. For example, both *Hail* and *Miracle* show a peculiar interest in the portrayal of cases of mistaken military identity.

In an untitled 1944 project for California Pictures, in which a Marine suffering from amnesia is welcomed in a small American town, Sturges explains:

> Little by little [the man] discovers his past life and the audience discovers it at the same time. He finds that he was the bad boy of the town, that he got a girl in trouble, that he committed a crime to raise money, that he was arrested, possibly sent to the penitentiary and that he escaped. He is no longer bad and he now wishes to expiate his crimes. As he is on his way back to the penitentiary, he is seized by the envoys of the San Diego Naval Hospital and we now discover the end of his story. After escaping he had enlisted in the Marines. He is a brave hero and the list of his decorations is very long. It is felt that his second adventure has wiped out his early record, and he is permitted to stay in the town with the girl and his son.[25]

Sturges's ideas, indeed, may well have influenced the later work of Frank Darabont, who explored the same themes and implications in *The Majestic* (2001), the story of a blacklisted Hollywood screenwriter who loses his memory and finds himself in a small town where he is mistaken for a decorated war hero. The opening of this film, set in a studio's headquarters where producers are modifying a dramatic screenplay to make it resemble a Lassie movie, echoes the beginning of *Sullivan's Travels*, with its fight between studio executives and Sullivan over the contents of his movie. But as soon as the screenwriter becomes involved in a car accident, loses his memory, and finds hospitality in a small rural town, it is Sturges's war movies that come to mind. As in *Hail the Conquering Hero* and in the 1944 project referred to above, the small American town badly needs a hero to foster its American ideals; and, as in *The Miracle of Morgan's Creek*, the townspeople are able to open their hearts to the man who has the courage to expose his non-heroic qualities.

The power of the uniform, together with the motif of mistaken identity, recurs obsessively in Sturges's work, as the draft of another unproduced project called *One Big Happy Family* shows. Here, Sturges proposes the story of a girl "who marries a young man in uniform ... or possibly a young man with money at some fashionable beach ... and later discovers that he is the scion of a great undertaking family."[26]

The usage of amnesia as a narrative expedient reoccurs also in a script draft dated 1950, with the title *Nothing Doing,* in which Sturges tells the story of an inventor-industrialist who suddenly loses his memory and is forced to re-evaluate his life. Once again, only the simple atmosphere of a country village and the love of a beautiful widow will get his memory back.

Interestingly, the first idea for *Les Carnets du Major Thompson* was a brand new story "about an author who creates a fictitious character ... who subsequently appears."[27] At the end, says James Curtis, "it came out that he was a war hero who had lost his memory fighting for France, and the French author admitted that he had taken his notebooks — which he hadn't of course — and gave this man who had no identity an authentic identity."[28]

War and Anesthesia

Sturges's cynicism about war and politics is visible even in a period movie such *The Great Moment*, finished in 1942, but re-edited by the studio and released in 1944. Despite the massive cuts, a subtle vein of anti-militarism is still left in the scene where Dr. Morton visits the president of the United States in order to have his award ratified. Morton says: "I certainly hate to have it look as if I were making the government pay to relieve wounded soldiers from..." and the president "snappishly" interrupts him: "Government pays for the guns, don't it?"[29]

This script (in all its different variations) shows a much more bitter and cynical attitude toward war and military institutions in general. The original opening, for example, contemplated a spoken foreword which sarcastically commented on Homo Sapiens as a "wise guy" who:

has stoned, crucified, burned [...] and rid himself of those who consecrated their lives to his further comfort and well being so that all his strength and cunning might be preserved for the erection of ever larger monuments, memorial shafts, triumphal arches, pyramids and obelisks to the eternal glory of generals on horseback, tyrants, usurpers, dictators, politicians and other heroes who led him, usually from the rear, to dismemberment and death.[30]

The monologue was supposed to accompany images of the cemetery where Dr. Morton was buried but, in his notes, Sturges says that he had planned to superimpose the voice onto "a vast plain, dotted with the wreckage of war — half a cannon, half a triumphal arch, half an equestrian statue (the rear half). There was no sign of life, the only movement coming from swirls of poison gas."[31]

Other minor scenes and dialogue eliminated from the final release contained sharp remarks on the contradictory behavior of the "wise guy" Sturges had mocked in the opening title card. For example, in a short sequence where Morton visits an Army colonel to sell him a massive quantity of ether inhalers to be used during operations on the battlefields, the colonel informs him that he has already bought the inhalers from a glassmaker, and he opens a drawer to show Morton the item. A detail of the drawer's content shows us a couple of weapons.[32] The screenplay continues:

> He puts down the inhaler and opens a drawer from which he takes an assortment of samples. The first thing he produces is an early revolver.
>
> THE COLONEL
> (Picking it up)
>
> Ever see one of these? A revolving pistol.
>
> (He demonstrates)
>
> You fire it, turn the barrel and there you are all ready to fire again. Neat, eh?
>
> He pulls out a few horrendous-looking saw-toothed bayonets. He picks up a bullet that opens out like a small umbrella.
>
> THE COLONEL
>
> Nasty little things these are. We don't believe in them. Of course if the other side should start using them ... here we are.

Masses and Individuals

Sturges's relativistic view of all values and judgments, together with his disillusionment towards the myth of the American hero, leads to a powerful deconstruction of the Classical Hollywood Cinema and its narrative paradigms, as is especially evident in his characters' dialogue.

Compared to Capra's all–American heroes, who speak with courage and inspiration about the great American values and aim at restoring the principles that the country has mislaid (*Mr. Deeds Goes to Town* [1936], *Mr. Smith Goes to Washington*, *Meet John Doe* [1941]), Sturges's characters never preach nor can they be regarded as the country's conscience. We noted that McGinty's timid attempts to bring his corrupted administration back on track is just the consequence of his wife's suggestions, and that both Woodrow Truesmith and Norval Jones are neither military nor civilian heroes. If these characters stand out in utter contrast to Capra's, it is not only because of their actions, but also for the words they speak.

The inspirational speeches that screenwriter Robert Riskin wrote for Capra's characters often paraphrase the writings of the Founding Fathers or passages of the Bible, translating them into everyday language. In the courtroom, when Longfellow Deeds talks about the disparity between those who are rich and those who are poor, his banal metaphors ("cars driving up the hill," "hot potatoes," "people rowing" and "people drowning") show all the traces of an over-simplified populist eloquence:

> It's like the road out in front of my house. It's on a steep hill. Every day I watch the cars climbing up. Some go lickety-split up that hill on high ... some have to shift into second — and some sputter and shake and slip back to the bottom again. Same cars — same gasoline — yet some make and some don't. And I say the fellow who can make the hill on high should stop once in a while and help those who can't.[33]

Later he adds:

> See all those fellows? They're the ones I'm trying to help. They need it! (pointing)
> Mr. Cedar and that Mr. Semple don't need anything. They've got plenty! It's like I'm out in a big boat and I see one fellow in a rowboat who's tired of rowing and wants a free ride — and another fellow who's drowning. Who would you expect me to rescue? Mr. Cedar, who just got tired of rowing and wants a free ride? Or those men out there who are drowning? Any ten-year-old child will give you the answer to that.[34]

Sturges's characters, instead, cannot afford to accuse others, persuade them to righteousness or make a case for honesty; they are not even allowed to revert to the words and tones of Riskin's oratory. Like Woodrow in *Hail the Conquering Hero*, Sturges's characters can merely excuse themselves for not fitting in, and they do it in the least rhetorical way:

> I would gladly have given my life to have earned just one of the many ribbons you see on these brave men's chests ... if I could have reached as high as my father's shoestrings, my whole life would be justified and I would stand here proudly before you ... instead of as the thief and coward that I am.... A coward because I postponed until now what I should have told you a year ago when I was discharged from the Marine Corps for medical unfitness ... a coward because I didn't want my mother to know ... well, it wasn't to save *her*, it was to save *me*.... I have never been in Guadalcanal or any place else ... I've been working in a shipyard for the last year. I've never received a medal of any description ... naturally, since I've never fought. Two days ago I decided to come home. Since I'd written to my mother I was overseas, I had to come home as a soldier ... I had to have some ribbons so Iya bought them in a hock shop. When I was all dressed up, I met some real Marines ... I brought them home with me to make things look better ... I fooled them as much as I did the rest of you, not that I really wanted to fool any of you ... I just wanted to come home ... I've told you all this because too many men

have bled and died for you ... and for me ... to live this lie any longer ... I *guess* that's why I told you ... I certainly didn't mean to when I came in ... I'm gonna pack my things now so this will probably be my last chance to say goodbye to you. I know my mother will give you back the mortgage ... and I hope you won't hold it against her that her son didn't ... quite come through.... There's no use telling you I'm sorry because I wish I was dead. I — that's all.[35]

We are obviously very far from the relentless inspirational speech that Jefferson Smith delivers to the Senate, with the intent of awakening his audience's conscience and provide them with a simple vision of politics (honesty versus corruption), life (country versus city), and language (direct emotional speech versus sophisticated manipulations of the word).

Compared to Woodrow's apologetic confession (almost a call for Vattimo's "weak thought"), Smith's debate with Senator Paine assumes the vibrant tones of a call for political activism:

I was ready to tell you that a certain man in my state, a Mr. James Taylor, wanted to put through this dam for his own profit — a man who controls a political machine and controls everything else worth controlling in my state. Yes, and a man even powerful enough to control Congressmen — and I saw three of them in his room the day I went up to see him.... And this same man, Mr. James Taylor, came down here and offered me a seat in this Senate for the next 20 years if I voted for a dam that he knew and I knew was a fraud. But if I dared to open my mouth against that dam, he promised to break me in two. All right, I got up here and I started to open my mouth and the long and powerful arm of Mr. James Taylor reached into this sacred chamber and grabbed me by the scruff of the neck...

I guess this is just another lost cause, Mr. Paine. All you people don't know about lost causes. Mr. Paine does. He said once they were the only causes worth fighting for. And he fought for them once for the only reason any man ever fights for them. Because of just one plain, simple rule: Love thy neighbor. And in this world today full of hatred, a man who knows that one rule has a great trust. You know that rule, Mr. Paine. And I loved you for it just as my father did. And you know that you fight for the lost causes harder than for any others. Yes, you even die for them — like a man we both knew, Mr. Paine.

You think I'm licked. You all think I'm licked! Well I'm not licked. And I'm going to stay right here and fight for this lost cause even if this room gets filled with lies like these; and the Taylors and all their armies come marching into this place. Somebody will listen to me.[36]

If, on the one hand, Dan McGinty or Woodrow Truesmith lack the moral integrity to indulge in this kind of talk, on the other hand, their apologies and good intentions prevent us from identifying them with Hollywood's anti-heroic types. Rather, they belong to a gray area where their objectionable behavior is determined by the circumstances and mitigated by their frankness.

Against Capra's populist idolization of the anti-intellectual hero, and his classical deployment of binary conflicts (such as the honest average man versus the corrupted sophisticated politician), Sturges suggests a disillusioned acceptance of a world populated by average men who are not immune to the corruption and dishonesty of the world, but who experience such conflict between high ideals and reality as a continuing dilemma.

If, for Capra, "the strength of America is in the kind of people who can plant a seed, sow the grass," and if his intentions really are "to glorify the average man, not the guy at the top, not the politician, not the banker, just the ordinary guy whose strength I admire, whose survivability I admire,"[37] for Sturges, the average man is an ordinary guy whose "survivability" consists in a pragmatic and difficult balance between principles and reality, and in a substantial weakness that makes him both victim and accomplice of the system.

This postmodern "weak thought" approach leads to a different conception of the masses: For Capra, they are good, honest, hard-working folks (as the townspeople in *Mr. Deeds Goes to Town* perfectly exemplify); for Sturges, they are respectful and persuaded of their own honesty, but not immune to selfishness and deception (as the townspeople of *The Miracle of Morgan's Creek* and *Hail the Conquering Hero,* or as the public opinion in *The Power and the Glory* and *The Great Moment*).

As Rozgonyi points out:

The entire population of Morgan's Creek seems to be involved in one game of deception after another…. Trudy and Ratzkiwatzki marry under a false name; Norval is persuaded to keep the truth from Officer Kockenlocker; Emmy and Trudy do not tell their father about Trudy's pregnancy; the sisters set up a plan to get Norval to propose to Trudy before he knows what has really happened; and Norval arranges a fake wedding, an act that is also illegal. The deceptions reach outside the family as well. Mr. Rafferty, for example, is forced — by the hypocrisy of the townspeople — to risk his own status by secretly looking after Trudy during her pregnancy, bringing the Kockenlockers food, and arranging for a doctor.[38]

One of the funniest and most cynical examples of deceit appears in the script but did not make it into the film, thanks to the cuts that removed the minister's sermon and the reading of the complete editorial on military marriages. The sermon, which Trudy and Emmy listen to from the pews, was lifted nearly word-for-word from the *Bugle*'s [the local newspaper] editorial.

It seems that in Morgan's Creek even clergymen cannot be trusted to be honest.[39]

The society that Sturges portrays (whether in the form of the pacific populace of a small village or in their incarnation as a crowd hungry for heroes) is made up of regular American folks loving their country, its myths and beliefs. However, we have seen how such people also demonstrate a profound inability in judging, interpreting, and telling the difference between fake and real heroes, corrupted politicians and honest men. In this sense, they are not only guilty of deception (as Rozgonyi points out) but, above all, of self-deception. These characters want to hear noble gestures that will fill them with pride so that, by rejoicing in the glory of one of their brethren, they can satisfy their own need for heroism — clearly a displacement of their own incapacity at performing heroic actions.

The words that Woodrow chooses to start his confession are the most apt at describing the pathological condition of this postmodern mass:

> You'd better save your hoorays for somebody else … for somebody who deserves them … like Doc Bissell here [the honest candidate running for mayor] … who has tried for so long to serve you … only you didn't know a good man when you saw one … so you always elected a phony instead.
> (he nods toward Mr. Noble [the present mayor])
> …Until a bigger phony came along … then you naturally wanted him.[40]

The fact that Woodrow's final confession moves the townspeople to want him as a mayor is but another sign of the mass's stupidity.

This example also reflects the sequence in *The Miracle of Morgan's Creek* where Norval (first arrested and sent to prison for bigamy) is forgiven and rehabilitated for the simple reason that his illegal wife gave birth to six babies (who are not even Norval's). The same group of puritans who chased Norval away now shows an unexpected flexibility in expanding their moral principles. The reason is the same as in *Hail the Conquering Hero*: Everything can be forgiven to an outcast member, as long as the appearance and the good name of the community can benefit from it.

If this anti-idealistic representation of the everyday man and Sturges's non-romantic vision of small towns and country folks helped give him the nickname "the anti–Capra,"[41] it is also true that Sturges's world is as far from the idealized vision offered by many Classical comedies of the 1930s and 1940s (Capra most obviously) as from the critical representation of the violent, irrational, destructive crowds depicted by a few movies of the period (*Fury* [1936], *They Won't Forget* [1937]).

Sturges, in fact, has no intention of exposing the dangerous ignorance of the masses, but he portrays them with ambiguous and multi-faceted traits. The benevolent neighborhood in *Christmas in July* is an example of simplicity and virtue, but also of narrow-mindedness, unawareness, and the inability to interpret reality. For these people, Jimmy wins the contest for the simple reason that he is a "good guy" whom they have known since he was born. Likewise, in *Hail the Conquering Hero,* nobody ever doubts that Woodrow is a decorated Marine because of the trust and respect they had for his father. In both cases, the people *want* to believe in their own illusions, no matter how absurd or unbelievable ("Christmas" in July or "miracles" in Morgan's Creek) they appear.

Sturges's crowds are hard to define and cannot be categorized in an either positive or negative way. The populace of Morgan's Creek, for instance, features a number of likable characters who also behave in the most disrespectful and even hypocritical way. Everybody in town, observes Rozgonyi, "seems to be involved in one game of deception after another.... The residents lie, cheat, steal, and treat each other miserably," and what is worse is that "all of these offenses ... are committed under the pretense of upholding the propriety and good name of their town."[42] Ironically, whether to celebrate the return of the war hero or the arrival of a new educator, Sturges's crowds often gather at the local train station to glorify what turns out being a con artist or an anti-hero.

Woodrow's arrival at the train station in *Hail the Conquering Hero* is probably the best and most illuminating example of Sturges's mixed feelings towards the crowd. Sturges, observes Henderson,

> cuts from one group to another after just a few lines of dialogue, seeming never to finish a scene but achieving a vivid sense of the interrelationship of all of the characters present and of the kaleidoscopic simultaneity of the event as a whole. One consequence of this treatment is a striking spatial dislocation of the viewer. It is impossible to determine in most cases where one group is standing in relation to the others, even when a character leaves one shot and enters the next. Sturges precedes his montage of the waiting townspeople with a very brief "establishing shot" of the crowd as a whole. This is the shot, itself a gag, that undermines the sergeant's description of a quiet return; but it is held too briefly to orient the viewer spatially, and, in any case, it is shot from too far away for the viewer to identify the characters.... The legendary serenity of small-town life is dissolved into a cacophony of four bands playing simultaneously.[43]

Dickos comments that:

The kinetic impact of Sturges's compositions — confused crowds pushing their way across the screen [...] — belie the delusion that there is much harmony in the world.[44]

The same implications are present in a similar scene from *The Beautiful Blonde from Bashful Bend,* in which saloon singer Freddie, running away from a vengeful judge whom she has accidentally shot in the rear, arrives in a small village where she is mistaken for the new schoolteacher. All the most respectable and prominent people of the town (symbolically named Snake City) are waiting for her at the train station. First, it is the music teacher who welcomes Freddie with his affected manners, followed by the mayor, his wife, the sheriff and other rich representatives who present their homage to the young lady, with rhetorical speeches and pompous ceremony. Sturges alternates this ridiculous spectacle with shots of the local cretins and troublemakers, who are snickering at their fellow citizens and wolf-whistling at Freddie and her girlfriend, Conchita.

In this way, Sturges adopts a detached perspective by putting on the same level two kinds of people that Capra would have placed in a conflicting good-poor versus bad-rich dichotomy. As a result, the sequence deconstructs not only the myths and visions of Americana otherwise glorified by Hollywood, but also the same system of binary oppositions of conflicting morals, values, and characters on which Classical cinema had solidly based its paradigm.

3

The Sturges Pastiche

In a world in which stylistic innovation is no longer possible, all that is left is to imitate dead styles, to speak through the masks and with the voices of the styles in the imaginary museum.

Frederic Jameson[1]

From simple internal citational games to more complicated extratextual cross-references, meta-linguistic narratives, genre contamination, and even footage manipulation, the cinema of Preston Sturges anticipates all these forms of postmodern pastiche — sometimes by hiding them in the most classically conceived Hollywood movies, sometimes by making the manipulation unexpectedly overt. So much so, that it is perhaps surprising that no one has ever coined a term such as "the Sturges Pastiche." More specific than "the Lubitsch Touch," such a label points at an aesthetics based on a unique combination of different genres, which — to be specific — ranged from cinematic comedy (slapstick, screwball, sophisticated) to popular forms of theater (farce and vaudeville), from the surreal world of cartoons (Warner Brothers' *Looney Tunes* and Tex Avery's caustic gags, above all) to more "serious" genres such as Hollywood melodramas, film noirs, and biopics.

Film scholars have used the concept of "pastiche" to refer to the ability to mix together pre-existing texts, styles and forms, and they have applied it to all sorts of movies and genres of the past three decades, from "nostalgia films" (*Amarcord* [1973]; *American Graffiti*; *The Big Chill* [1983]; *Stand by Me* [1986]; *Peggy Sue Got Married* [1986]; *Hope and Glory* [1987]), to remakes (*Always* [1989]; *Cape Fear* [1991]; *Psycho* [1998]; *The Ladykillers* [2004]), from homages to classical genres (*Dead Men Don't Wear Plaid*;

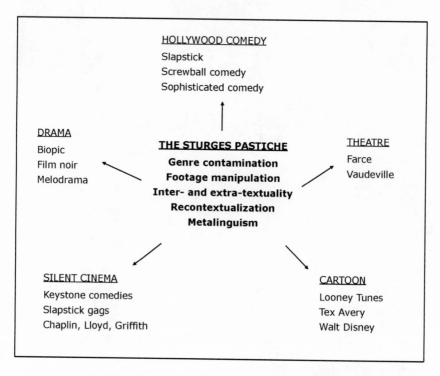

Young Frankenstein; Mars Attacks!; Far from Heaven [2002]) to articulated meta-linguistic operations[2] (*The Purple Rose of Cairo; Who Framed Roger Rabbit; Pleasantville* [1998]).

What these heterogeneous groups of texts and categories have in common is the requirement of a quite postmodern type of audience: a spectator who interprets the fictional universe that the movie constructs not only against his or her real-life experiences, but also against his/her film history knowledge; a movie expert, whose cinematic culture is ultimately needed for the signification of the quotations and cross-references in the text. Postmodern cinema, in fact, uses "strategies of disruption like self-reflexivity, intertextuality, bricolage, multiplicity, and simulation through parody and pastiche," in order to produce texts that are "concerned with the very act of telling/showing stories and remembering told/shown stories."[3] This complicated game that the final text engages in with its reader does not play on the spectator's knowledge of reality, but — more specifically — on his/her familiarity with classical cinema.

Regardless of the kind of film discussed, the extra-textual references produced by the pastiche demand an expertise and a sophistication of analysis that are much higher than those needed for a classic movie. A very simple postmodern farce such as *Dead Men Don't Wear Plaid*, for example, seamlessly combines footage from classical film noirs with new footage and dialogues, in a narrative that — to be fully enjoyed and appreciated — calls for a specifically cinematic competence.

Movies such as *Zelig* (1983) and *Forrest Gump* (1994) exploit the possibilities of optical and digital manipulation of previous footage, in order to place side by side, in the same shot, fictional characters together with historical figures such as Roosevelt, Hitler, Nixon, John Lennon, JFK and Elvis Presley. But the enterprise would be completely wasted if the audience did not have the necessary "culture" to decipher all these referents. Mel Brooks' spoofs of westerns (*Blazing Saddles*), horror movies (*Young Frankenstein*), musicals (*Life Stinks* [1991]), and the Hitchcock style (*High Anxiety*) would hardly be funny at all if the spectator did not have some basic knowledge of the genres Brooks is parodying.

The same applies to Sturges's insertion and manipulation of footage from a previous movie in the opening of his *The Sin of Harold Diddlebock*, or to his articulated combination of different cinematic styles, genres and quotations in movies such as *Sullivan's Travels* or *Unfaithfully Yours*. These require, from the spectator, a knowledge of their cinematic and musical referents.

Postmodern cinema (particularly the one of independent and non–Hollywood filmmakers) tends to push such requirements to the point of narrowing their audience to a restricted number of film buffs. In *The Dreamers* (2003), for example, Bernardo Bertolucci recreates the 1968 protests following the dismissal of the director of the Cinemathèque Française, Henri Langlois, by alternating new images of Jean-Pierre Léaud handing out leaflets at the Palais de Chaillot in Place Trocadèro, with vintage black-and-white footage showing Henri Langlois and François Truffaut addressing the crowd. However, the sequence does not provide any contextual reference, and spectators who are not familiar with the events are left confused. The rest of the movie turns the cinematic pastiche into a sort of postmodern movie trivia, where the frequent inserts of old movies parallel the narrative, in a continuous homage to both "classical" cinema and to the "modern" French passion for it.

Whether destined for a restricted number of devotees or a broader mass audience, the postmodern pastiche shows a tendency to self-sufficiency, so much so that the game of text contamination does not even need to be explained or narratively justified any more. *Natural Born Killers*

(1994), for example, blends the characters' optical point of view with the audience's, by using dashing and unmotivated alternations of dissimilar photographic styles and image qualities — from black-and-white movies to amateurish videos, from TV news to sitcoms. Steven Spielberg's *Artificial Intelligence: AI* refers to conventions, structures, and motifs from different types of science-fiction genres, and combines them with other classical models (comedy, melodrama, childhood cinema, adventure, cartoons), while deconstructing and reconstructing other texts (like Carlo Collodi's *Pinocchio*, whose plot constantly parallels and interacts with the movie as an active subtext).

Similar games of text combination were already present in the modern cinema of the 1960s, when Jean-Luc Godard's or François Truffaut's provocative cinematic quotations aimed at an audience of *cinephiles*, and Sergio Leone's overt deconstruction of the western genre were exposing cinema's awareness of its own past.

Postmodern cinema, however, gives pastiche a narrative functionality that goes beyond the merely provocative quotation, in a final *synthesis* between classic narratives and modernist self-indulging practices. It is not surprising if the most representative postmodern American filmmakers, such as Allen, Coppola, Scorsese, and Spielberg, share a similar attraction towards both the European new waves and the Classical Hollywood Cinema.

As Kenneth Von Gunden puts it:

> Born in the thirties, forties, and fifties, the young lions were *consumers* of popular culture long before they were *producers* of it. They grew up with television's recycling of Hollywood's films of the thirties and forties and the vast outpouring of multimedia entertainment directed primarily at youthful audiences. Hence the lions and *their* audiences share an easy familiarity with the same inter-multitextual elements.[4]

Preston Sturges and Genre Contamination

Sturges's interest in the appropriation of different styles produced playful interactions between different Hollywood genres, often within the same movie. In the drama *The Great Moment*, the biopic of Dr. William Morton and his discovery of anesthesia, Sturges takes advantage of any potentially comic element to develop comedy situations, slapstick gags, and narrative techniques extraneous to biographical and melodramatic genres. Morton's first experiments with analgesics are turned into a conjugal comedy of misunderstandings, when the dentist gets intoxicated by the fumes of a bottle of ether accidentally left by the fire and behaves like a drunk as his wife enters the room. In the same movie, the character of Eben Frost, Dr. Morton's devoted spokesman, keeps repeating the story of his successfully painless tooth extraction to any person he meets, so much so that his lines become the repetitive slogans of an annoying farcical character. Throughout the movie, Sturges makes him clumsy and groggy, and accompanies his malapropisms with spectacular pratfalls. When mistakenly administered a dose of non-rectified ether, for example, Frost jumps off the dentist's chair and destroys the entire office in a state of excitement.[5]

Here, as in many other comic scenes, Sturges draws from the whole repertoire of slapstick comedies about dentists' sadism and patients' phobias, and recontextualizes, in a dramatic movie, comedy routines developed by, among others, a popular W. C. Fields' short entitled *The Dentist* (1932).[6] The result is a quite unusual (and, for many commentators, odd) combination of melodrama and farce, where the dramatic and melancholic moods cohabit with pratfalls and belly laughs.

Likewise, in *The Great McGinty*, Sturges devises an unusual concoction of screwball comedy and political melodrama — the latter being a genre that lived for a brief period after the Wall Street crash with films such as *The Dark Horse, Gabriel Over the White House,* and *The President Vanishes.*

The movie tells the story of Dan McGinty, a bum recruited by a mob boss to help with fraudulent activities, who becomes a puppet city mayor for a corrupt administration. Politics and romance blend together, as McGinty is convinced to marry his secretary Catherine in order to raise his popularity among women. The political issues are constantly filled with comic situations and sight gags, which involve both McGinty and his political boss, but also Catherine and her husband.

The contamination of genres is even more interesting if we consider that the movie was produced in the early 1940s — that is, when the screwball comedy had already started to decline, and the political melodrama had long shown itself to be an unpopular subgenre. Sturges, in reality, was playing with Hollywood's recent past.

"Where *Easy Living* [1937] and *The Lady Eve* mix farce and comedy," observes Diane Jacobs, "*Miracle of Morgan's Creek* mixes farce and melodrama, maximizing the pain and violence inherent in both forms."[7] *The Miracle of Morgan's Creek*, in fact, tells the story of a highly dysfunctional family in a highly dysfunctional town, where Mr. Kockenlocker and his daughters Trudy and Emmy often come to blows. The characters are as wild and instinctive as those in a Tex Avery cartoon: Trudy comes home after a wild party for the American troops to remember that she has married a soldier, whose name she has completely forgotten. When she finds out that she is pregnant, she convinces her best friend Norval Jones to marry her. The following chain of events is one of the most absurd and unrestrained ever devised in a "classic" comedy. Slapstick, farce and a sharp parody of small-town values co-exist in a spoof of the Andy Hardy series, whose values such as "listen to your parents, obey the rules, do not question the status quo" are completely overturned. "Far from venerating family life," observes Jay Rozgonyi, "Sturges pulls the rug out from under the institution, offering us one example after another of unhappy family members and disdainful observers."[8] As Diane Jacobs notes, "In farce, with its antisocial message, the characters are volatile and powerless; in comedy, they are stable and strong. [...] Sturges's films would begin challenging these distinctions."[9]

Unfaithfully Yours is an extraordinary example of contamination between sophisticated comedy, film noir, and (at least in Sturges's original intentions) burlesque.[10] In this three-act fantasy, jealous orchestra conductor Sir Alfred DeCarter suspects his wife Daphne of infidelity; we see Sir Alfred imagining three different ways of dealing with the situation — each one matching the mood of the musical piece he is conducting.

Sturges used different photographic styles in each piece, in order to underline the different cinematic genres each fantasy sequence refers to. For the tragic-comic resolution of the first "act," based on Rossini's "Overture" from Semiramide, Sturges opts for a concoction of noir-esque low-key lighting and shadows, alternated with a high-key lighting photography, typical of sophisticated comedies.

For the disillusioned resolution of the second "act" (based on Wagner's "Reconciliation Theme" from Tannhaüser), and the dramatic conclusion of the third (on the notes of Tchaikovsky's Francesca da Rimini), the cinematography assumes the much more somber and elegant style of a Twentieth Century–Fox period movie.

A typically noir kind of photography dominates the movie, and creates interesting conflicts with the comic plot and its characters. Many shots dedicated to Sir Alfred directing the orchestra, for example, include sinister projections of shadows, which add an ironic trait to the character's personality.

Top: Concoction of styles: low-key lighting in the noir-esque fantasy sequence from *Unfaithfully Yours.* Pictured: Sir Alfred (Rex Harrison). *Bottom:* Concoction of styles: high-key lighting in the sophisticated comedy fantasy sequence from *Unfaithfully Yours.* Pictured: Sir Alfred (Rex Harrison) and Daphne (Linda Darnell).

Concoction of photographic styles: the Fox melodrama in *Unfaithfully Yours.*
Pictured: Sir Alfred (Rex Harrison) and Daphne (Linda Darnell).

The result appeared so "spotty and uneven" to the studio, and far from
"the standard of the photography of our other pictures,"[11] that producer
Darryl Zanuck requested several visual and narrative changes. The final
movie, however, still shows clear references to various Hollywood genres
in a complex pastiche of different styles. In this way, *Unfaithfully Yours*
clearly anticipates movies such as *Young Frankenstein* and *Dead Men Don't
Wear Plaid*, postmodern spoofs that mock the classic genres by poking fun
at their photographic attributes.

It is probably in *Sullivan's Travels* that Sturges manages to combine
the most dissimilar classical film styles. Throughout the film, we constantly move from Depression drama to slapstick moments, from farce to
sophisticated comedy, from Keystone chases and pie-in-the-face routines
to a dramatic depiction of the human and social condition of homeless
people and prisoners.

The screenplay, after all, is filled with verbal references to directors
(Capra and Lubitsch often recur in Sullivan's dialogues), and visual quo-
tations from previous movies — Charles Chaplin's *The Immigrant* (1917) and
City Lights (1931), Mervyn LeRoy's *I Am a Fugitive from a Chain Gang* (1932),

William Wellman's *Wild Boys of the Road* (1933), King Vidor's *The Crowd* (1928) and *Hallelujah* (1929).

When, thirty years later, postmodern filmmakers would blend together farce, romantic comedy and slapstick humor in movies such as *What's Up Doc*, they would essentially work on the same kind of pastiche, but in a much more blatant and self-conscious way. For *What's Up Doc*, Peter Bogdanovich and screenwriters Buck Henry, David Newman, and Robert Benton would re-elaborate rules and conventions of the classic screwball comedy, and reshape archetypal couples such as Rosalind Russell–Cary Grant and Spencer Tracy–Katharine Hepburn, into the modern duo Barbra Streisand–Ryan O'Neil. Classic skirmishes and motifs (from suitcase mismatch to identity exchanges) would be brought back to life together with a good dose of physical gags and slapstick humor —filtered through the experience of the "hotel bedroom-farce," a subgenre from which Hollywood had already drawn in the Sixties (for example, in the Blake Edwards *Pink Panther* series).

In respect to *What's Up Doc*, Sturges's comedies can be regarded both as classic "sources" for Bogdanovich's pastiche, and as anticipative examples of postmodern contamination. On the one hand, the couple Streisand-O'Neil is clearly modeled on the Sturgesian pair Stanwyck-Fonda from *The Lady Eve* (Streisand's character being the same kind of con artist, able to choose, control, and manipulate her naïve male companion). On the other hand, the postmodern concoction of sophisticated and physical comedy, romanticism and slapstick action, and the series of quotations that go from Capra to Hawks, from Harold Lloyd to Buster Keaton, from *Casablanca* (1942) to the *Looney Tunes,* indicate in Sturges's practice of textual deconstruction and quotation the main model for this kind of referential game.

Silent Cinema

Among the different and often incompatible cinematic styles that Sturges combines in his pastiches, there emerges a certain predominance of allusions to silent cinema. From Mack Sennett's physical gags to Keystone Cops chase sequences, from Lloyd's satirical routines to melodramatic Chaplinesque pantomimes, Sturges makes silent cinema one of the key referents in his appropriation of Hollywood genres.

Silent slapstick moments characterize Sturges's work starting with his early screenplays. In *The Good Fairy* (1935), Luisa falls off a ladder in an attempt to act out the fairy tale she is telling and is left hanging from a chandelier. *Never Say Die* (1939) is so packed with chases, pratfalls, and sight gags as to make the movie almost a manual of slapstick comedy — one, moreover, that Sturges would quote and re-use in the movies he would later direct.[12]

Eddie Bracken falls off his bed, is knocked on his head by an opening door, and trips over his own pants in *Hail the Conquering Hero*, while in *The Miracle of Morgan's Creek* he is involved in most of the fights of the Kockenlocker family. *Easy Living*, one of the most famous comedies written by Sturges in the Thirties, starts with Mr. Ball falling down the stairs after a black cat crosses his path, and is followed by a hilarious conjugal chase studded with pratfalls, which ends up with Mr. Ball throwing his wife's fur coat from the roof. The coat's accidental landing on a girl's head sets off a plot filled with fights, scuffles, and sight gags — such as the hilarious slapstick sequence at the automat, where Mr. Ball's son starts a fight with a security guard, and breaks open all the vending machines of the automated diner, setting the hungry customers free to attack the food.

It is not surprising that *Time* reviewer Frank S. Nugent criticized the movie for being "frequently overwhelmed by Sennett touches,"[13] while several years later, Alexander King would still refer to Sturges as the "Toscanini of pratfalls."[14] Sturges himself showed his affection for silent comedy in his "eleven rules for box-office appeal," drawn up in 1941:

1. A pretty girl is better than an ugly one.
2. A leg is better than an arm.
3. A bedroom is better than a living room.
4. An arrival is better than a departure.
5. A birth is better than a death.
6. A chase is better than a chat.
7. A dog is better than a landscape.
8. A kitten is better than a dog.
9. A baby is better than a kitten.
10. A kiss is better than a baby.
11. A pratfall is better than anything.[15]

Pratfalls and other forms of graphic violence dot even more sophisticated comedies such as *The Palm Beach Story*. From the vertiginous silent routine of the opening credits, to the long "Ale and Quail" shooting sequence on the train (as narratively useless as it is visually exhilarating), Sturges inserts chases and physical gags into the structure of a typical

Pratfalls and other forms of graphic violence dot even Sturges's more sophisticated comedies. In *The Palm Beach Story*, Tom Jeffers (Joel McCrea) runs out of the apartment in his pajamas, trips several times over a big comforter, and then collides with a revolving window.

screwball comedy of the late 1930s. Examples include Geraldine stepping onto John's pince-nez, and Tom running out of the apartment in his pajamas, tripping several times over a big comforter he had wrapped around himself, and then colliding with a revolving window.

The leading couple is surrounded by completely farcical characters such as Toto, whose clumsy behavior and Chaplinesque dialogue made of "yitz"es and "nitz"es are reminiscent of Hinkel's monologues in Chaplin's *The Great Dictator* (1940) and the Tramp's song in mock speech from *City Lights*.

In this film, Sturges sometimes passes from a primordial Keystone farce to the indirect elegance of the Lubitsch Touch (especially in the high-class *milieu* depicted in the final part), in a perfect concoction of silent slapstick and 1930s sophistication. See a simple sequence like the kiss between Claudette Colbert and Joel McCrea, where the camera focuses on the woman's feet curling up: a farcical, physical element of sexual humor slipped into a highly romantic scene.

Sturges makes light of almost every kind of cinematic comic sub-genre from the typical screwball comedy of misunderstandings and remar-riage (that is, a happy marriage followed by a temporary separation and crowned with the final reunion), to the comedy of eccentrics of the early 1930s (*Love Me Tonight*, 1932 and *My Man Godfrey*, 1936) — here perfectly revived by the eccentric couple of millionaire siblings interpreted by Rudy Vallee and Mary Astor. And, once again, the final result is a very post-modern look at the Hollywood genres of the previous decades: a parade of what classical comedy had been in all its forms since its silent heyday.

Sturges's fascination with pratfalls, sight gags and other elements of silent comedy goes beyond the simple aesthetics of citational games, as it usually serves graphically to underline the violence behind relationships, or to produce metaphorical downfalls.

In *The Palm Beach Story*, for example, pratfalls and other physical gags

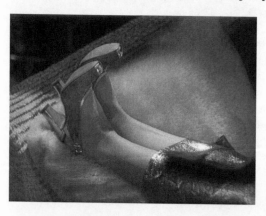

are reserved for clumsy male characters who, like silent comedians, are constantly hit by objects, trip over their own clothes, or have their glasses broken. By contrast, female characters, with their verbal skills, seductive power, and confident attitude, seem to belong to the classier universe of sophisticated comedies.

Farcical and physical elements of sexual humor slip into romantic scenes: Geraldine's (Claudette Colbert) feet curling during a kiss, in *The Palm Beach Story*.

Likewise, in *The Lady Eve*, while Jean's sophisticated behavior goes along with her manipulative powers, Charles's continuous pratfalls enrich the depiction of his weak and naive personality with metaphorical images of falling. As Diane Jacobs points out:

From the second he sets eyes on Jean, Charles gets buffeted about like a silent comic: sprawled flat on his face when Jean trips him in the boat dining room; coaxed onto a chair in her stateroom, only to get swatted off and driven wild as she runs her hand through his hair ... Charles' most stupen-dous descent is from the train steps into the mud as he flees Eve's wedding night revelations, but Charles also races down flight after flight of stairs to

In the scene from *The Sin of Harold Diddlebock* where Jackie the lion takes a walk on the ledge of a tall building, dragging along Harold and his pal Wormy, Sturges's principal reference is *Safety Last!* (1923), the silent comedy in which Harold Lloyd climbs a skyscraper and winds up dangling off windows, poles and the iconic clock's hands.

consummate his passion in the film's exhilarating end. Beyond their metaphorical subtext (man's falling in love, out of grace, off his high horse), Charles's plunges reflect the nature of this particular romance and also Sturges's view of success.[16]

Finally, Sturges's fascination with silent cinema is overtly stated in *The Sin of Harold Diddlebock*, the movie that opens on the footage from the silent comedy *The Freshman*. For the scene where Jackie the lion decides to take a walk on the ledge of a tall building, dragging along Harold and his pal Wormy, Sturges's principal reference is *Safety Last!* (1923), the silent comedy in which Lloyd climbs a skyscraper and winds up dangling off windows, poles and the iconic clock's hands.

The Sturges Pastiche, however, does not limit the assimilation of silent cinema to slapstick aspects only, but it absorbs and reformulates the most interesting techniques of silent narration. *Sullivan's Travels*, for exam-

Top: The Miracle of Morgan's Creek Norval (Edie Bracken) asks Emmy (Diana Lynn) "Which of these six kids is mine?" in *The Miracle of Morgan's Creek.* *Bottom:* Emmy's response: "They all are!"

ple (besides its famously incredible chase sequence — for which Sturges had hired actors and crew who had previously worked with Mack Sennett), contains a long sequence that can easily be regarded as one of the best postmodern homages ever paid to silent melodrama. The third "travel" that Hollywood director John Sullivan makes into the "valley of the shadows of adversity," in order to draw inspiration for his next movie, is entirely narrated without dialogue or noises, except for an appositely composed musical piece called the "Hobo Symphony."

Both the visual elements (a dramatic depiction of the world of homeless people, dotted with a few gags involving Joel McCrea and Veronica Lake), and a score that alternates romanticism with onomatopoeic effects for the silent gags, remind us of Chaplin's most balanced silent mixtures of comedy and grief, optimism and misery, in movies such as *The Immigrant, Easy Street* (1917), and, above all, *City Lights*. In particular, the scene where "a meek looking orator" addresses an audience of bums with emphatic gestures, underlined by an overdramatic orchestration and by a series of onomatopoeic effects, is an explicit homage to the opening sequence in *City Lights* where Chaplin used unusual instruments to parody the voices of a mayor and of a female leader who pompously introduce the unveiling of a city statue dedicated to "Peace and Prosperity."[17]

Sturges returns to silent mode in the climax of *Miracle of Morgan's Creek*, when Norval finds out that his wife has given birth to six kids. With the camera placed inside the nursery room, we observe Norval looking at six cribs, and pantomiming the question, "Which of these six kids is mine?" When Emmy waves her hands to indicate that they are all his, Norval's reaction turns into a panic attack — with a consequent slapstick routine of chases and pratfalls.

Likewise, *Unfaithfully Yours* constructs most of its final sequence (Sir Alfred coming home and trying to apply the schemes he has daydreamed about) as a silent movie, by showing Sir Alfred literally destroying his house and cutting his finger in a long series of silent actions.

Even William Wyler's *Roman Holiday* (1953) — a movie written and modified by several screenwriters, including Sturges — contains a good example of Sturges's silent narration, in a passage that we can find in his original script: When princess Anne and Joe Bradley are taken to the police station after a comic chase through the Roman streets, the music takes over, and the questioning and the explanations are simply pantomimed.

Norval's (Edie Bracken) reaction to the news that he's the father of sextuplets, in *The Miracle of Morgan's Creek.*

The Cartoon Elements

One of the few postmodern elements that contemporary critics and commentators have extensively attributed to Sturges's "classical" movies is the presence of cartoon-like elements. From the designs in *Never Say Die* and the animated credits of *The Lady Eve* to the Disney short that the prisoners watch in *Sullivan's Travels,* from cartoonesque character names (Muggsy, Bugsy, Hopsie, Warmie, Toto, the Wienie King, and even Tom and Jerry—the main couple from *The Palm Beach Story*) to slapstick gags pushed to the extent of physical impossibility, Sturges's movies are filled with references to the history of classical Hollywood animation.

Beside its relevance in the pastiche context, this cartoon approach is also of primary importance in the shaping of narrative events and characters' personalities. Andrew Dickos, for example, notes that in *The Great McGinty* Sturges recreates a specific American idiom, "indebted to the tradition of the political satire of cartoonist Thomas Nast. McGinty, The Boss, and Catherine—all acquire the black-white qualities that, despite

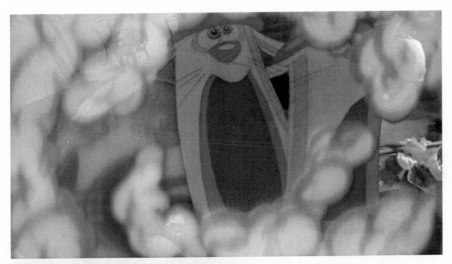

Top: Howling Roger in *Who Framed Roger Rabbit? Bottom:* Howling Harold (Harold Lloyd) in *The Sin of Harold Diddlebock.*

the characters into which they develop, are typed according to the virtues and evils they represent." Hence the simplification of political dialogues to a "cartoon strip exchange."[18]

In an essay dedicated to "Cartoon and Narrative in the Films of Frank Tashlin and Preston Sturges," Brian Henderson points out that in *The Sin of Harold Diddlebock,* "Harold resembles a cartoon character not only in not changing but also in mechanically repeating the same behavior patterns despite experience that invalidates them. (Likewise, Elmer Fudd goes hunting for Bugs Bunny despite countless prior failures.)" The scene where Harold gets drunk is a good example: "Harold alternates saying he feels nothing with howling like a wild man, a sound his sane self hears but cannot connect with himself. Such a reaction to a strong substance, often called Tabasco or red hot sauce, is familiar from cartoons — Roger Rabbit's paroxysms at the taste of a strong drink quotes a long-standing cartoon tradition."[19]

When cartoons are included in the movie, they usually acquire a narrative function. For example, *Playful Pluto* (1934), the Disney animated short that a group of convicts hysterically enjoys in *Sullivan's Travels*, assumes the function of the story's epiphany, as it reveals to Sullivan himself the importance of laughs for people who have nothing else in their lives.

Even the cartoon in the opening credits of *The Lady Eve* works as a narrative reading-key and a powerful allegory of the movie's main theme. James Ursini maintains that the "grinning snake slithering vulgarly through every opening at hand and around several strategically placed apples" actually summarizes the combination of "allegory and humor with an Aristophanes-like blending" on which the whole story is based.[20] For Stanley Cavell, these animated title cards suggest that "Preston Sturges is going to present us with some comic version of the story of the expulsion from the Garden of Eden"—an interpretation which seems confirmed by several other elements in the story, such as the fact that "the leading lady attracts the young man's attention by clunking him on the head with an apple,"[21] or the fact that the man keeps a snake in his cabin, which shows up right when Jean is trying to seduce Charles. In this sense, the opening cartoon really establishes "the myth about the creation of woman and temptability of man" as the main theme of the movie.[22]

The Beautiful Blonde from Bashful Bend, Sturges's most cartoonesque movie, is a concoction of comedy, farce, and a meta-linguistic spoof of a short-lived subgenre known as "Western Comedy," full of references to the narrative conventions of animated cinema.[23] In this movie, Sturges creates a series of simple gags, based on pratfalls and other forms of physical humor: a judge repeatedly shot in his rear end by a beautiful blonde who loses her dress in the middle of a gunfight, two boys howling like Tex Avery's wolf, and—even if Henderson holds that Sturges does not use "gags of physical impossibility"[24]—a physically impossible, cartoon-like gunfight in which no one gets hurt:

> A man shooting from a roof is shot, falls off, and climbs back onto the roof, shoots again and is shot off the roof again, climbs back on again, and so on — four times in all. Another man kneeling in front of a water trough gets a face full of water every time he shoots; after this happens four times, he holds his pistol higher, and the splash, which he seems to have avoided, is merely delayed. After this he shoots into the water itself and gets a huge water jet in the face, after which he throws his gun away and gives up. Another gag has a nearly bald man ready to shoot a rifle, only to have his hat blown away. A one-time cartoon gag has a man aiming and firing a shotgun

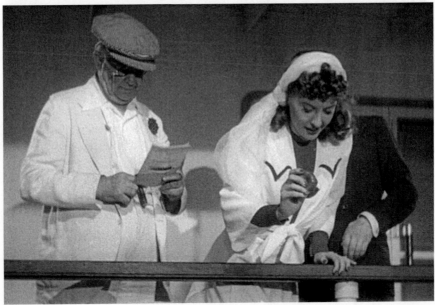

Top: Cartoon snake in the Garden of Eden from *The Lady Eve. Bottom:* Eve (Barbara Stanwyck) dropping an apple onto Adam's head, under the distracted eye of Colonel Harrington (Charles Coburn) in *The Lady Eve.*

only to have it blow up his face — we see his shotgun in black radiating shards and his face black, just like Elmer Fudd's shotgun and face after Bugs Bunny has put his finger or cork in the barrel or has twisted the barrel in a knot just before Elmer fires. In the midst of the shootout, who should stick their heads around a corner but the Basserman boys themselves? "What's the shootin' fer?" howls one. "Can we shoot too?" howls the other. Freddie says why not, then realizes who they are and asks what happened. They pretended to be dead, says one, the other then continuing the story stuttering like Porgy Pig: "When that big B-B-B-Blackie tried to kill us."[25]

Whether Sturges's citational intentions are aimed at creating "slap-stick-probable" more than "cartoon-impossible" situations (as Henderson argues), what is relevant here is that we are once again facing the same meta-linguistic awareness and the same principles of style contamination that we have traced behind Sturges's pastiche of Hollywood genres: an extremely (if prematurely) postmodern attitude to quote, fragment, absorb and recontextualize texts and narrative techniques that we will find again, forty years later, in Robert Zemeckis' meta-cartoon *Who Framed Roger Rabbit*, where the rules that govern the classical Hollywood cartoons will be explicitly exposed in all their absurdity.

Meta-linguism and Cross-reference

Cross-references and Recontextualization

Classical Hollywood comedies, with their parodies of a high-class *milieu*, often provided the best occasion for a meta-linguistic reflection, as the satire of social rules often involved a spoof of the cinematic conventions associated with "serious" genres. Mack Sennett's comedies, for examples, were, after all, a demystification of dramatic cinema (both in terms of contents and forms); Buster Keaton's relationship with objects of modernity assumes a highly meta-linguistic function in *Sherlock Jr.* (1924), in which his character dreams of entering the fictional world projected on the screen, and exposes the arbitrary rules of continuity editing, by falling down every time a shot and its setting unexpectedly change behind him.

In general, silent comedies based on *screen personas* (Charlie Chaplin, Buster Keaton, Harold Lloyd, Stan Laurel and Oliver Hardy) are mainly based on a recontextualization of the same characters and their competences in new situations, where the comic effect relies on the audience's knowledge of the actor's previous movies and gags.

With the coming of sound, Hollywood smoothed over meta-linguism, hid recontextualization, and confined disruptive solutions such as camera looks and gags of physical impossibility to specific genres (musicals and cartoons, respectively). Parody, however, remained focused on targeting both the high-class *milieu* and the cinematic norms of representation associated with it, and it managed to retain a certain degree of cinematic self-consciousness.

The studio system, after all, relied on the recycling of actors, music, and narrative sources, and on the audience's ability to recognize them. Paramount, for example, recycled the Lorenz Hart-Richard Rodgers love song "Isn't it Romantic" in different movies (from Rouben Mamoulian's *Love Me Tonight* and Billy Wilder's *A Foreign Affair* [1948] to Sturges's *The Lady Eve*) with the same purpose of mocking love scenes that were not so romantic after all. The same thing happened to the Victor Schertzinger-Clifford Guy waltz "Dream Lover," leitmotiv for Ernst Lubitsch's *The Love Parade* (1929), Mitchell Leisen's *Arise My Love* (1940), Billy Wilder's *The Major and the Minor* (1942), and several other classic comedies.

Some of the cross-references that we find in Sturges's movies and scripts fit perfectly in this studio system "allowance." In *Remember the Night* (1940), for example, Barbara Stanwyck and Fred MacMurray go to dinner on the notes of "Easy Living" (the song that gives the title to a previous Sturges's screenplay), and we can hear the same leitmotiv in the "love scene" at Niagara Falls. When Harold Diddlebock asks the man who sold him his circus if he would consider repossessing his business, the man answers: "I'd like to be 9,000 miles away: *Home in the Arms of Mother*," which is the title of the song that Sturges wrote and used in the opening of *Hail the Conquering Hero*. The scene where Harold decides to bring Jackie the lion with him to the bank, in order to intimidate reluctant bankers into granting him a loan, clearly mirrors a similar situation in *Easy Living*, when Mary visits financial tycoon J.B. Ball with two intimidating dogs.

Other hidden examples of classical self-references, in Sturges's cinema, rely on characters' names: businessman Mr. Waggleberry from *The Sin of Harold Diddlebock* sounds very similar to the bookkeeper Mr. Waterbury from *Christmas in July*, a transformation of the name Lomax Whortleberry, the bookkeeper from Sturges's unproduced play *A Cup of Coffee*; in an early draft of *Unfaithfully Yours*, Sturges originally named Sir Alfred's brother-in-law August Henschler III[26]— the Roman number drawing an obvious parallel to the similar eccentric dandy J. E. Hackensacker III, played by the same actor (Rudy Vallee), in another Sturges movie, *The Palm Beach Story*.

Often, however, Sturges's pastiche overcomes Hollywood invisible self-consciousness, and pushes the practice of cross-reference in the postmodern realm of overt intertextuality, meta-linguism, and self-reflexivity. One example of this process at work is *Safeguarding Military Information* (1941), a rare wartime propaganda short, written by Sturges and produced by Paramount for the U.S. War Office. In contrast to Frank Capra's educational series *Why We Fight*, mainly based on U.S. army footage and enemy newsreels commented on by a compelling voice-over, *Safeguarding Military Information* is structured around a few fictional episodes, linked to each other by "pedagogic" sequences, drawing conclusions on what the audience has seen. The final goal is to warn military and civilian personnel that "a careless word, a seemingly harmless boast, may cost the lives of hundreds of countrymen and jeopardize the security of your homeland." In order to prove this, Sturges creates a few short fictional episodes, connected by brief military lectures about the dangers of giving away even the most apparently harmless information.

In the first episode, it is easy to recognize exactly the same setting, characters, and situations that we will find three years later in the opening sequence of *Hail the Conquering Hero*: Eddie Bracken sits at the counter, trying to explain to his lover that he will not be able to take her to the beach tomorrow. The girl questions his explanations and accuses him of having an affair with another woman. Upon the insistence of his jealous fiancée, Bracken ends up revealing that his division is sailing for Hawaii in the morning, and gives her the name of the boat and time of departure. At this point, a camera movement reveals another man sitting at the counter, overhearing the whole conversation, while sophisticated equipment is transmitting the dialogue to a remote location. The following sequence shows us the ship being bombed, while we hear Bracken's voice-over repeating, in a loop, the information to his fiancée. In order to illustrate how "a tactless talkative person can destroy months of careful planning and endanger the security of the nation," Sturges shows Bracken's mother receiving news of the death of her son. The message is clear: "a careless word, a slip of the tongue may mean the difference between victory and defeat. [...] Think before you speak!"[27]

Hail the Conquering Hero will show that Eddie Bracken's character has learned his lesson, in a sequence in which he answers to his mother's requests: "I can't tell you that, Mama ... that's military information."[28]

Sturges, here, resurrects his character, places him at the same bar counter, but assigns him opposite "competences," in a typical postmodern game of intertextual reference and recontextualization: The tactless but courageous marine of *Safeguarding Military Information,* in fact, becomes here the son of a World War I hero discharged from the Marines for chronic hay fever, who is too ashamed to return home.

The start of World War II, with the imperativeness of its events and Hollywood's commitment to propaganda, certainly helped open up the diegetic boundaries of fiction to extra-textual elements. War events became part of the narrative in many contemporary dramas, homefront movies, comedies, and even musicals, often resulting in the widespread enclosure of real-life footage from newsreels and documentaries. Hollywood fiction became so sensitive to the latest news and propaganda directives that producers would often require some rewriting and re-editing before the final release.[29]

After Pearl Harbor, Hollywood's classic conception of a "closed" fictional universe, which allowed limited references to the external context, was dramatically shattered. Sturges made the most of this new receptivity, and pushed the interaction between fiction and reality towards a postmodern reduction of History to its cinematic documents. In *The Miracle of Morgan's Creek,* for example, we see the reaction of the world to the news of the birth of Trudy's sextuplets, through a montage sequence that superimposes shots of typing hands with funny headlines such as "Canada Protests" and "'Possible But Not Probable,' Says Premier," or where the humor displays a distinctive wartime influence: "Nature Answers War," "Platoon Born in Midwest." A shot of Mussolini slamming his fist on a desk while screaming "Non è vero" dissolves into the headline "Mussolini Resigns. 'Enough is sufficiency,' Screams Il Duce," while the image of a very short Führer shouting at his tall henchmen is labeled: "Hitler Demands Recount."

Writing of the postmodern movie *Forrest Gump,* Steven D. Scott points out that:

> The treatment of history as a malleable story (one that accommodates Gump's appearance alongside George Wallace) is one of the more distinctive elements of the film; and it is, indeed, one of the points of postmodernism. If one theoretical position of postmodernism is that history is a narrative like any other, then a corollary is that that narrative can always be played with.[30]

Postmodern cinema will play extensively with this "malleability" of history, so much so that citational games and their extra-textual referents

Hitler (Bobby Watson) demands a recount of Norval's sextuplets in *The Miracle of Morgan's Creek*.

will become more important than the plot itself. From *Back to the Future* (1985) to *Who Framed Roger Rabbit*, from *Dead Men Don't Wear Plaid* to *Pleasantville*, playful interactions among different spatial, temporal, and media dimensions represent the main attraction for the audience.

As already noted, in order to decipher such contexts we need new "levels of spectatorial competence" based on an "active and indispensable participation" to the accumulation of information and memory games that the movie constructs.[31] It is exactly this kind of active participation that Sturges's gags about wartime require, for example, in *The Miracle of Morgan's Creek*.

Sturges's citational aesthetics, however, were not limited to the war period and its cultural references; the practice characterizes his entire career, involving more sophisticated forms of extra- and inter-textuality. *The Miracle of Morgan's Creek*, for example, features two secondary characters named Dan McGinty and "The Boss," who were already the leading characters in *The Great McGinty*. Not only does Sturges use the same two actors (respectively Brian Donlevy and Akim Tamiroff) to play the same two roles he had created four years before, but he also makes Dan McGinty a state governor, referring to a specific moment in the timeline of *The Great McGinty*'s plot (precisely between McGinty's appointment as a governor and his incarceration). The inter-textual bridge that Sturges casts between the two movies, therefore, becomes so specific and explicit that it breaks the compartmental closure typical of classical cinematic texts.[32]

More extensively, Sturges creates narratively relevant inter-textual connections in *The Sin of Harold Diddelbock*, his first independent movie after leaving Paramount in 1943. Entirely built on the recontextualization of Harold Lloyd's screen persona, his cinematic recognizability, and his previous characters and gags, *The Sin of Harold Diddelbock* includes a long silent sequence from Lloyd's *The Freshman*—the one where college student and water boy Harold "Speedy" Lambs is sent onto a football field to replace injured players and miraculously wins the game.

The sequence (dubbed with sound effects) is intertwined with new footage showing a man in the audience who is particularly excited over the play. When Harold wins the game, the newly shot footage takes over and shows the excited man in the changing rooms, giving Harold his card and promising him a job after graduation.

Similarly to postmodern movies such as *Forrest Gump* and *Zelig*, where fictional elements morph together with real facts and actual footage, *The Sin of Harold Diddlebock* throws us in the postmodern realm of "rereading and rewriting of things," that Cristina Degli-Esposti identifies as being at the roots of postmodern cinema.[33]

Again, Sturges' work of recontextualization is different from the classic usage of cinematic quotations. In contrast to Billy Wilder's usage of the silent movie *Queen Kelly* (1929) in *Sunset Blvd.* (1950), Sturges does not make of the extra-textual footage a fictional text-within-the-text (in *Sunset Blvd.* the clip from *Queen Kelly* is projected in Norma Desmond's private screening room as a movie made by the characters of *Sunset Blvd.*). Sturges, instead, appropriates the extra-textual silent clip with new audio-visual insertions, and he blends it seamlessly into his movie's narrative. *The Sin of Harold Diddlebock* smoothes and adjusts the difference between old and new footage, in order to make the alternation as even as possible, but it also expects that the audience recognize the playful aspect of this manipulative game. That is why the film opens with an expository title stating: "The football game you're about to see was actually photographed in 1923 as part of Harold Lloyd's picture *The Freshman*."

Cinematically, the result is similar to what Carl Reiner did in *Dead*

Men Don't Wear Plaid (where bits of classic films noir blend with new black-and-white footage to give birth to a new story) or to a postmodern movie such as *The Limey* (1999), where Wilson's (Terence Stamp) flashbacks are portrayed by resorting to footage from Ken Loach's *Poor Cow* (1967), featuring images of a young Terence Stamp.

Conceptually, the whole process is very similar to the one applied by postmodern British musician Gavin Bryars in his composition *Jesus' Blood Never Failed Me Yet* (1971), for which he used the audio clip of a homeless person singing a religious hymn, put it on loop, and built a brand new orchestral accompaniment around it. Like *The Sin of Harold Diddlebock*, Bryars's composition is based on the enclosure and modification of a previous text into a new original work, the appreciation of which relies mainly on the listener's knowledge of the creative process behind it. Bryars explains the whole process in the cover notes of his record, exactly as Sturges did in the opening credits of his movie.

Top: Postmodernism at work in *Forrest Gump*: Fictional elements (Forrest Gump, played by Tom Hanks) morph together with actual footage of Richard Nixon. *Bottom:* Postmodernism at work in *Zelig*: Fictional elements (Zelig, played by Woody Allen) morph together with footage of Adolf Hitler.

It is interesting to note that Sturges actually misdates his source: *The Freshman*, in fact, was not "photographed in 1923," as the opening credits mention, but in 1925. Nineteen twenty-three, however is the year of Lloyd's *Safety Last!*, another movie that Sturges indirectly refers to in the already-mentioned sequence with the lion on the ledge of a tall building. The inaccuracy assumes the aspect of a voluntary form of postmodern slip-up, as it is reconfirmed by another divergence involving the extra-textual relationship between Harold, the character (who tells a bartender that he was born in Nebraska in 1901), and Harold, the actor, who was actually born in Nebraska, but in 1893.

Meta-linguism

Since its early days, the Seventh Art has often showed a meta-linguistic tendency to spoof the rules and conventions behind the cinematic practice and its texts. Some of the simplest one-shot movies of early cinema already included stories about operators taking pictures or shooting movies, and silent directors such as Buster Keaton, Charlie Chaplin or King Vidor turned to cinematic self-reflections for their stories (*The Cameraman* [1928]; *Sherlock Jr.*; *Behind the Screen* [1916]; *Show People* [1928]).

Between these movies and the postmodern meta-reflections of Allen, Brooks, and Zemeckis (where characters interact with the "virtual" characters and environments from other movies, TV shows, and cartoons), there lies a group of classical Hollywood-on-Hollywood movies such as *Going Hollywood* (1933), *A Star Is Born* (1937 and 1954), *The Bad and the Beautiful* (1952), and *Singin' in the Rain* (1952), where the meta-linguistic aspect relies mainly on the make-it-in-the-business plot. Sturges's impulse to expose the rules of the game, however, goes beyond the conventions of this group, and it turns genre spoof and film-within-a-film situations into a much more serious threat to the classical invisibility of Hollywood storytelling.

The Beautiful Blonde from Bashful Bend, for example, contains many unsettling examples of "genre spoof" in a way that clearly anticipates more disruptive postmodern parodies (such as Mel Brooks' *Blazing Saddles*). In this pretty unusual western, with neither good nor bad characters and featuring a long shooting scene where no one gets hurt, Sturges exposes the structure of the western and overturns its main features: Freddie, the leading character, is a hot-tempered independent woman with a jealous heart and a passion for shooting (the movie opens on her old grandfather teaching the young girl to shoot at a line of cans). The woman's manipulative skills and shooting techniques ridicule men's abilities to obtain their goals. Throughout the movie, women appear to be better fighters, whether they are handling a gun or turning dishes and kitchen utensils into weapons, while men seem a caricature of the archetypical Western macho roles: the supreme male authority figure (the town's judge) is an unlucky fellow repeatedly shot in his rear, while the man who starts

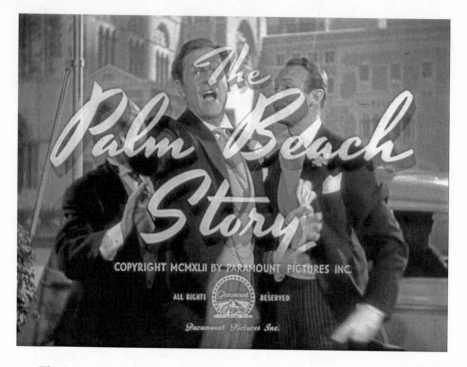

The Sturges Pastiche: opening sequence in the style of a 1940s movie trailer.

the final shooting ends up admitting that he has "plum forgotten" the reason.[34]

It has already been shown how *The Palm Beach Story* makes fun of Hollywood comedies, by contaminating stereotypes, structures, and mechanisms from all its subgenres. This meta-linguistic approach becomes overtly explicit in the opening and the ending of the movie — a frantic silent montage of typical screwball comedy actions and misunderstandings occurring to a couple, and leading to their final wedding. In less than three minutes, Sturges puts up not only an overt spoof of the genre to which the movie belongs, but he structures it in the style of a 1940s movie trailer, replacing the superimposed publicity slogans with the film's credits. This "coming attraction" montage ends on an ironic "and they lived happily ever after" card, followed by another one questioning: "Or did they?"

The ending of the movie will carry out such gag by presenting a new wedding involving the leading couple,[35] side by side with their twin brother and sister, who are getting married to the movie's secondary couple. Once again, a title card states "They lived happily ever after," but it is soon followed by the same question as at the beginning: "Or did they?" By connecting prologue and epilogue with such rhetorical repetition, Sturges exposes the *clichés* of the genre, by making fun of its method based on the repetition of events and situations, which can be recombined ad infinitum.

The whole film, with its exaggerated accumulation of misunderstandings and imbroglios pushed to the extreme, can be interpreted as a meta-linguistic essay on the schemes that govern the screwball comedy — so much so that the events and the meaning of the story almost become of secondary importance. That is why, when Gerry tries to explain how she and Tom got married in the first place (that is, the series of confusing events that we saw in the opening "trailer"), she dismisses the importance of such a narrative kernel by saying: "That was another plot entirely."[36]

In *The Good Fairy*, an early screenplay written for William Wyler, Sturges's meta-linguistic intentions are even more explicit. The narrative spring behind this classical comedy of misunderstandings is an episode that seems to anticipate by fifty years the sociological discourses on the dream factory that are indulged in by directors such as Federico Fellini and Woody Allen. Luisa is a poor orphan, hired by an eccentric movie theater manager as an usherette because all the professional ones end up flirting with customers and giving the theater a bad reputation. Once in the theater, Luisa becomes a sort of "primordial viewer" who gets so deeply enraptured with the magic of the silver screen that she forgets her duties and sits down among the audience. Sturges dedicates a consistent sequence to portraying different typologies of movie-goers — from a wholly absorbed viewer who interacts with the characters' lines, to a snoring spectator, to a father who decides to leave right in the middle of the film, while his son complains: "This isn't where we came in, papa."

In this sequence, foreshadowing similar situations portrayed in Fellini's *Roma* (1972) as well as in *Amarcord*, Sturges also lampoons the typical Hollywood melodramas (a genre to which he had himself previously contributed), by putting on the "internal" big screen a fake Hollywood drama, where a desperate woman is begging her lover for compassion.

As Diane Jacobs comments:

> On the screen, two lovers named Mitzi and Meredith are in the throes of a histrionic separation. "Go!" Meredith orders Mitzi, while Mitzi pleads, "Go? Oh, you don't mean that, Meredith!" "Go!" says Meredith. "Oh, you don't mean 'go,' Meredith! Reconsider...," says Mitzi. "Go!" says Meredith. "Meredith," says Mitzi. "Go!" suddenly chimes in a man watching the

Top: Luisa (Margaret Sullavan) imitating Mitzi's melodramatic pose in *The Good Fairy. Bottom:* Mitzi (June Clayworth) overacting in the film within *The Good Fairy.*

Portrayal of the movie-watching experience in *The Good Fairy*. Pictured: Luisa (Margaret Sullavan) and unidentified actor.

Cecilia (Mia Farrow) watching a film in *The Purple Rose of Cairo*.

Portrayal of the movie-watching experience in *The Good Fairy.*

movie, who Sturges now shows us in looming close-up. And after a few more "go's" from the screen, a family in the audience, whispering among themselves, begin unconsciously repeating the movie dialogue.[37]

It is not only "the idea that art can infiltrate life" as Jacobs points out, comparing this scene with the cartoon scene in *Sullivan's Travels*. More than a mere plot contrivance, the sequence in the movie theater represents a subtle and ironic reflection on both the textual and the communicational aspects of cinema. In fact, later on in the movie, when Luisa tries on a fancy "Foxine" stole in the changing room of a department store, Sturges captures her between two opposite mirrors, where she starts imitating Mitzi's attitude, poses, and lines from the movie she watched.

In this way, *The Good Fairy* anticipates the relationship between cinematic fiction and reality, screen and audience, celluloid dreams and shabby reality that Woody Allen amplifies in a postmodern movie such as *The Purple Rose of Cairo*. There, Cecilia, like Luisa, is a simple-minded woman living a hopeless life, fascinated by the charm of the silver screen that reveals to her the fantastic and inaccessible world of high-society eccentrics. Like Sturges's character, Allen's finds refuge in a movie theater, and draws inspiration from a funny parody of a 1930s movie. Allen, however, will push the film-within-a-film structure further, by having the screen character, Tom Baxter, step out of his movie and interact with Cecilia, while the other on-screen characters stop acting and begin conversing about the script, the reels, and the audience.

Sturges's Meta-movie

It is with *Sullivan's Travels* that Sturges elaborates his most explicitly meta-linguistic discourse on cinema. Set at the headquarters of the Hollywood dream factory, the movie tells the story of John Lloyd Sullivan, a successful director of comedies such as *Ants in Your Pants of 1939*, who feels uncomfortable with the lack of social and moral commitment in his work, and sets out to make a picture about human misery called *O Brother, Where Art Thou?* In order to research his characters' roles, he decides to dress like a hobo, to travel among the poor people and experience their suffering. After getting more than he bargains for (he loses his memory and ends up in a prison camp), Sullivan will turn his quest for socio-polit-ical aesthetics into a more "therapeutic" vision: Cinema needs to alleviate people's preoccupations and lighten their burden.

The movie starts as a film-within-a-film, with an action scene in which two men are fighting atop a moving train. When one of the two falls into the river, the words "The End" appear on the screen. At this point is revealed a screening room with a director and two producers who start talking about social, moral, and economic issues related to the movie(s). The meta-lin-guistic discussion that takes place immediately introduces *Sullivan's Trav-els* as a movie that reflects overtly on the contents and forms of the cinematic text, and opposes the view of an artistic director who wants to make a movie "that would realize the potentialities of film as the socio-logical and artistic medium that it is," to the view of a producer who would rather make another musical, a comedy, or a drama "with a little sex in it."[38]

Deceptive film-within-a-film openings had already appeared on the big screen in the 1930s, sometimes with ironic purposes (see, for exam-ple, the opening of Rouben Mamoulian's *The Gay Desperado* [1936] which starts as a gangster movie *a la Scarface* [1932] projected in a movie the-ater). What is different here is the context in which the opening film is placed: not a film theater, but a producer's screening room, not the place of cinematic fruition, but the command center that presides over the cre-ation of the cinematic text. By violating one of the most solid guidelines of Classical Hollywood Cinema (the invisibility of the storytelling process), Sturges turns the cinematic text into a meta-linguistic essay, and trans-forms the viewer's experience into a study of cinematic production.

In contrast to previous Hollywood-on-Hollywood movies such as *What Price Hollywood?* (1932) and *A Star Is Born*, where the meta-linguis-tic aspect relied mainly on a make-it-in-the-business plot and on back-stage dynamics, *Sullivan's Travels* states, from its opening sequence, a much broader range of intentions, bringing up issues related to cinematic fruition, such as the taste of the audience, its demands, and its control and manipulation through marketing plans based on formulas and gen-res.

According to the producers, only intellectuals would be interested in a social analysis of society, while women — the largest group of spectators—would certainly go for another musical, a romance or a drama "with a little sex in it." There is certainly an autobiographical element behind this conflict—one that relates to Sturges's difficulty in selling and directing *The Great McGinty* at Paramount, because of the movie's political subject. However, the resolution of such controversy unveils an approach that overcomes the traditional dichotomy of directors versus producers.

From its opening, *Sullivan's Travels* sets Sturges's film poetics as a conflict between two sociological ideas of cinema: the idea of movies as a socially conscious mirror of real life *versus* the idea of cinema as a form of escapism from real life (that is, *O Brother, Where Art Thou?* versus *Ants in Your Pants of 1939*). The monologue on which the movie closes seems to substantiate the victory of the latter over the former: "There's a lot to be said for making people laugh ... did you know that's all some people have? It isn't much ... but it's better than nothing in this cockeyed caravan..."[39]

However, it could be argued that *Sullivan's Travels* itself, with its peculiar concoction of comedy and drama, farce and sociological analysis, slapstick and politics, sets Sturges's interpretation apart from Sullivan's, in a more complex synthesis between the two initial conflicting positions.

Most critics have centered their examinations of the movie around this aspect, talking about a moral directed against comedy directors who ventured into new genres (Capra, Chaplin), or even as a forecast of Sturges's own fall and ruin. But Sturges only apparently rejects the idea of cinema as a means of social change,[40] as proved in the church scene, where convicts and devotees sit together in front of a Disney cartoon, united in a unique religious experience that cancels any moral and penal discrepancy—in the same way that the screening experience in *The Good Fairy* reset social and class disparities among the different members of the audience. As Jacobs points out, "The comic experience is—like religion for the faithful—a profound, if temporary release from suffering. It won't change the world, but it will make life more tolerable."[41]

Sturges does not limit his meta-linguistic discourse to the explicit statements placed at the beginning and the end of the screenplay. In fact, the whole movie is filled with all sorts of references to classical cinema: Capra and Lubitsch are verbally quoted by Sullivan himself, while explicit homages to the Keystone silent chases and to Chaplin's melodramatic comedies are disseminated all through the film. A parody of the Lubitsch touch can easily be recognized in the scenes with butlers and servants—

for example, when the butler tries to talk Sullivan out of dressing as a hobo, showing his socially conservative viewpoint, as was usually articulated in such Lubitsch's movies as *Angel* (1937) and *Ninotchka* (1939). Other examples include the phone call that the two servants make to the train station, to inquire how the hobos usually jump on a train, pretending to be two gentlemen at a club betting on the subject.

The movies directed by Sullivan bear titles that make fun of the typical slapstick comedies of the early 1930s (*Ants in Your Pants* and *Hey, Hey in the Hayloft*), while even funnier titles are given to the Hollywood melodramas that Sullivan is forced to watch, disguised as a hobo, in the local theater of a country town: The evening programs include titles such as *The Valley of the Shadow, The Buzzard of Berlin* and *Beyond These Tears.* Sturges even places himself in a Hitchcockian cameo: He plays the movie director on a set where The Girl is reading a newspaper that breaks the news that Sullivan is alive. But, above all, it is the spectacular chase with Sullivan trying to shake off the caravan of assistants and producers that represents the movie's ultimate meta-linguistic statement. When Sullivan decides to flee in a car driven by a young kid (an obvious homage to William A. Wellman's *Wild Boys of the Road*), Sturges creates a slapstick montage full of those "Keystone chases, bathing beauties, custard pie operas," that Sullivan had been complaining about with his producers at the beginning of the movie, and that becomes here a statement of Sturges's passion for silent cinema and of his poetics of style contamination.[42]

Sturges is able to make viewers aware of the fictional aspects of the movie, often through simple verbal jokes. For example, when the sergeant at the Beverly Hills police station asks Sullivan: "How does the girl fit into this picture?" Sullivan answers: "There's *always* a girl in the picture ... Haven't you ever been to the movies?"[43] At the prison camp, after the "Mr." sends Sullivan to a sweatbox, he orders the other convicts to go back to work, and adds: "What do you think this is, a vaudeville show?"[44] Later on, when Sullivan regains his memory he tells Trusty: "If ever a plot needed a twist, this one does."[45]

Long before *Sullivan's Travels*, Sturges had already written a completely meta-linguistic movie entitled *Song of Joy.* Conceived in 1935, and never produced, the movie was a bitter satire on the Hollywood star and studio systems, with the president of the "Apex Film Company" needing to put together a movie in order to exploit a star on temporary loan to the studio.

"Complete with shots of the extras' dressing rooms, of daily rushes and a production number of the sound stage," observes Diane Jacobs,

Sturges's Hitchcockian cameo in *Sullivan's Travels*: Preston Sturges watches Veronica Lake as The Girl.

"*Song of Joy*, for all its outrageousness, is very much a behind-the-scenes film about the process of film-making."[46] Jacobs emphasizes that it is also a movie about Hollywood egoism and its power struggles: "From Apex, to his screenwriter Jasper (whose "face with one single expression reflects all the grievance of the Writers Guild"), to the pompous foreign director, Vladimir, who brags that he "don't make no pictures vit' accents," all *Song of Joy*'s characters emerge as Hollywood types: absurd but wholly credible."[47]

In Jasper's intentions, the movie-within-a-movie tells the story of "phony producers luring innocent girls to Hollywood,"[48] in a game of Chinese boxes that predates by thirty years Federico Fellini's *8 1/2* (1963), in which a director who is suffering from a lack of inspiration decides to make a movie about a director who is going through the same crisis.

Internal and External Narrators

Whether overtly explicit, as in *Sullivan's Travels* and *Song of Joy*, or more indirectly, as in *The Palm Beach Story*, Sturges shows a recurrent interest in revealing the structures and mechanisms that Hollywood hides behind its texts. Sturges plays with the structure of the comedy, displays its nuts and bolts, unveils its mere skeleton to the public, to the point that many unrealistic situations make sense (or create laughs) only if compared to an imaginary catalogue of stereotypical cinematic situations. At the beginning of *Unfaithfully Yours*, for example, the characters of Sir Alfred and his wife Daphne are funny only because they act as highly stereotyped romantic characters from a Hollywood melodrama, while Daphne's sister Barbara mocks them with her husband, with an anticipation of the attitude of a detached, postmodern spectator who looks down on the clichés of classical cinema.

Unfaithfully Yours pushes Sturges's meta-linguistic reflections on narrative to the point of telling the story of three possible alternatives to the same story (an orchestra conductor's fantasy about his wife's betrayal). As a result, the movie is so focused on its meta-narrative aspect as to appear completely deprived of any real-life context — a characteristic that we can find in the postmodern cinema of Sergio Leone or Robert Zemeckis, where the referential context is no longer represented by real-life events, but by other movies.[49]

Unfaithfully Yours is a movie that stresses the distinction between what Gaudreault calls "mega-narrator" (that is, the sum of mechanisms that supersede the act of narration)[50] and the notion of internal narrators (characters or devices which assume the temporary and limited function of telling a story from their point of view). In *Citizen Kane* (1941), for example, the narrative is related by six different internal narrators, whose partial knowledge is exposed by a final camera movement which reveals the word "Rosebud" in a close-up of a burning sled, thereby also uncovering the presence of a mega-narrator. Likewise, in *Unfaithfully Yours*, Sir Alfred's daydreaming fantasies are only the partial hypotheses of an internal narrator, against which mega-narrator Preston Sturges will soon take over, by way of a final sequence proving that Sir Alfred's wife had actually never betrayed him.

That Sir Alfred's point of view is kept separate from the one of mega-narrator Sturges is also proved during the movie, when Sir Alfred has a fight with his wife and, in answer to her threat of going to the movies instead of his concert, he screams: "Culturally, that'll suit you better."[51]

Mega-narrator Sturges takes a distance from the internal narrator Sir Alfred by also introducing his character's fantasies with a camera movement that shifts from a medium shot of Sir Alfred conducting the orchestra to the pupil of his eye, literally entering Sir Alfred's optical and cognitive point of view. Sturges described this idea already in a 1933 draft: "We move closer to him until his face fills the whole screen. Closer yet until one eye fills the screen. Still closer 'til the pupil of his eye, infinitely magnified, turns the screen black. The music rises to a crescendo now. We

Entering Sir Alfred's (Rex Harrison) vision in *Unfaithfully Yours*.

FADE IN slowly on the living room [...]." The same thing happens in the next episode: "Again we pass into the interior of his mind and his thoughts return us to his apartment."[52]

Sturges's narrative, instead, starts on a long crane shot that moves close to the conductor's back, literally entering his body from behind, and dissolving into an airplane shot in which he is flying. However, not only do we not see the conductor's face, but also his hair looks shorter than Rex Harrison's in the rest of the movie, and when the camera reaches the back of the conductor, Preston Sturges's name appears in big letters as writer, director and producer. In other words, the opening of the movie seems to suggest that the conductor is not Sir Alfred, but a more symbolic representation of the mega-narrator, from whose mind the whole movie springs. In the original screenplay, Sturges himself describes the opening credits as a sequence, even numbering it as the first scene of the movie, and when he refers to the conductor he does not name him "Sir Alfred."

The opening credits of *Unfaithfully Yours* also push that "moderately self-conscious" narration that Bordwell identifies behind Hollywood's classic credit sequences,[53] to an "extremely" explicit narrative self-awareness. Better than any narratologic essay on narrative, Sturges makes us reflect on the existence of the invisible "narrative entity" concealed behind Classical Hollywood Cinema, and illustrates the difference between the director's supreme narrative power and the character's temporary one, as the difference between a creator and a simple conductor of someone else's symphony. The rest of the movie will confirm this interpretation, by showing that Sir Alfred's knowledge of the events is actually limited and incorrect. In other words, in *Unfaithfully Yours,* the meta-narrative reflection takes over the love-jealousy plot, and turns the gap between different points of view among characters, narrator and spectators into the real theme of the movie.

Sullivan's Movie

It has been pointed out that postmodernism is a practice that does not really have previous structural models, but only previous texts (sources) to be used in its own practice. (Degli-Esposti, in fact, explains, "Pastiche, quotation and cross-references are a way to compensate for postmodernism's lack of a history of its own."[54])

The fact that postmodern directors have regarded Sturges's cinema as a classic model, rather than a matrix of postmodern text composition, further reinforces such argument. In *The Ladykillers,* for example, the Coen

Recontextualizing Sullivan's experience: *O Brother, Where Art Thou?* is filled with "situations" that seem to spring directly out of Sullivan's experiences: When Everett, Pete, and Delmar try to jump on a train, they are ridiculed by a group of perplexed homeless, as happens to Sullivan and The Girl when they are labeled "amateurs" by a group of real hobos. *Opposite page top:* Tramps on a train in *O Brother, Where Art Thou? Opposite page middle:* Tramps on a train: Chick Collins and Jimmy Dundee in *Sullivan's Travels. Opposite page bottom:* Everett (George Clooney) in *O Brother, Where Art Thou? Above:* The Girl (Veronica Lake) and John Sullivan (Joel McCrea) in *Sullivan's Travels.*

Brothers quote and recontextualize a sequence from *Sullivan's Travels* in which the portrait of a dead husband changes his expression — a choice that clearly indicates an appropriation of Sturges's movie as a classic source.

However, in *O Brother, Where Art Thou?* (2000), the Coen Brothers' postmodern homage to *Sullivan's Travels* (and certainly one of the most interesting examples in the history of cinematic pastiche and the evolution of postmodern cinema), Sturges's movie is not only considered as a classic reference to play with, but it becomes the object of a complicated game of intertextual cross-references.

As the title suggests, the Coens' movie is supposed to be based on the

The screenplay for "O Brother, Where Art Thou?" as it appears at the end of *Sullivan's Travels.*

"virtual" screenplay that Sullivan wants to shoot, after having travelled in the world of desperate prisoners and homeless people. As we can see at the end of *Sullivan's Travels,* a script precisely called "O Brother, Where Art Thou" has been virtually written, but is discarded after Sullivan's dramatic experience convinces him that cinema's purpose is the relief of people's suffering through humor and comedy.

In *O Brother, Where Art Thou?* the Coens imagine what Sullivan's screenplay would have included, based on the experiences that he had gone through during his travels. In this way, while avoiding any direct quotation from Sturges's movie, they work on reconstructing the fictional screenplay ("O Brother, Where Art Thou?") that a fictional character (Sullivan) writes in a fiction movie (*Sullivan's Travels*). And they do so, not only by analyzing Sullivan's experience, but also by envisaging the artistic process through which he has to go, when recombining his life happenings into a text.

That is why *O Brother, Where Art Thou?* is filled with "situations" that seem to spring directly out of Sullivan's experiences: When Everett, Pete, and Delmar try to jump on a train, they are ridiculed by a group of perplexed homeless, as happened to Sullivan and The Girl when they were labeled "amateurs" by a group of real hoboes.

The young kid who rescues the three fugitives from the burning barn in *O Brother* is something that Sullivan would have included in his screenplay after having experienced the crazy driving of the 13-year-old boy in a sequence of *Sullivan's Travels*. Every sequence involving prisoners constantly reminds us of the final Sullivan's travel among convicts — see, for example, the scene in which the three fugitives hide in a movie theater.

The Coens' ability with postmodern pastiche lies in this recontextualization of Sullivan's experiences which give birth to "pale" references to *Sullivan's Travels*, instead of banal explicit quotations. *O Brother*, in fact, is neither the sociological project that Sullivan never realized, nor a remake of Sturges's movie, but a more complex cinematic text that goes beyond any consolidated schemata of postmodern pastiche. After all, the movie is filled with other "pale references" to all sorts of texts (the *Odyssey*, the social and political movies from the New Deal era, gangster cinema, and the Coen brothers' cinema itself).

Quotation, meta-linguism, pastiche, and remake are, here, moved to a totally new level, and — as the title suggests — Sturges's work is not treated as a classical source for postmodern games, but as a postmodern text-within-the-text.

Meta-television

> The strange thing about television is that it doesn't tell you everything. It shows you everything there is to know about life on earth. Yet the mysteries remain.
> Thomas Newton in *The Man Who Fell to Earth* (1976)

Among the most interesting examples of postmodern meta-language that Sturges offered in his career, lies one of the least studied aspects of his work: the series of television projects that he developed in the early 1950s, when his career as a Hollywood director was officially over.

As mentioned in chapter one, Sturges's interest in the new medium was partly due to the necessity of reinventing himself and finding new sources of income, and partly the result of aesthetic considerations on the creative possibilities offered by the small screen. As Sandy Sturges recalls, Preston thought that television "was a fantastic invention, just

Top: Recontextualizing Sullivan's experience in *O Brother, Where Art Thou?*: Boy Hogwallop (Quinn Gasaway), the young driver. *Bottom:* Sullivan's experience in *Sullivan's Travels*: Bud (Robert Winkler), the young driver.

incredible.... He thought that ... it might be a powerful force in the world."[55]

In an unpublished letter to John Hertz, dated 1951, Sturges recounts how he discovered the creative and comic potential of the new medium in these terms:

Top: Sullivan's experience in *Sullivan's Travels:* convict John Sullivan (Joel McCrea) in a movie theater. *Bottom:* Recontextualizing Sullivan's experience in *O Brother, Where Art Thou?:* Convict Pete (John Turturro) in a movie theater.

About a year and a half ago I was in a store that sells television sets. I saw two things ... and I saw the light. The first thing I saw was the hair on the back of a man's hand. He was giving a drawing lesson. The second thing was a panning shot across some dress models, winding up on the cloak-and-suiter himself, who didn't know he was in the shot and was scratching his pants.... I hurried out of the shop knowing that I could tell any story on television.[56]

As twenty years earlier, when he approached cinema as a young screenwriter, technical aspects and difficulties of the new medium did not seem to bother him at all:

> I knew all about the screen size arguments already, because Karl Freund had taught me seventeen years ago that motion picture film need be sharp enough only to stand a 2.5 enlargement, i.e., a blowup 1⅞ inches, because that is the size of the average motion picture screen if measured between the fingers at reading distance: fourteen inches. In other words a television screen approximately two inches high, fourteen inches from the eyes, is the same size as the screen in the Rivoli theater from an average seat.[57]

In a way, Sturges's fascination with television shows the influence of a cinematic mind:

> I continued to think about television ... and all at once, the other night, a lot of thoughts came together and jelled: a film format I invented twenty years ago, a lot of ways to cut cost, some beliefs about keeping up quality and dignity, my opinions about proper pace, and a lot of other things. I knew that I had found one of the things I was looking for: a continuing show of the finest dramatic quality, designed exclusively for television, that would never run out of material or, for that matter, have the slightest difficulty in finding it, that would take all of my time and could also, quite easily, pay me a satisfactory wage.[58]

The "format" that Sturges refers to is the one that he had developed a few months earlier in a project called *The Show* — later referred to as *The Preston Sturges Show* and *The Preston Sturges Stories*. The teleplay, complete with dialogue and detailed camera movements, is very similar to a Hollywood screenplay, and highly cinematic in its layout. Its contents, however, focus almost entirely on television aesthetics. Sturges, in fact, had designed the pilot in the form of a show-about-a-show, set at his restaurant-theater the Players, where the camera would record not only the actions on stage, but also the audience's reactions and behind-the-scenes inconveniences, in order to provide an inside look at the mechanisms of TV production and broadcast. (See detailed excerpts in Appendix C.)

The teleplay begins with Sturges' description:

> The show would start with a drawing of the exterior of the Players at night. Activity in the form of shadows would be seen past the windows and out of these same windows would come music and laughter. As many times as required we would push into a close shot of a door which, opening magically, would reveal a necessary credit. We now dissolve to a cue of people presenting tickets at the door. A saturnine gentleman of fifty is taking the tickets.... Now a man in uniform taps the saturnine gentleman on the shoulder and

says, "All ready with the show, Mr. S." "How is it going to be," says Mr. S. "Terrific," says the man in uniform...

DISSOLVE TO trademark on the main curtain. CAMERA number 2.
We hear very lovely music ... and the camera pans down to the back of the orchestra leader...

CUT TO CAMERA number 1
The apron behind the curtain ... Mr. S. appears from the stage door, rather nervously checks the props on his desk, still more nervously consults his watch.... [He] goes to the curtain of the small proscenium six feet behind the first proscenium and sticks his head through the curtain.

CUT TO CAMERA number 3
This catches Mr. S.'s head sticking through the curtains. Nervously he says, "All ready?" CAMERA pans to the can-can girls dressing and making up at a wheeled dressing table. One of the girls says, "We're always ready ... you know that ... like the Marine Corps ... Semper Fidelis."

Sturges does not limit his meta-linguistic approach to this "educational" unveiling of the mechanisms of *mise-en-scène* and broadcast. The aesthetic reflection on the medium is expanded further when the "real" show starts, and Sturges in person jumps on stage to address his televiewers:

That's right, thank you very much, Herman. We will take as our text for tonight: Television! What is it? Do we like it? Will it endure? To tackle first things first: until such time as a successful method is devised enabling the viewers of television and other air shows to pay directly for what they receive ... as you pay for a bushel of corn or even for a television set ... the indirect form of payment will continue and you will pay ... as you are paying now ... through the nose...

In perfect Sturgesian style, the meta-linguistic approach is functional in its comic effect, and becomes the occasion for a parody of the production system, its rules and requirements, very similar to that of *Sullivan's Travels*. For example, when three announcers interrupt the show for "a few well chosen words from our sponsor without whom this marvelous show would never reach you," a fourth announcer hurries on stage with the following "advice":

The top of the evening to you, ladies and gentlemen ... I bring you greetings from REXLAXO, Nature's relaxant ... spelled R-E-X-L-A-X-O.... Do you suffer from gas? Bilious attacks ... dizziness ... flatulence ... flat feet ... obesity ... back ache ... front ache.... You don't have to ... Merely dissolve six big, fat REXLAXO ... tablets in a quart of hot spring water and toss it off! *Then* see how you feel! Hear the words of pretty little Mrs. Amandine L. DeBosquet of 369 Genessee Street, Purple City, Nebraska....

Mrs. DeBosquet then enters with an "unsolicited testimonial": she drops the tube of REXLAXO into her wash and the clothes "come out whiter than they ever done before."

The extensive usage of meta-linguistic jokes and overt discussions over the conventions of the TV medium is certainly one of the main reasons the show was never produced. Executives and investors drawn to new forms of media in their early stages of development have always looked with suspicion at the meta-linguistic approach — as the unveiling of the medium's language and its rules runs counter to the audience's fundamental need to enjoy the text without critical involvement. Besides, as with photography and cinema, it would take the distance of decades before television could begin looking, and laughing, at itself.

It is hardly surprising that the ideas behind Sturges's futuristic pilot would not find their full realization until 1992, when postmodern director David Lynch wrote and directed a TV series very similar to *The Preston Sturges Show*. The program, entitled *On the Air*, is a situation comedy set in a 1950s TV studio where the Zoblotnick Broadcasting Company (ZBC) produces a live TV variety program called *The Lester Guy Show*. The show-within-the-show turns out to be an unqualified catastrophe for all involved, causing professional grief and mental suffering to actors, directors and producers alike. As in Sturges's meta-show, the television commercials utterly fail to prove the quality of the advertised products, and the cameramen's mistakes bring unexpected events to the televiewers in a hilarious cascade of blunders. Given its vantage point, Lynch's television series could afford to play extensively with the retro values of the 1950s era and deploy a pastiche of different TV styles. But the conceptual premise behind the show and its similarities with *The Preston Sturges Show* confirm the degree to which Sturges's ideas were ahead of their times.

Other Sturges TV projects ranged from this kind of experimental meta-show to more "classical" programs, such as a series of televised plays which had not been performed on the stage for some time or "panel shows," like the one he envisioned for *They Still Live*:

> A panel show, based upon the thoroughly logical but seldom thought of fact that our lives are ruled by those who went before us ... in other words, by the dead. The name of the show stems from the theory then that since these men still rule us and their words and philosophies and laws are part of our everyday life, in a sense, THEY STILL LIVE.
>
> ...Thus a man might be executed today for the violation of a law originating in the Code Napoleon, adopted by the thirty-eighth Congress, ratified by the then Senate, upheld by Supreme Court Justice, Oliver Wendell Holmes (I may be a little off on my dates) and signed by Abraham Lincoln. He might

have been unsuccessfully defended by quotations from Blackstone, cases of long defunct personages would have been mentioned at the trial and the prayer what might have been said over his body was probably written two thousand years ago.[59]

Whether about theater, philosophy, history, or television itself, all Preston's ideas for television shared a similar educational goal. *Station F.A.T.E.,* for example, focused on the mechanisms and contradictions of change and destiny, while *It Happened Exactly Here* provided an approach to history through a connection with everyday life. As Sandy Sturges described it:

> You go to a particular part of the sidewalk in Paris, and that's exactly where Joan of Arc was burnt at the stake....[60] A comparison between what it looks like now and what it must have looked like then, and what happened there.... Very interesting because, of course you walk the streets and the last thing you're thinking about is Joan of Arc.[61]

That these projects did not exactly match the light and frivolous kind of entertainment that most TV shows were offering at the time was obvious to Sturges himself. Most of his treatments, in fact, bear notes such as "to end the show in a lighter vein...,"[62] or "after this depressing preamble I hasten to state that the show itself would be quite gay."[63]

The reasons that all these projects remained unproduced, however, have more to do with their futuristic conception of TV entertainment than with their serious didacticism: If *The Preston Sturges Show* anticipates David Lynch's meta–TV shows, *It Happened Exactly Here* predicts a "pop" approach to history based on simple dramatization which is now fully adopted by The History Channel, while *You Be Witness,*[64] a live trial featuring direct interaction with the televiewers, clearly paves the way for the ideas behind reality shows and court shows.

In a primordial phase of television like the early 1950s, when studio executives were working on defining its essence and shaping its genres (news, quiz shows, TV series), a man like Preston Sturges might as well have been seen as a man who fell to earth from another planet. Besides, Sturges's extravagant "cinematic" approach certainly did not help in the task of attracting sponsors or investors. His expensive productions, featuring fifteen set changes in one show, were exactly the opposite of the "classical" television model based on static visuals, in which movement was provided neither by varying settings, nor by virtuoso camerawork, but by a simple alternation of multiple cameras capturing long shots, medium shots, and close-ups simultaneously. Sturges's television was light years ahead of all this.

Questioning the Internal Narrator:
Sturges and the Mise-en-scène
of Classic Cinema's Narrative Functions

The same interest that Sturges shows in the display of the mechanisms of storytelling that are usually hidden in a classic TV show appears
also in his cinematic work and its relationship with Classical Hollywood
Cinema. While dealing with standardized genres, narrative structures and
techniques, in fact, Sturges always found a way to expose the mechanisms
hidden behind the invisibility of classical storytelling. In *Christmas in
July*, for example, when a black cat crosses Jimmy's path, Ellen asks a jan-
itor if that is a sign of good or bad luck. The man answers: "It depends
on what happens afterwards"[65] — a subtle and indirect way of commenting on the condition in which the characters of the movie (and of any
Classical Hollywood comedy) are confined. The movie, in fact, is structured around a typical game of misunderstandings, in which gags arise
from the gap between the characters' wrong interpretation of the events,
and the spectator's full knowledge of the context. Immersed in a world of
signs and situations they cannot decipher correctly, the characters of *Christmas in July* suffer from a "classical Hollywood" condition that Sturges
exposes.[66]

During his work in Hollywood, moreover, Sturges did not simply
limit himself to displaying the mechanisms behind the classical text, but
he often assigned his characters relevant narrative functions as well.

Film theorists and narratologists have often insisted on the ability of
the cinematic text to display its own narrative agents, by having characters implicitly acting as narrators or narratees. *Citizen Kane*, for example,
has often been quoted as the perfect example of such games, due to the
presence of characters such as Thompson, the journalist who represents
the implicit spectator — the addressee of an act of communication whose
addressers are the characters (implicit narrators) he interviews.

Sturges uses the same pattern in movies in which the narrative structure centers on a character recollecting events from the past, with another
character acting as a listener. Often, he even challenges such role play, and
makes the spectator reflect on the partiality of the Hollywood storytelling
process and its agents, by having the narratee question the truthfulness of
the narrator.

In *The Power and the Glory*, for example, Henry's flashbacks are constantly put to the test by his wife, whose skeptical and prejudicial interpretation of the events at the heart of the film makes her a particularly "active" kind of narratee. In this way, it is not only the classic narration that is challenged, but also the notion of the Hollywood spectator as a passive onlooker. In Sturges's hands, the spectator becomes a much more active figure in textual communication. While Henry tells his wife the story of the life of Tom, she does not act as a simple listener, but as an interpreter who first matches Henry's recollections against her own interpretative schemes, and then contradicts them. In Henry's words, Tom was an "honest man" pushed to ambition by his first wife, and brought to ruin by his second one. Henry's wife, instead, paints a totally different picture, apparently based on gossip and hearsay: In this view, Tom was "a good-for-nothing," a murderer, a cheater who did not deserve a better life.[67]

Henry's rejection of this view sounds like a warning directed against simplistic readings. Similar to Thompson's comments on Rosebud ("It wouldn't have explained anything. I don't think any word can explain a man's life"[68]), Henry's admonition sounds as indisputable as the "no trespassing" sign placed on the fence of Charles Foster Kane's estate: "You can't judge him by ordinary standards. They wouldn't fit him. He was too ... too big."[69] The interpretative skills of Henry's wife, however, are more complex than they appear. On the one hand, she seems to rely on those "schemata" and "mental sets" that — as Gombrich explains — the classical reader uses to formulate hypotheses on the text, based on expectation and probability.[70] On the other hand, unlike someone who is simply a "passive onlooker," Henry's wife proves to be a more attentive interpreter, as the last sequence in the movie (absent in the screenplay) shows her benevolently putting her hand on Henry's shoulder, as a sign of agreement and re-consideration of her first hypothesis.

These and other hermeneutical issues become even more explicit in *The Great McGinty*, in which Sturges doubles the figure of the implicit spectator into two narratees: a nameless Dancing Girl and a customer with suicidal tendencies named Tommy Thompson, who listen to the narration of the bartender, Dan McGinty.

In the long opening sequence that precedes the first flashback, Sturges gives more importance to the character who will become the narratee (the sequence focuses on Tommy and his attempt to commit suicide), making it difficult for the audience to anticipate which of the two will tell his narrative and become the protagonist. Even the opening credits place the two characters on the same level by stating, "This is the story of two men who met in a banana republic. One of them was honest all his life except one crazy minute. The other was dishonest all his life except one crazy minute. They both had to get out of the country."[71]

The Great McGinty, even more than *The Power and the Glory*, challenges the trust that the audience of a classical Hollywood movie usually places in its storyteller. Towards the end of the movie, in fact, one of the narratees (the Dancing Girl) will accuse McGinty of being "a big liar ... about the whole thing." McGinty replies (even more ambiguously), "Okay, sister, you have it your way," and then asks the other narratee (Tommy, the paying customer) to be paid for the drinks he served, "as though demanding payment for his story/film."[72]

The movie ends with an unexpected shift towards a moment of "zero focalization," where the external narrator Sturges relieves the internal narrator McGinty from his task, and unveils for us, in the framing story, the presence of the main characters who populated McGinty's narrative. But such reassurance over the truthfulness of McGinty's recount is only briefly apparent: Far from being sustained, the honesty of the internal narrator is left shadowy, as such characters could simply represent the source material on which McGinty built up his fictional tale. Far from Hollywood's narrative closure, such an ending is much closer to the "open finale" of a postmodern movie such as Tim Burton's *Big Fish* (2003), in which the truth behind the absurd stories of a very imaginative storyteller remains questionable even if his fictional characters unexpectedly show up at his funeral.

A similar attempt to question the classical spectator's faith in the internal narrator is carried out in *Triumph Over Pain*, Sturges's original script for a movie that was re-edited and released by Paramount as *The Great Moment*. In the script (and in the original cut), Sturges had created a complex non-chronological flashback structure that shifted back and forth between flashback and framing story, with Lizzie Morton and Eben Frost taking turns both as narrator and narratee.

Sturges uses both cinematic flashbacks and verbal recollections (Lizzie's recount of Morton's death, for example) and he has Lizzie and Eben shift position right in the middle of their narratives. In sequence D, for example, Eben recollects a parade in Morton's honor, and the flashback shows him walking with Morton from the parade to the mansion where Morton lives, where he says goodbye. Morton and Lizzie are then shown in their bedroom, suggesting that the narrative voice has obviously passed from Eben to Lizzie. Also, in both the script and the first cut, Sturges gives space to a third narratee figure, the more "passive" kind of spectator represented by Betty Morton, Lizzie's little daughter, who listens to part of the story distractedly.

The movie's final release cut out not only most of the dialogue and framing sequences between Lizzie and Eben, but it also put off the introduction of the character of Betty until a later point in the movie.[73]

Sturges's desire to overcome the strict boundaries of the classical flashback structure is also demonstrated by the fact that, in the original script and in the first cut, Lizzie states that she has been asked to write an article about Morton for a magazine, and Eben starts reading her draft. In other words, all the flashbacks that take place coincide with the article that Lizzie has written, and we witness them filtered through Eben's "reading."

Sturges's assignment of narrative functions to his characters surfaces also in movies that do not rely on the flashback structure. A typically classic comedy such as *The Lady Eve*, which is entirely based on conventions of double and mistaken identity derived from both Classical Hollywood Cinema and classical theater, betrays an attempt to reflect explicitly on the mechanisms of narration, and to make of its main character an extraordinary example of an implied narrator. In fact, Jean Harrington and Lady Eve Sidwich (the two characters interpreted by Barbara Stanwyck) are not only able to manipulate naïve Charles Pike and to con him into believing anything they want, but their decisions and actions become the spring of almost every narrative kernel in the story.

Classical Hollywood narratives seldom gave such supreme narrative powers to their characters (let alone women). In *The Lady Eve*, instead, the female character is given the faculty to see, tell and change most of the plot events: It is Jean who trips up Charles, making him fall to the floor, in order to grab his attention; her verbal skills drag him to her cabin; her games of seduction have him fall in love with her and eventually propose; and the apple she drops from the ship's deck onto Charles' head, at the beginning of the film, clearly establishes her "narrative" competences.

Jean is aware of such powers when she says: "If you waited for a man to propose to you from natural causes, you'd die of old maidenhood. That's why I let you try my slippers on ... and then I made you put your arms around me and hold me tight."[74]

And when an unexpected chance event, such as Charles's discovery of Jean's true identity, seems to threaten her narrative powers, she manages to regain control by conning Charles into believing that she has had many lovers, and thus manipulating him into leaving her. This will allow her to resurrect herself as a new narrator-character (Lady Eve), and begin her manipulative games all over again. As a perfect narrator, Jean/Lady Eve teaches her narratee Charles the most important lesson in text interpretation:

> [You] cannot acknowledge that passion may have a past of flesh and blood; very well, I'll show you the reality of your ideal; I'll give you a new perspective in Connecticut [...] I'll give you something you will feel compelled to believe; you thought you believed the worst about me before, here is something you will find worse.[75]

Beside Jean's extraordinary cognitive competence, Sturges also bestowed upon her extraordinary visual faculties (often referred to as ocularization) which are quite unusual for a female in a classic Hollywood movie. The sequence in which Jean meets Charles in the ship's dining room begins with Jean observing, through her purse mirror, other women trying to catch Charles's attention. When Charles does not pick up a handkerchief that a corpulent girl drops on the floor, Jean begins to describe, comment, and even anticipate the events that we see reflected in her mirror:

> The dropped kerchief! That hasn't been used since Lily Langtry ... you'll have to pick it up yourself, madam ... it's a shame, but he doesn't care for the flesh, he'll never see it. [...] That's right ... pick it up ... it was worth trying anyway, wasn't it? ... Look at the girl over to his left ... look over to his left, look over to your left, bookworm ... there's a girl pining for you ... a little further just a little further. *There!* Now wasn't that worth looking for? See those nice store teeth, all beaming at you. Why, she recognizes you! She's up ... she's down, she can't make up her mind, she's up again! She recognizes you! She's coming over to speak to you. The suspense is killing me. "Why, for heaven's sake, aren't you [the] Fuzzy Oathammer I went to manual training school with in Louisville? Oh, you're not? Well, you certainly look exactly like him ... it's certainly a remarkable resemblance, but if you're not going to ask me to sit down I suppose you're not going to ask me to sit down ... I'm very sorry. I certainly hope I haven't caused you any embarrassment, you so-and-so," so here goes back to the table. Imagine thinking she could get away with anything like that with me ... I wonder if my tie's on straight ... I certainly upset them, don't I? Now who else is after me? Ah! The lady champion wrestler, wouldn't she make an armful.... Oh, you don't like her either.... Well, what are you going to do about it....[76]

Jean's position in this long voice-over narrative shifts effortlessly from external observations to a Joyce-like "stream of consciousness" that assumes all the functions and the possible grades of focalization a narrator is normally asked to assume.

The mirror she holds in her fingers does not simply reflect what is happening in the background, it becomes a screen-within-a-screen that selects, pans across, tracks, and magnifies the narrative space, with the same powers of selection and ubiquity as a camera. Jean even dubs the dialogue that Charles and a girl are having, in a way that only the voice-over narrator in *The Power and the Glory* could do.

Charles, on the other hand, represents an extremely passive kind of narratee. From the moment Jean sets eyes on him, he becomes "her" character, completely trapped into that fictional, mirrored world that she selects and manipulates. Reduced to the stereotype of the naïve and gullible character that Henry Fonda played in so many movies (and that Sturges seems to parody by having Jean's father define him as "a fine specimen of the sucker sapiens"[77]), Charles represents the ultimate "passive" spectator: a viewer always happy to fall for the fictional tale of a narrator; a participant eager to activate the so-called suspension of disbelief, in order to enjoy the spectacle created by the *grand imagier*. In fact, when at the end of the movie he meets Jean again, he runs to embrace her and kiss her as if nothing has happened, without looking for any kind of explanation, like a spectator who runs back to the movie theater to enjoy, once again, a fictional act, and who has to pretend to believe it, in order to enjoy it again. When Jean points out that he "still" does not understand, Charles answers: "I don't want to understand ... I don't want to know.... Whatever it is, keep it to yourself.... All I know is that I adore you, that I'll never leave you again."[78]

4

Time Representation

Many film scholars have seen what Frederic Jameson terms "a peculiar way with time" as characteristic of the postmodern outlook.[1] Yet such manipulations of time did not begin with *Twelve Monkeys* (1995), *Memento* (2000), *21 Grams* (2003), or other films often seen as "postmodern," and not even with the modernist experiments of *Hiroshima Mon Amour* (1959), *L'Année dernière à Marienbad* (*Last Year in Marienbad*) (1961) or *Pierrot le fou* (1965). In some of Sturges's earliest films, such as *The Power and the Glory*, as well as in later works such as *Unfaithfully Yours*, his interest in the exploration of the narrative mechanisms produced anticipatory results.

As discussed in the previous chapter, Sturges's narratives rely greatly on the usage of classical flashback structures, based on the recollections of characters-narrators. A typical characteristic of narrative cinema, the flashback is the filmic translation of the literary "analepsis"—a narrative mechanism that fills in narrative gaps and ellipses. From *Das Kabinett des Doktor Caligari* (*The Cabinet of Dr. Caligari* [1919])—where the main narrative unexpectedly turns out to have been a flashback—to Alain Resnais's *L'Année dernière à Marienbad*, where main and framing stories are mixed up in a continuous overlapping of present recollection and past events, narrative cinema has demonstrated a stronger interest in the analepsis, leaving the prolepsis (or flash-forward) to a few isolated movies and situations. In Classical Hollywood Cinema, analepses are mainly based on the standardized "recollection model," which keeps the present tense of the framing story separate from the present tense used to portray the events remembered. From *Citizen Kane* to *Sunset Blvd.*, from *How Green Was My Valley* (1941) to *All About Eve* (1950), Hollywood disguised the anachronisms produced by the flashbacks in the form of perfectly chronological narratives interrupted by brief returns to the framing story.

What sets Sturges's movies apart from this Classical model is the peculiar disposition of the flashbacks in non-chronological terms. In *The Power and the Glory*, for example, the biography of self-made man Tom Garner is divided into three narrative blocks that coincide with the main stages of Tom's life and career. Since the story unfolds through the recollections of Henry (a character with the functions of an internal narrator), the events are all mixed up, contravening the linearity and continuity of classical editing and narrative, so as to reproduce the mechanisms of memory sifting through the past. From a first flashback showing Henry and Tom playing together as children, the film moves to another one showing Tom discussing his business strategies, and working with Henry, who has now become his secretary. Then we shift back to the chance encounter between Tom and his wife-to-be Sally, followed by their courtship and marriage, to go forward again to the moment when Tom buys the Santa Clara railroad, meets his lover Eve, and begins fighting with his son. Henry's tale and his voice-over will keep shifting between recollections of Tom's and Sally's life as newlyweds, and the love story between Tom and Eve, until the moment when Sally commits suicide. At that point, we move back to the beginning of Tom's career and the birth of his first baby, and then forward again to the events that will lead to Tom's death — in a way that reminds us more of Edith Piaf's postmodern biopic *La môme* (*La vie en Rose*) (2007) than the classic recollection of the life and career of an opera singer such as *Maytime* (1937).

If, in the Classical Hollywood Cinema, the flashback is "the only permissible manipulation of story order"[2] (a concept against which the new waves of the Sixties would react with highly disruptive, non-chronological representations of time[3]), Sturges's experiment falls somewhere in between classicism and modernism. On the one hand, he makes the most of the classic confinement of recollections within a well-defined framing story; on the other hand, he challenges Hollywood's prohibition on overt manipulations of the story order. As usual, in Sturges, such choice has nothing to do with subverting and exposing the conventions of classical cinema (as modernist directors such as Godard or Resnais did), but is dictated by the need to find more adequate tools to express concepts otherwise difficult to convey through the strict rules of the classical paradigm.

Sturges himself claimed that the peculiar structure of *The Power and the Glory* was chosen because he noticed that "when Eleanor[4] would recount adventures, the lack of chronology interfered not at all with one's pleasure in the stories and that, in fact, its absence often sharpened the impact of the tale."[5]

Sturges's management of timelines and chronology is extremely prophetic also in terms of cinematic enunciation. In *The Miracle of Morgan's Creek* and *The Great Moment*, the passage from the framing story to the flashbacks is obtained through an unusual series of very quick dissolves. Classical Hollywood Cinema (and earlier Sturges movies as well) traditionally indicated such passages with much more distinctive enunciation marks, in order to render the time-shifting as clear as possible. Usually introduced by close-ups of characters looking off-screen, the entrance into the flashback was followed by optical devices such as blurs, masks, or long dissolves, and accompanied by evocative crescendos of music. "Classical cinema," observes Brian Henderson, "reacts to a tense shift as though to a cataclysm; the viewer must be warned at every level of cinematic expression, in sounds, in images, and in written language, lest he/she be disoriented."[6] American cinema retained such practices throughout the Forties — that is, until the audiences began familiarizing themselves with the more economic editing of the European "New Waves," which would slowly bring Hollywood to trim down its tense-shifting rhetoric.

Sturges's management of time structures and their enunciative marks differs once again from the standard Hollywood practice, and it shows a certain resemblance to non–Hollywood experiments in storytelling. In this sense, Sturges's first version of *Triumph Over Pain* is a perfect case study. As mentioned before, the movie underwent several changes and cuts, until its official release as *The Great Moment*. According to Sturges's biographers, Paramount feared the audience's rejection of what appeared to be an unappealing subject at that time: a recounting of the experiments that led Dr. William Morton to the discovery of anesthesia.[7]

However, a comparison between Paramount's release (the only version that has survived) and Sturges's original script shows how the studio's re-editing was mainly intended to "correct" the non-chronological order of flashbacks, in order to normalize the narrative structure.

As David Bordwell points out, "The classical film normally shows story events in a 1–2–3 order," even when they are given as flashbacks in a framing story. "Advance notice of the future," he observes, "is especially forbidden, since a flash-*forward* would make the narration's omniscience and suppressiveness overt."[8] Even if Sturges's original script does not really utilize flash-forwards, it begins with two non-diegetic sequences set in contemporary times. In the first one, set on a battlefield, a voice-over points out the contradictory characteristics of Homo Sapiens, who "has stoned, crucified, burned at the stake" doctors and scientists "who consecrated their lives to his further comfort and well being," while he has erected monuments and memorial statues "to the eternal glory of generals on horseback, tyrants, usurpers, dictators, politicians and other heroes who led him, usually from the rear, to dismemberment and death."[9]

This clear pedagogic intent is carried on in the second sequence, featuring a present-day operation where a little boy is reassured by his parents, "Of course it isn't going to hurt!"[10] The narration then moves to the moment where Lizzie (Morton's wife) and Frost (Morton's friend) meet and remember earlier events. Lizzie starts with a verbal recollection of the last moments of Morton's life, his subsequent death, and the reactions of the newspapers. Then she jumps back to the brief moment of success, when Dr. Morton was hailed as a great discoverer. The narrative continues on the long descending phase leading to Morton's death, then returns to the beginning of his career, his studies, his meeting with Lizzie, his first experiments and legal battles, until the moment where he decides to give up the secret of its formula to spare a suffering girl the pain of her operation.

Sturges explained the reason for this peculiar order of events as follows:

> I believe a biographer has two obligations: He must be true to his subject and he must not bore his public. Since ... he cannot change the chronology of events, he can only change the order of their presentation. Dr. Morton's life, as lived, was a very bad piece of dramatic construction. He had a few months of excitement, ending in triumph and twenty years of disillusionment, boredom and, increasingly bitterness.[11]

The studio version removed the two non-diegetic sequences and abridged the first part of the movie describing the last events in Morton's life, so that the classical chronological flashback could start as soon as possible, as was customary in the most traditional Hollywood biopics.

That Sturges intended to stay clear of this kind of biographical flashback is made explicit in a letter he wrote to one of his viewers, in which he rejects the "Pasteur manner" (referring to a William Dieterle movie of 1935), "where every character knows already his place in History and acts as if carved in marble."[12] Sturges, instead, intended to show not only the ambiguities behind Dr. Morton's achievements, but also the difficulties behind their posthumous interpretation, as underlined by Lizzie early in the framing story when, talking about the doctors who claimed to have invented anesthesia, she admits: "Maybe they all *did* discover the use of ether before him."[13]

Sturges's characters are often dropped into narratives that question the objectivity of their recollections and mechanisms. This interest in the reproduction of the mechanisms of memory, its subjectivity and its flaws, is as far from the Hollywood "present tense" representation of the past as it is close to a postmodern sensibility. In this sense, the usage of framing stories as moments of reflection on the mechanisms of storytelling are also an occasion to reflect on the subjectivity of memory, and the gap between the real past and the recollected one. The result, in a way, is very similar to that of *Distant Voices, Still Lives* (1988) and *The Neon Bible* (1995) by British filmmaker Terence Davies, in which a pastiche of nostalgic recollections, evanescent images, and popular songs are arranged into a series of loosely connected episodes, with the ultimate goal of portraying of the act of remembering, instead of the events remembered.

Sturges's fragmentation of the classical linear flashback moves in a similar direction, as it ends up questioning the mechanisms of memory with highly disruptive results for the Hollywood narrative.

The studios' preoccupation with Sturges's manipulations of time seems to be at the roots of another sensational cut: the elimination of a long flashback sequence included in the original script for *Unfaithfully Yours*. It has already been noted that this movie is organized into three hypothetical narratives, all taking place in Sir Alfred's mind, which sifts back and forth between the present and an unusual kind of "future possible." One of the three fantasy sequences originally incorporated a flashback about Sir Alfred's first meeting with his wife-to-be, Daphne, at a charity concert in Michigan. The episode — usually referred to as "The Porthaul Story"— recurred at least three times: first as a verbal analepsis, in a conversation between Sir Alfred and Daphne,[14] then in a drafted dialogue between Sir Alfred and his brother-in-law,[15] and finally as a real flashback inside the second hypothetical narrative[16]— the one wherein Sir Alfred imagines his wife admitting her betrayal, and writes her a check to set her free. Fearing that an excessively complicated timeline would jeopardize the easy comprehension of these events, producer Darryl F. Zanuck decided to cut it, making the second fantasy sequence the shortest (and weakest) of the three.

However, what for Hollywood seemed confusing and unacceptable was actually a fascinating experiment in cinematic time, far from both the linear structure of the classical Hollywood flashback, and from the modern narrative fragmentations of Godard or Resnais; a choice that proved, once again, how Sturges's departure from Classical Hollywood Cinema does not imply any of the provocative modernist disruptions, but appears much closer to those perfectly intelligible manipulations of storylines that we can find in postmodern movies.

In this way, more than Godard's *Pierrot Le Fou*, Marker's *La Jetée* (1962), and Resnais's *L'Année dernière à Marienbad*, Preston Sturges's *Unfaithfully Yours*, *The Power and the Glory*, and *The Great Moment* anticipate works such as Neil Jordan's *The End of the Affair* (1999), in which the timeline of Graham Greene's original novel is completely reworked in a narrative structure that shifts back and forth through non-chronological flashbacks, in order to increase the efficacy of the narration by multiplying the perspective on the story's events.

Sixty years before, Sturges was doing exactly the same, by employing the flashback "not so much to express the selfish subjectivity of memory," as Andrew Sarris noted, "but to reorganize, restructure, and resequence reality so that all its ironies, comic and tragic can be more effectively expressed."[17]

5

Possible Narratives and Hypothetical Tales

I said "If."

Sir Alfred in *Unfaithfully Yours*

The Art and Method of Variation

That Classical Hollywood Cinema established its rigorous paradigm on the repetition and variation of the same narrative syntagms is a concept that the film industry itself seemed to be aware of. As a famous aphorism from the early 1930s, attributed to MGM producer Irving Thalberg, goes: "We don't make movies, we remake them!"[1]

Of course, textual and inter-textual variations of structures and themes had already marked the history of literature, theater, music and painting, from the remote classical past to the modern experimental present — the comedies of Shakespeare, the experiments of Borges, Faulkner, and Queneau in literature; the series of Cézanne and Matisse in painting; Bach's "Goldberg" Variations and Beethoven's "Diabelli" Variations in music.

If variation in traditional arts became for Hollywood a convenient model with which to create narrative templates which were easily developable into a series of cost-cutting replicas, classical variation was regarded by creative directors and screenwriters as a source of inspiration for experiments with narrative composition. Filmmakers such as Alfred Hitchcock, John Ford, Robert Siodmak, Preston Sturges and, above all, Ernst Lubitsch made the most of this method by creating a dense web of connections among similar stories. In this way, their filmographies can be interpreted as vast hypertexts, where inter- and extra-textual variations chase each other from one movie to the next one.

Sturges himself worked extensively on the variation of themes, motifs, plots and narrative situations. For example, he defined *Hail the Conquering Hero* as a variation on the theme of *Monsieur Beaucaire*:

> As I wanted to do something with a wartime background, I thought for a month or so along the lines of what I call Monsieur Beaucaire in modern clothes. By that I mean a hero who is believed by all to be a villain but who in the end is introduced as a man of great honor with a long list of decorations.[2]

Sturges's working method was entirely based on the consideration, in logical terms, of every possible narrative alternative. As one of his biographers comments:

> Sturges often went back and forth between prose notes on a story and dramatized scenes or fragment of scenes. Once he had sketched a plot more or less to his satisfaction, he occasionally resorted to brief prose notes ... to decide which of several pathways to follow to a preconceived end.[3]

For *The Miracle of Morgan's Creek*, for example, the accident that induces Trudy to get married, pregnant, and to forget where, how and with whom all that happened, takes three different shapes, as we can see in a note he wrote on July 15, 1942:

> 1) She could get tight, get married, forget where she was married and the name of her husband, and presently be in the situation.
>
> 2) She could get married to a soldier on the spur of the moment and, through the medium of a slight automobile accident, get a conk on the head and find herself in the same situation as in 1)....
>
> 3) She could get married secretly, fearing the wrath of her parents, intending to reveal the fact much later on. Finding herself pregnant, she would reveal the fact immediately, and needing proof, go to the county clerk's office only to find it had just burned to the ground. Next she would go to the army authorities to ask the whereabouts of her husband, but as we are at war, the whereabouts of her husband could not be revealed. (Some other element is needed, however, for the townspeople to believe that she is *not* married.)[4]

In constructing his plot, Sturges seems to proceed with the logic of a narratologist (rather than with the intuition of an artist), through a lucid consideration in terms of possibilities and consequences. His draft for the conclusion of *The Miracle of Morgan's Creek* shows the same approach:

> a. [Trudy] thinks she recognizes the picture of the husband in the newspapers.

b. She thinks she recognizes the picture of her husband in the newspaper as just having been arrested for bigamy.

c. She remembers her husband's name. It was "Smith."

d. Her father comes looking for her, having just talked to the lawyer.[5]

In other words, it is as if Sturges were choosing among a system of signs, a grammar of syntagms — to use a terminology devised by linguists and semioticians several years later — combinable on logical bases. In this way, Sturges's draft for *The Sin of Harold Diddlebock* is so abstract that it resembles Vladimir Propp's formula for identifying the structure of the Russian folktale[6]:

Harold Lloyd story:

> Unsuccessful worm.
> Drink and many difficulties.
> Difficulties force resourcefulness.
> Resourcefulness brings success.
> Success brings confidence.[7]

Like Propp's functions,[8] the abstract events that Sturges identifies in his outline are nothing else than schematic "functions," that could be recombined *ad infinitum* into a series of classical Hollywood comedies.

Several other classical Hollywood screenwriters such as Billy Wilder, Samson Raphaelson, Ben Hecht, and I.A.L. Diamond, have intuitively worked on a system of combinations and variations of narratives, themes and motif, especially in the realm of comedy. What distinguishes Sturges from them is the lucid theoretical awareness that emerges from the story outlines, the comments, and the marginal notes to his own scripts. Regarding *The Miracle of Morgan's Creek*, for example, he wrote:

> The classic form of this type of comedy is to plunge the heroine into trouble and keep her in ever-increasing trouble until she triumphs over all by the very degree of her trouble.[9]

Possible Narratives and Hypothetical Tales

If variation of standardized structures was a common technique in classical screenwriting practice, hypothetical and parallel narratives were, instead, truly exceptional. Few movies ventured to embrace hypothetical narrative: In Siodmak's *The Strange Affair of Uncle Harry* (1945), the studio censorship imposed a "happy ending" that would reduce the incestu-

ous connotations of the main story: The tragic, melodramatic dilemma of
a man who has to choose between a life with his sister and a marriage with
the woman he loves, is quickly sorted out by a last scene showing the man
awakened by his girlfriend from a bad dream (that is, the narrative we followed until that moment). Another filmmaker who had attempted to
exploit the meta-linguistic implications of hypothetical narratives was
Harold Lloyd in *Girl Shy* (1924), a film in which pages of the book "The
Secret of Making Love," written by a shy tailor, take the form of fantasy
sequences, and become the occasion for a reflection on the needs of
escapism from reality into fiction.[10]

It is true that hypothetical narratives frequently occur in the musical
genre as pretexts for "production numbers," but an explicit variation of
the same story in three micro-stories, coherently connected in a broader
macro-narrative, was unheard of in Hollywood until Sturges's *Unfaithfully
Yours*.

As mentioned earlier, the movie tells the story of Sir Alfred, an orchestra conductor who, in the midst of performing three different musical
pieces, plans three different variations on the idea of taking revenge against
his wife Daphne and her presumed lover Tony. When conducting Rossini's
Overture to *Semiramide*, he fantasizes about murdering Daphne and plant-
ing false evidence that will incriminate Tony. For the second piece in the
program, Wagner's "Reconciliation" theme from *Tannhaüser*, he somberly
accepts his wife's betrayal and writes her a check, as a sign of forgiveness.
For the last piece, Tchaikovsky's symphonic poem *Francesca da Rimini*, he
conjures up a direct confrontation with Tony and a game of Russian
roulette that will provoke his own death.

The "postmodern" side of *Unfaithfully Yours* lies, first of all, in this
staging of the hypothetical mechanisms that other classical movies centered on subjectivity merely suggest. Differently to other classical directors and screenwriters, Sturges does not limit himself to creating a subtle
game of variations (from which we can abstract a model), but he puts the
model itself on stage, showing the mechanisms that generate hypotheses
(and which exist even if the hypotheses do not become real).

Even before the three fantastic narratives take place, we can hear Sir
Alfred formulating hypothetical narratives verbally: The dialogues with his
brother-in-law, and with the private eye he has hired, are full of assump-
tions and studded with interjections such as "I said 'if,'"[11] "Suppose I did,"[12]
and "I presume."[13] Addressing his valet Jules, he asks him directly: "What
would you do if you found out your wife was untrue to you?"[14]

In this way, Sturges anticipates not only the dilemma that will haunt Sir Alfred's mind throughout the movie, but also his incapacity at reading between the variations of the betrayal theme he is presented with. Sir Alfred, after all, is unable to confront and interpret even the simplest piece of information (he rejects his brother-in-law's insinuations, tears to pieces the detective's report, and he mistakes a tailor for a detective).

A very similar "jealousy" comedy, Pietro Germi's *Divorzio all'italiana* (*Divorce Italian Style*) (1961), centered on the schemes of a Sicilian baron to kill his wife, shows how Sturges was really ahead of his time in developing a discourse on the subjective mechanisms of hypothetic narration. In Germi's movie, in fact, the series of brief "daydreams" through which the baron fantasizes about getting rid of his spouse do not represent alternatives of the same micro-tale, nor become an occasion for a reflection on the mechanisms of the hypothetical narration itself.[15] The baron's hypothetical narratives are simply pretexts for gags that punctuate a different kind of discourse: a political reflection on the paradoxical condition of married couples in a specific historical context.

Sturges's usage of hypothetical narratives and their variations, indeed, suggests comparisons with more experimental narratives, such as Akira Kurosawa's *Rashômon*, Alain Resnais's *Smoking/No Smoking* (1993), and the literary experiments of Raymond Queneau and Alain Robbe-Grillet.

In *Rashômon*, for example, Kurosawa tells a story of rape and murder from the viewpoint of four different characters, in a series of multiple overlapping hypothetical narratives which all turn out to be unreliable. In the same way that Sturges uses the hypothetical narratives to show his character's insecurities and lack of interpretative skills, Kurosawa uses the same narrative mechanism to reflect on the fallacy of the perception of the human mind. In this way, the spectators are left questioning not only the truthfulness of the internal narrator(s), but also that of their own eyes, ears, and mind.

In 1950 (that is, three years after *Unfaithfully Yours* and one year before the release of *Rashômon*), Sturges devised a project for a television show called *You Be Witness,* based on premises similar to those in *Rashômon*:

> This show is based on the undeniable fact that most people are unable to recall, with any degree of accuracy, any given event they may witness. Proof of this fact can best be illustrated in the almost daily occurrences in courtrooms, when honest, well meaning people are called upon to reconstruct some scenes and then give such conflicting testimony. To err is only

human — but in this show a simulated scene of violence will be enacted, three (or more) persons selected from the audience will witness a scene, then they will be questioned on the witness stand by a man who will conduct his interrogation in a manner not unlike regular courtroom procedure.

...

The opening scene takes place in a courtroom. (long shot) A young woman is being called by the court clerk to come to the witness stand. A close shot reveals her to be rather attractive and a bit frightened and confused. With the camera on her, the voice of the prosecuting attorney (o.s.) begins — NOW MISS LANE WILL YOU TELL TO THE BEST OF YOUR ABILITY EXACTLY WHAT HAPPENED ON THE NIGHT OF JUNE 14 AT APPROXIMATELY NINE etc. Dissolve to — contestants and the interrogator of the show *You Be the Witness*. The witnesses are introduced to the audience. The interrogator gives a brief talk on the responsibility of a witness in giving correct testimony. He cites some cases where accused persons have been convicted on incorrect testimony. After explaining to the witnesses to observe closely a scene which will be enacted for them, the curtains part and a quickly enacted scene of violence transpires. One by one the witnesses are grilled. A blackboard in the background keeps a tally of the correctness of the testimony. After two or possibly three different scenes have been presented the scores are compared and the winner receives his reward. To end the show in a lighter vein, the interrogator suggests that the witnesses now assume that they are the jury and he gives a brief synopsis of a law case that actually happened, one that is quite ridiculous in content and asks each one exactly how he would judge the case. After each passes judgment, he comes forth with the ridiculous judgment which was actually handed down in the case.[16]

In *La Jalousie* (Robbe-Grillet's novel that proved most representative of the so-called *nouveau roman*), long, repetitive descriptive "scenes" involving a woman and a man are given to the reader without further explanation. The title, and a few other hints, merely suggest that the obsessive repetition and variation of the same actions are due to the presence of an internal narrator (the husband) who is spying on his wife and her alleged lover through the openings of a *jalousie* (the French term for Venetian blind), and to whom the apparently impersonal descriptions belong.[17]

The combination of variation and hypothetical narration in *Unfaithfully Yours* also anticipates the structure of films such as Tom Tykwer's *Lola rennt* (*Run Lola Run*) (1998) and *Smoking/No Smoking*— a movie in which Alain Resnais used Alan Ayckbourn's play *Intimate Exchanges* (1982) as the basis for a series of hypothetical variations of a story that stops, at every relevant narrative kernel, to go back and show "what might have happened" if the characters had made, or failed to make, a specific choice.

Likewise, in *Przypadek* (*Blind Chance*) (1987), Polish director Krzysztof Kieslowski presents three variations of the same story, but in this case the developments do not depend on the main character's will, but on unplanned factors such as chance events and banal incidents. The accidental hitting of a passerby, wasting time queuing in line, or not being able to find the exact change will affect his future life:

> Witek runs after a train. Three variations follow on how such a seemingly banal incident could influence the rest of Witek's life. One: he catches the train, meets an honest Communist and himself becomes a Party activist. Two: while running for the train he bumps into a railway guard, is arrested, brought to trial and sent to unpaid labor in a park where he meets someone from the opposition. He, in turn, becomes a militant member of the opposition. Three: he simply misses the train, meets a girl from his studies, returns to his interrupted studies, marries the girl and leads a peaceful life as a doctor unwilling to get mixed up in politics. He is sent abroad with his work. In mid-air, the plane he is on explodes.[18]

We can also find a simplified version of this system of possible narratives and multiple outcomes in *Sliding Doors* (1998), in which the creation of a second alternative plot is justified in terms of parallel reality. In all these examples, whether the narrative interrupts the action to represent actions that might happen, or that might have happened, the final result is equally non-classical, in the sense that hypotheses about the future are usually forbidden in Classical Hollywood movies. That is why, when a classical director such as George Cukor tries to repeat Sturges's and Kurosawa's experiments in *Les Girls* (1957), the story involves three non-overlapping flashbacks, told by three different internal narrators, and it requires a fourth party to straighten things out by providing the audience with a reassuring explanation about what "really" happened.

As Classical Hollywood narratives often cast glances at the past, but hardly ever anticipate the future (let alone the idea of making hypotheses about it), it is not surprising that, for *Unfaithfully Yours*, Spyros Skouras (chairman of the board of directors at Fox) urged Zanuck and Sturges to add explicatory subtitles before each fantasy sequence in order "to explain that the murder and Russian Roulette scenes were merely fantasies." Likewise, when discussing the narrative structure of the movie with Sturges, Zanuck himself referred to the scenes that take place in Sir Alfred's head in terms of "retrospects."[19] Sturges preferred the alternative term "prospects," which, as Brian Henderson points out, is "a far better word than theorists of narrative have come up with for what might be called future possible."[20]

Theme and Variation: A Musical Approach

The narrative structure of *Unfaithfully Yours* shows several signs of the musical influence that has contributed to its construction of repetitions and variants. In music, variation is a technique widely applied to all sorts of styles and periods, the process by which a certain unit (from a simple phrase to an entire movement) is altered through repetition and changes — harmonic, melodic, contrapuntal or rhythmic. Musical forms such as symphonies, sonatas, and concertos all rely on the repetition of motifs, and the "theme-and-variation" form has interested composers such as Handel (the "Harmonious Blacksmith" set), Bach (the "Goldberg Variations"), Beethoven (the "Diabelli Variations"), Brahms and his variations on themes by previous composers, Schoenberg ("Variations for Orchestra"), and Britten ("Young Person's Guide to the Orchestra — Variations and Fugue on a Theme by Purcell").

That Sturges adopted the archetypical musical form of "theme-and-variation" as the main compositional principle of *Unfaithfully Yours* is made explicit in several ways: by creating three different variations (revenge, forgiveness, duel) on the same narrative theme (jealousy), by associating musical pieces of different styles to each narrative variation, and by having each narrative develop in exactly the time that it takes Sir Alfred to direct a musical piece.

Sturges also chooses musical works whose narrative subjects are variations of the same theme of love and betrayal on which the film focuses: In Rossini's *Semiramide,* the queen and her lover kill her husband; Tannhäuser is torn between the pleasures of passion (Venus) and the faithfulness of pure love (Elizabeth), and in *Francesca da Rimini,* the main character is a beautiful girl who cheats on her husband with a younger lover.

Sturges also stresses the different style and tone of each musical fantasy by dedicating several shots to the reactions of the audience at the end of each performance: Hugo, Sir Alfred's manager, is so happy with the passionate interpretation of Rossini's piece that he runs backstage and congratulates the conductor; Daphne is visibly moved at the end of the second piece, and is shown drying her tears with a handkerchief; the two "music lovers" (Mr. Sweeney and the tailor) alternate euphoric and ecstatic reactions according to the composition/fantasy being performed.

Sturges mirrors the correspondence between music and narrative in several other ways: When Sir Alfred tells his wife, "You look exceptionally pretty tonight," she answers, "Maybe it's the music." And when Sir

Alfred accidentally sets fire to his room, another Rossini's Overture (from *Guillaume Tell*) is used as backcloth to the gag. Sturges, in fact, had originally dedicated much longer sequences to Sir Alfred's rehearsals with his orchestra, stressing the central role of music behind Sir Alfred's reasoning and his mental mechanisms.[21]

That Sturges's main reference in terms of iteration and variation is music emerges also in an anecdote the director told about his source of inspiration for the movie. Sturges had been thinking of writing the screenplay since as early as 1932,[22] while he was writing *The Power and the Glory*. "I had a scene all written," he recalled,

> and had only to put it down on paper.... To my surprise, it came out quite unlike what I had planned. I sat back wondering what the hell had happened, then noticed that someone had left the radio on in the next room and realized that I had been listening to a symphony broadcast from New York and that this, added to my thoughts, had changed the total.[23]

Also, as Diane Jacobs notes, while Sturges

> made a point of playing the Philistine in public (assuring reporters that his musical tastes were "low" and he relied totally on his music director, Alfred Newman), he had showed considerable expertise in selecting Sir Alfred's concert program. Together with [his girlfriend] Francie [Ramsden], a music lover, he compiled three pages of suggestions for the revenge and Russian roulette fantasies (including Debussy's *Danses sacrées et profanes* and César Franck's *Symphony in D Minor*). But from the start Preston was set on using the reconciliation theme from *Tannhäuser* for the forgiveness fantasy, which is recapitulated when Alfred embraces Daphne in the final scene.[24]

Sturges also capitalizes on the ambiguity that background music can create. At the beginning of each piece, in fact, we track from the images of Sir Alfred conducting the orchestra to the ones he is fantasizing through a dissolve into the pupil of his eye, and the music softens to the background. At this point, the music changes its narrative status from "sound off" (a diegetic sound whose source is left off-screen) to "internal sound over" (a mental sound perceived by the character only), but it can easily be misinterpreted as "external sound over" (the common non-diegetic background music that accompanies the diegetic action in any movie). In this way, the softening of the sound cons the spectator into wondering if the dissolve into Sir Alfred's mind was a sign of introspection, or rather of narrative ellipsis, and if what follows is a hypothetical narrative (highly unusual in classical cinema) or a jump-cut to the next step in the linear chronology of the events. These doubts will be cleared up at the end of the first fantasy sequence, where, right at the moment Sir Alfred seems trapped in a dramatic-grotesque conclusion, he appears again conducting his orchestra, on the verge of ending his performance.

Classical movies rarely lead their spectators to question their own perception of the events narrated, and when an unexpected twist happens, it simply unveils the reticence of the external narrator, who hid (until that moment) a specific piece of information. In this way, for example, in Alfred Hitchcock's *Suspicion* (1941), Lina's hypotheses are the result of a series of suppositions based on a range of clues that she and the audience are given. When an unexpected event overturns her/our most logic expectations, we do not feel tricked for not having been able to interpret the signs; in fact, we are aware, since the very beginning, that we can access only the same amount of information the character is given (internal focalization), and we expect, throughout the movie, an extra piece of information that will complete the jigsaw. Hitchcock will undermine the traditional trust that the audience places in an internal narrator in *Stage Fright* (1950), by revealing that the events we have seen through the focalization of an internal narrator were actually the product of his lies. Even in this case, however, what is being questioned is not the audience's incapacity at reading signs (as, instead, happens sometimes in postmodern movies — see 1999's *The Sixth Sense*): it is the external narrator to be blamed for having withheld the necessary information that would have made it possible to unmask the internal narrator.

Instead, during the first fantasy sequence of *Unfaithfully Yours*, the audience is left questioning if the music should be considered non-diegetic or diegetic, and, consequently, if the events belong to the "reality" of the storyline, or to the parallel hypothetical universe of Sir Alfred's mind. This ambiguity Sturges instills in the spectator's mind mirrors Sir Alfred's own difficulty in telling the difference between suspects and facts, daydreaming and reality, and in deciding what to believe. Sir Alfred experiences, in a parallel universe, those risks that he is not able to experience directly in his actual life, learning from the mistakes made by his imagination. That is why, in the third fantasy sequence, Sir Alfred confesses to Daphne and Tony the strategies he had devised in the previous ones — and he refers to them using the past tense:

I thought of killing you, my dear ... I cut your throat with my razor ... your head nearly came off...
(he turns to Tony)
...but it was *your* fingerprints they found on the razor, Tony, and you they

burned ... screaming your innocence ... it's a relief to hear that in the past tense, isn't it?

Then he turns to Daphne, to inform her of what he had planned during his second fantasy sequence:

...then ... such is human idiocy ... I forgave you...
...wrote you an enormous check ... and grew maudlin over the necessity of youth for youth.

This type of interaction among separate narratives anticipates the postmodern inter-textuality of TV movies such as *Scener ur ett äktenskap* (*Scenes from a Marriage*) (1973) and *Dekalog* (*The Decalogue*) (1987). In these works, Ingmar Bergman and Krzysztof Kieslowski, respectively, took advantage of the serial possibilities of television to design multiple texts that can be experienced either as separate independent entities or as one long articulated work.

Sir Alfred's transfers of experience from one narrative to the other is also reminiscent of the *Back to the Future* trilogy (1985–1990), in which the construction of the story in serial texts allows the main character to revisit sequences from a previous movie. In *Back to the Future Part II* (1989), in fact, Marty travels back in time to moments he had already gone through in the first movie — to the point that he can literally see his previous self in action. This allows him not only to live again, in a sequel, the same situations he had experienced in the first episode, but also to benefit from such experiences, exactly as Sir Alfred can benefit from what he has learned in each separate micro-story.

The Oulipian Aspects of Unfaithfully Yours

Besides anticipating the postmodern interest in hypothetical narratives and variations, *Unfaithfully Yours* also anticipates the idea of writing by logical bases, with multiple outcomes, that can be found in literary experiments by Queneau, Calvino and other scholars-authors from the artistic-scientific movement Oulipo (*Ouvroir de littérature potentielle* — Workshop of Potential Literature). Founded in 1960 by Raymond Queneau and François Le Lionnais, the movement counted, in its ranks, writers and mathematicians such as Jacques Roubaud, Georges Perec, and Italo Calvino, who composed poems, stories, and novels under self-imposed constraints (palindromes, lipograms, algorithms, homomorphisms, "false" translations, and combinatories).

In Queneau's *Exercises de style*, published in France in 1947 (the same year *Unfaithfully Yours* was being produced), a two-paragraph story about two chance encounters by a man with an annoying character is retold 99 times, each time in a different "style" (prose, free verse, sonnet, telegram, pig Latin, simple exclamations, and so on). *Unfaithfully Yours* uses the same concept, by transforming its theme through variations (the revenge is fulfilled with a murder, the revenge is substituted by forgiveness, the revenge is left unfulfilled because of the irony of fate), and by developing a model of logical possibilities and variations, explicitly interrelated with already made (or successively make-able) texts. Far from being classically closed, in fact, Sturges's film shows several traces of potential, unexpressed variations: Daphne's sister and her husband, for example, double and counterpoint the main couple (and their story) in terms of subtext (and not as a deviation from the hypothetical plan). The story of Sir Alfred and Daphne itself, after all, can be considered as a comic variation on the story of Othello and Desdemona (Sir Alfred's schemes are nothing but a parody of Othello's dilemma).

Sturges's own *exercise in style* expresses itself in his ability to justify for the spectator the presence of variations, by sewing them to each other in a narrative continuity that overcomes their immediate perception as alternatives. In this respect, however, *Unfaithfully Yours* takes its distance also from Queneau's *Exercises de Style* and moves closer to the practice of postmodern mainstream cinema based on a narrative interaction among the variants. That is why, as noted above, Sir Alfred's hypothetical narratives keep in consideration the "experiences" from his previous fantasies, to the point of confessing to Daphne and Tony, in the third fantasy sequence, the schemes he had devised to get rid of them in the previous ones.

In Queneau's meta-texts, by contrast, the links between the "exercises" are not narrative — that is, they cannot be ordered in a sequentiality to create a story. Every exercise is autonomous, compared to the others, and it represents, with them, a system of variations based on stylistic norms — the final result being a manual of rhetoric that could be expanded into an encyclopedic form, but not into a narrative.

In Sturges, the creative constriction, as in an Oulipian text, expresses itself in the ability to build a story by episodes through variations of the same episode. However, at the same time, the creation of a model of variations and hypotheses has pragmatic narrative purposes: Besides transforming each episode into a part of the whole, in a chapter of a whole story (a macro-story made of micro-stories), it is a strategy for the main character to reach his ultimate goal (getting revenge for his wife's presumed betrayal) and to come to terms with his inability to act.

Sir Alfred's imaginative attitude, in fact, allows him to see himself as better than he is, and to create imaginary doubles of himself that can experiment with his ambitions and frustrations, in ways that are precluded in his real life. The outcome is more ambiguous that it might seem because, if his imaginary double does incarnate his desires, it also makes his limits even more explicit, as the character remains unable, even on the imaginative level, to conduct his own life as he is able to conduct his orchestra.

In this way, *Unfaithfully Yours* is not only an experiment in possible narratives and variations, but a precursor of the postmodern movie whose plot can be interpreted as a meta-discourse on the irreconcilability between success in art and success in life.

6

A Style Without a Style

Le style, c'est l'oubli de tous les styles.

Jules Renard

In the course of his career, Preston Sturges employed the simplest cinematic syntax to convey the hypothetical stories, achronological timelines, and meta-linguistic reflections that we have analyzed thus far. While some of the most prominent Hollywood filmmakers of the 1930s and 1940s were adopting deep-focus, tracking shots, montage sequences, masks and other striking visual solutions, Sturges's lack of cinematic virtuosity was so blatant as to appear almost in conflict with his complex narrative style.

This absence of easily recognizable cinematic marks has often been interpreted as a deficiency in terms of aesthetics that prevented Sturges from making it into Andrew Sarris's "first line" of *auteurs* because — as Sarris himself wrote — he "may have been contributed more to the American language than to the American cinema."[1]

A more attentive analysis, however, reveals how Sturges's predisposition to conceal the cinematic technique cannot be dismissed as an absence of style, or as a capitulation to some sort of "zero degree" of classical narration. Rather, it can be explained as a conscious stylistic choice (neutrality instead of virtuosity), so that the incredibly rich and experimental narrative and the disarming neutrality of his cinematic style end up being the two sides of the same coin.

The modest, unobtrusive visual style of Sturges's movies, in fact, is perfectly functional in relation to a narrative structure and comic style that are mostly based on "external focalization" — the case in which (to use a literary terminology introduced by Gérard Genette[2]) the events seem to

105

happen before the spectator's eyes, without the intrusion of an internal focalizer (a character's viewpoint) or an external narrator's viewpoint (zero focalization). Sturges's comic style relies entirely on an unpreventable chain of self-triggered events that unfold "naturally" before our eyes and rely on fast-paced, witty dialogue, fully appreciable only through a high degree of technical transparency.

The usage of visible cinematic syntagms, instead, would mean "calling attention to a work's own artfulness," and challenging the "'invisible' or 'transparent' representational regime" — which usually coincides with a shift in terms of focalization.[3] In this way, Hitchcock's complex tracking shots, Welles's long takes, Mamoulian's rhythmic alternations of close-ups, Lubitsch's windows and door shots, and Wyler's deep-focus constructions are figures of speech that imply the surfacing of an implicit narrator and a shift to zero focalization. *Notorious*'s (1946) famous crane movement that reveals to spectators the key in Alicia's hand, for example, marks an important passage to zero focalization, as it allows the implicit narrator to provide us with an important piece of information that, otherwise, we would be missing. Likewise, the long take that opens Welles's *Touch of Evil* (1958) is a suspenseful moment of zero focalization, in which the implicit narrator shows the audience a man placing a bomb in the trunk of a car.

Sturges's cinematic transparency and external focalization are as functional and as necessary to the comic value of his narrative as Hitchcock's or Welles's non-focalized virtuosity are crucial to the dramatic and suspense values of their movies. In this way, Sturges's lack of powerful cinematic marks becomes a stylistic signature, a choice of transparency as functional to the narrative content as the formal visibility of other Hollywood *auteurs*: a "style without a style" that reminds us, once again, of the cinema of postmodern directors, whose aesthetics often emerge through the impalpable usage of a very basic cinematic grammar. In the case of Steven Spielberg, for example, his simple close-ups of characters looking off-screen depict their gaze as just a projection of their inner thoughts, as if they were dealing with a sort of metaphysical "look over." Likewise, Stanley Kubrick uses slow tracking shots to keep characters walking through enormous spaces at the center of the image. The goal is to cancel the characters' movement, to make them motionless, to comment on the characters' journey in an environment — the society in *Barry Lyndon* (1975) and *A Clockwork Orange* (1971), the military in *Full Metal Jacket* (1987) and *Paths of Glory* (1957), outer space in *2001: A Space Odyssey* (1968), and the supernatural in *The Shining* (1980) — that tends to crush the individual.

In *Barry Lyndon*, for example, both Barry and his son-in-law, Lord Bulling-don, move constantly through rooms and palaces, while the camera antic-ipates their movement, and keeps their figures stationary at the center of the shot. In *A Clockwork Orange*, the apparently strong and ferocious Alex is often kept at the center of the shot while he is moving, driving, or walk-ing. *The Shining* is entirely built on this principle: Characters move all the time through the deserted corridors of the Overlook hotel, trapped inside a spatial-temporal dimension from which there is no way out. Both *Full Metal Jacket* and *Paths of Glory* use the same device (the "following shot") in the same contexts (an anti-militarist look at the army): Long tracking shots anticipate the review of a pitiless sergeant who screams and insults his GIs, while his slow walk is rendered motionless by his being framed at the center of the screen.

Sturges's usage of a basic cinematic grammar, whose undetectable signs accompany similar situations in different movies, goes exactly in the same direction. One illustration of this process at work is the recurrence of long takes or single-shot sequences, combined with following shots, in situations where two characters are walking in the street.[4] It is a pattern that recurs several times in *The Miracle of Morgan's Creek*: when Trudy is trying to talk Norval into covering for her, when she confesses to him what had happened the night before, and when she discusses what to do next with her sister Emmy. The same happens in *Hail the Conquering Hero*, when the mayor's son walks Libby home from the office, and the camera follows them in a one-shot sequence of almost three minutes.

Almost in compliance with Bazin's dictates concerning "forbidden editing,"[5] Sturges rules out *découpage* even in those moments when the external focalization becomes more urgent and needs to be visually rein-forced with a transparent device, appropriate to the situation: Long takes and following shots are necessary not only to portray the characters' walks in realistic continuity, but also to allow the audience to concentrate on an important narrative kernel, which is provided through the dialogue.

This mutual correspondence between form and content has nothing to concede to more virtuoso combinations of long takes and following shots, such as the one in the abovementioned opening of *Touch of Evil*. In Welles's movie, in fact, the interaction between camera position and *mise-en-scène*, combined with zero focalization, is necessary for the creation of suspense: The implicit narrator shows us anonymous hands placing a bomb in the trunk of a car, and has us follow the car moving in a crowded street through a complicated crane movement. The continuity and the fluid mobility of the camera are both necessary to add suspense to the fact that the car could explode at any moment, right before our eyes, killing the two characters who are walking nearby.

As Welles's baroque long takes display a cinematic virtuosity that is perfect for his own suspenseful narrative, Sturges's invisible long takes point at a transparency similarly functional to his story: There are no bombs, no mysterious characters, no secrets to be unveiled through the omniscience of an external narrator. In Sturges's films, gags and events unfold before our eyes. And even if sometimes an internal focalizer might emerge (a character whose point of view is used as a representational filter — for example, Jean commenting on Pike's behavior through her mirror in *The Lady Eve*), or if the dormant implicit narrator unexpectedly appears (as in the silent music sequences from *Sullivan's Travels* previously analyzed, or the "narratage" technique that will shortly be discussed), external focalization remains the main narrative strategy used by Sturges to make us laugh.

It is for this reason that Sturges's cinema is characterized by an extraordinary frequency of long takes and one-shot sequences that usually punctuate the most verbose and motionless sequences: the long discussion between Sullivan and the producers, at the beginning of *Sullivan's Travels*, is introduced by a brief shot in the screening room, and followed by a four-minute take in the producer's office; moreover, the scene from *The Lady Eve* in which Jean tries to seduce Charles in her cabin features a three-minute static close-up. In general, Sturges reserves long takes for discussions between couples, like the four-minute single-shot sequence between Claudette Colbert and Joel McCrea having dinner in *The Palm Beach Story*, or the second daydreaming scene in *Unfaithfully Yours* (a three-minute sequence including a two-minute long take).[6]

In all these examples, the long take appears every time Sturges wants his audiences to sit back and concentrate on what his characters have to say (which is usually a relevant piece of narrative information). Examples of this characteristic include the first meeting between Woodrow and the Marines in *Hail the Conquering Hero* (a five-minute take that includes a tracking shot onto Woodrow's face, to intensify his monologue about the Marines) and the hysterical existential reflections of Harold in *The Sin of Harold Diddlebock*—the Sturges movie that featured the highest number of long takes.

Narratage

Underlining the point that Sturges's cinematic techniques are entirely subordinated to his screenplays and their narratives is the fact that, as its name suggests, his most famous stylistic invention is extremely "literary." Simply put, "narratage" is a voice-over narration superimposed on silent images, a technique by which the narrator comments on the characters' actions, and sometimes even loans his voice to the actors concerned.

Nowadays, the overall result might look like an odd residue from the silent period, but when Sturges experimented with it for the first time in his screenplay for *The Power and the Glory,* Paramount decided to launch a massive promotional campaign in which "Narratage" was advertised as a "radical change," a method of "pictorial narration ... destined soon to spread throughout many of the film center's product."[7] According to the studio, such a technique "resembles, though it emphatically does not parallel, the literary method of the novel,"[8] and it is "a means of filmic story telling that is not only a device manufactured in a laboratory but a combination of devices, originally suggested by the author, mulled over by the photographer and perfected by the director and the cutter."[9] Sturges employed such a technique only in two sequences. The first is when the internal narrator Henry "dubs" both Tom and Sally's voices in a comic proposal scene; the second in relation to Sally's suicide when, shocked at the discovery of her husband's affair with another woman, she walks as a ghost into the crowd, talking to beggars and cab drivers through the voice of the internal narrator, in a powerful "alienation effect" worth of Bertolt Brecht.

Narratage will find its most functional application twenty years later, in *Les Carnets du Major Thomson,* where Sturges used the "diary form" to portray a series of sketches about French manners and customs, as described by the voice-over of a character. Other than that, Sturges rarely employed such a technique, and he preferred to disguise it in more discrete ways. In *The Lady Eve,* for example, Jean comments on Charles's embarrassment before a group of unmarried ladies who are desperately trying to grab his attention, and she voice-dubs all their virtual dialogue while observing the scene through her mirror. In *The Great Moment,* Sturges adapts this technique to portray Dr. Morton's mental process while he is researching anesthesia, but instead of returning to an internal voice-over, the silent shots of him reading the pages of a medical encyclopedia are overlain with graphic titles reproducing written words and sentences whose font size increases every time a relevant concept enlightens Morton's mind.

Film critics and historians have reassessed the importance of nar-ratage, pointing out the extreme naïveté of the whole process, which is — after all — nothing more than a simple application of verbal narration over silent images. It neither influenced Hollywood's wider models of narra-tion nor came to represent a stylistic mark of Sturges's auteurism. Holly-wood, in fact, would rarely employ this technique, other than in newsreels, comedy shorts, and cartoons. In a short entitled *So You Think You're a Nervous Wreck* (1946), for example, an employee's fears and phobias are commented on by a voice-over narrator who fastidiously describes every movement, facial expression, and related thought of the main character. A radical narrative experimenter like Orson Welles would develop his own version of narratage for television, especially in a never-aired pilot enti-tled *The Fountain of Youth* (1958) for a program in which Welles appeared on screen as an omniscient external narrator controlling his characters' actions, dialogues, and voices as if he were a powerful puppeteer. Walt Dis-ney used narratage in some animated movies; in *Melody Time* (1948), for example, Dennis Day's voice dubs the narrator and all the characters of the segment "The Legend of Johnny Appleseed."

Apart from these few exceptions, full-length features got rid of such a visible technique and returned to it, as a last resort, only for "whodunit" movies where a final explanatory flashback would solve the mystery by quickly reviewing the events presented in the film from a new angle. At the end of Renè Clair's *And There Were None* (1945), for example, the killer himself explains to the only two survivors what happened to the other victims by superimposing his voice onto a montage of events and character's actions, and even by dubbing the voices of his own victims.

The legacy of narratage is probably to be uncovered *outside* Holly-wood, for example in that literary trend that affected the French Cinema of the 1950s and 1960s. It was certainly anticipated by Alexandre Astruc's 1948 manifesto of the *"camera-stylo,"* which bore an impressive resem-blance to the above-mentioned advertising campaign for *The Power and the Glory*:

> Cinema will gradually break free from the tyranny of what is visual, from the image for its own sake, from the immediate and concrete demands of the narrative, to become a means of writing just as flexible and subtle as written language.... It will soon be possible to write ideas directly on film without even having to resort to those heavy associations of images that were the delight of the silent cinema.[10]

The French *nouvelle vague* would mobilize most of these suggestions, showing a literary (and yet functional) tendency to express thoughts through the spoken word. This showed itself in a renewed interest in the usage of overwhelming voice-over narrators in movies such as *Journal d'un curé de campagne* (*Diary of a Country Priest*) (1951), *Hiroshima Mon Amour,* *L'Année dernière à Marienbad, Jules et Jim* (*Jules and Jim*) (1962), and *Les deux anglaises et le continent* (*Anne and Muriel*) (1971)—with results (for example, the dubbing of characters) often very close to what Sturges had experimented within his own narratage.

It is by no means coincidental, therefore, that Sturges's usage of narratage resurfaced in 1955 in *Les Carnets du Major Thomson*—his last film and the only one he ever wrote, produced, and directed in France.

7

Post-Hollywood

If Sturges's experiments with narrative structures suggest a rebellious, anti-classical attitude towards Hollywood rules and aesthetics, we have noted how the story of Sturges's own life indicates an opposite tendency to fit in, and a general awareness that his artistic temperament could not live outside the system. "I loved Paramount and did not wish to leave," Sturges repeated several times. "My leaving Paramount, which was my home, the faces on the men, the good-byes in the commissary, all these things come back to me, far from cheerfully."[1]

When Sturges's venture into independent cinema (the California Picture Company, co-founded with Howard Hughes in 1944) failed miserably after only a couple of movies, Sturges ran back to the studios, signing contracts with Fox and MGM, and even trying to negotiate a return to Paramount. It was too late, as the system had rapidly changed: The end of the war, the loss of profits, the beginning of serious competition from television and, soon after, the Paramount Decision (1948) of the Supreme Court forcing the studios to divest themselves of their theater chains had forced Hollywood to restructure its modes of production and to re-focus on more alluring aspects. The studios were placing all their energies into elements of immediate visibility — actors, costumes, and set decorations — and would soon begin investing their finances in technical innovations that would enhance the spectacular value of the product (widescreen, stereophonic sound, 3-D). The importance of writing and directing began to be underplayed, and with creative geniuses once hailed like movie stars now often regarded as potential trouble-makers, the system was slowly replacing them with mediocre writers and pedestrian *metteurs en scène*, able to put together quick and inexpensive vehicles for the star or the technical innovation of the moment.

That this change affected Sturges's creative freedom is quite clear, if we compare the 1933 advertising campaign for *The Power and the Glory* with the 1949 one for *The Beautiful Blonde from Bashful Bend*—the former pinpointing the "radical innovation" of Sturges's "story telling technique,"[2] the latter focusing on the essential value of Betty Grable's legs.

Sturges was perfectly aware of the change and prepared to adapt himself to the "new" studio system. As Diane Jacobs argues, this is clear from the letters that he wrote at this time to

> Henry Ginsberg and Frank Freeman at Paramount, assuring them he was able and willing to make the same sort of films he'd made half a decade before and describing elaborate methods he'd contrived for working cheaply. Preston likened his reputation for being difficult with the plight of a dentist who can't get work because he's known to be painful. He was determined to prove he was a reasonable man.[3]

Sturges tried to adapt his creativity, by structuring his script for *The Beautiful Blonde from Bashful Bend* entirely around the character of Betty Grable, with a storyline and a series of gags centered on her body and her musical numbers.

As already observed, when the Internal Revenue Service froze his assets, Sturges moved back to France, reversing the historical trend of European émigrés going Hollywood. In the country of his childhood, Sturges was received with all the honors and the consideration due a Hollywood rebel, but rather than representing a deliberate reaction to the studio system, his departure from Hollywood was the forced exile of a "classic experimenter" who still needed to interact with the classical paradigm in order to produce his alternatives — an ambiguous condition very close in many ways to a postmodern sensibility.

Sturges's own career shows a continuous intention to fit in inside the system. Even the image that he created of himself at the end of his life, as "'Hollywood's Bad Boy' run off to Paris" saying that "he was fed up with crass American businessmen and announcing ... that in twenty years he'd managed to antagonize every studio boss in Hollywood," was, after all, Diane Jacobs judges, really just "a way to salvage pride."[4]

In terms of cultural exchange, French culture and cinema had already surfaced in Sturges's work. His Hollywood pastiche, in fact, had provided an interaction between narrative structures, modes and forms belonging to both "national" sensibilities: From the French tradition of farce and vaudeville (André Deed, Max Linder, and other silent comedians whom Sturges had become familiar with, during his French childhood) to the

American practice of slapstick comedy (Mack Sennett, Fatty Arbuckle, and Harold Lloyd), Sturges's comedies from the 1930s and 1940s had showed a peculiar concoction of French and American elements. His mix of sociological analyses and physical comedy are often charged with surrealist touches *a la* Émile Cohl, and it is not difficult to recognize the same subtle criticism of bourgeois respectability and decorum that one can find in the caustic humor of Deed and Linder. In this way, Sturges's American work certainly represents an important contribution to that too-often-overlooked relationship between French and American film comedy, which goes from Linder to Chaplin and from Keaton to Tati.

On the other hand, Sturges's unconcealed interest in physical comedy is primarily indebted to the American tradition of pratfalls, bathing beauties and Keystone Cops, made of cross-cut chases and alternate editing. As Sturges said to his friend Marcel Pagnol: "At best my efforts have been a French point of humor filtered through an American vocabulary."[5]

That the pre–Truffaut French cinema was completely uninterested in this postmodern concoction of different cinematic styles and comic genres is obvious in an anecdote that Sturges recounted in an unpublished article about working with French producers:

"I am enchanted with the idea of making an *adult* subject. Few have been offered me. If you will agree with me, however, that even an adult likes to be amused once in a while, give me a hell of a cast, let me add a story of sorts with jokes, a little sex and maybe some suspense; then sprinkle it all with a few pratfalls, I think I can give you back something."

"What is it Le Pratfall?" asked my puzzled friends.

"You know," I replied, "tomber ... Bang! Sur le derrière ... Boom!"

"Ah," said my friends, "Le gag!"

"That's right," I said, "Le gag sur le Prat!"

"This is enjoyed in your countries?" asked my friends sadly.

"Relished," I replied.

"Slightly childish," said my friends.

"You never said a truer thing," I replied. "You have to be young in heart."

"But what," asked one of the gentlemen, "is Le Gag sur le Prat to do in this adultish picture?"

"It's the sugar," I said. "You know, like they put on pills."[6]

Sturges's interlocutor in this amusing anecdote was Alain Poire, an executive producer for Gaumont. Poire had contacted Sturges as soon as he arrived in Paris, to offer him the opportunity to adapt a movie from a popular *Figaro* column, written by Pierre Daninos under the pen name of Major William Marmaduke Thompson. Thompson, a fictional English character who had been living in Paris for twenty years, was still bemused by the French mentality. Sturges accepted Poire's proposal and wrote an original screenplay.

As he later remembered;

> We had hardly begun to count our unhatched chickens when a new book titled *Les Carnets du Major Thompson* by Pierre Daninos, compiled from his columns in *Le Figaro,* became a best-seller.
>
> The studio got very nervous. They imagined the audiences coming to see on film the incidents they had read in *Le Figaro* or in the book. They imagined the fury of those audiences if they did not get what they expected.
>
> They asked me to write another script.
>
> The new script was to incorporate, as much as possible, the random reflections on the habits of the French made by the Major Thompson of Mr. Daninos' columns. The columns of Mr. Daninos did not tell a story, nor were they intended to; I told Monsieur Poiret of Gaumont that one could as easily make a film based on the telephone directory.
>
> I was in no position to refuse work, however.
>
> My solution was to give the English major, living in France, a French wife and a seven-year-old son. The major and his wife differ violently on whether the child should be raised with a pride in his English forebears or a pride in their hereditary enemies, his French forebears. From this matrix, the major's observations on the French drawn from the columns, would then be illustrated on the screen.[7]

As Sandy Sturges recalls,

> The funny thing about *Les Carnets* was that Gaumont hired him because the story was about an English major married to a French wife, and the observation of the Englishman about French idiosyncrasies. So, they hired Preston because we were in London at the time, and they thought he was an Englishman.[8]

Sturges recounts this experience as if it had happened in one of his comedies:

> "What do you mean you're not English!" said my producer, stunned. "It was because you were English that we engaged you to *make* this picture in the first place!"
>
> "I'm awfully sorry to disappoint you," I said, "I was born in Chicago and it's pretty late to do anything about it now! I could buy a suit that was a little tight in the armholes if you like, and tuck my handkerchief up my sleeve, but I don't think it would fool anybody."
>
> "But you came to lunch with me the first time in a Rolls Royce," said my producer accusingly.
>
> "That's right," I said, "and you ate Ravioli! But I didn't draw any conclusions from it."[9]

In the end, Sturges's American perspective helped to provide an equally detached approach to both the French and the British culture. However, it is obviously the French customs he was more interested in satirizing. Sturges even extends the parody of French types from the movie to his personal (that is, extratextual) experience with the French producers. In his same unpublished article, in fact, Sturges recalls:

> "I was thinking of making the picture in two languages," I said, "English and French. In fact, if I make this picture at all, I think it will be in two languages. I would not care to put in all the time and effort it is going to take to turn this book into a picture, and then show it in France only!"
>
> "There is also Belgium," said my French friends, "and don't forget Switzerland."
>
> "I won't," I said, "I went to school there."
>
> "Canada is also a very large market," said the producers, "the *French* part, naturally. The rest is so illiterate!"
>
> "I didn't realize it was so big," I said. I had visited Quebec because my mother was born there.
>
> "Then there is North Africa," said my friends, "not to mention Madagascar and several of the Antilles!"
>
> "Look," I said, "during my years in this industry I have quite often read the world-wide box-office reports of pictures I had a piece of. I have a fair idea of where the money comes from, and whereas I agree completely with you that anyone who does not speak fluent French is not only an analphabet, but a louse, I still wouldn't care to make a picture that didn't have a chance in the English-speaking countries."
>
> "But could one *make* an Anglo-American picture out of this subject?" asked the producer.
>
> "If one could make a picture out of it all," I said, "one could do it just as well in English as in French. The fascination about this subject is that it opens up great vistas. If I can make a picture out of this, I plan also to make a picture out of the Dictionary of the Academy, Fanny Farmer's Cook Book and Doctor Phyffe's Twenty Thousand Words Often Mispronounced."
>
> "You are being humorous," said my friends, "you doubt the subject."[10]

Les Carnets du Major Thompson

Far from the severity and efficiency of the Hollywood studio system, Sturges had to face not only a more primitive mode of production, suffering from the lack of equipment and of permanent prop departments, but he also had to cope with different creative requirements, such as the need to make a bilingual movie. When the producers decided to shoot both a French and an English version, they requested that Sturges write two screenplays and shoot each scene twice, in English and French, without at the same time any move towards doubling the budget.

Sandy Sturges recalls many occasions when Preston had to overcome the deficiencies of the French studio system — from borrowing stockings from the crew to replace Martine Carole's ones, to the usage of manhole covers to reproduce vertical tracking shots[11]:

> One of the difficulties he had on the film was that Martine Carole said she spoke perfect English, and Jack Buchanan said he spoke perfect French. And so when Preston started shooting the scene at the breakfast table, and they're talking about the little boy, Martine says her line. Silence! "Cut." And Preston asks: "Jack, do you know your line?" And he replies: "Of course, of course!" So, they'd start over. Jack responds, and now it's Martine's turn ... Total silence! It turned out that neither one of them would recognize their cues in a different language. So Preston had Martine sitting in Jack's lap for that part of the scene. And when the characters were having a discussion, Jack would talk to Martine, and when he was finished talking he would give her a poke — and that was her cue. Then she would give Jack a poke in his back — and that was his cue. They knew their lines perfectly, they just didn't know *when* to say them![12]

Film historians (and Oulipian writers) have emphasized that it is often out of restrictions that the most original and expressive solutions are born. It was under these restraining circumstances that Sturges developed an updated version of his narratage technique, as the possibility of adding a voice-over onto a series of pantomimed actions would avoid the need for a retake in a different language. Narratage, however, was more than a cost-cutting strategy for Sturges: It was the most appropriate way of transposing the diary-form chronicle of Daninos's book into a cinematic text, and a way to set free, once and for all, the concoction of silent gags, conjugal farce, and slapstick humor that had subtly punctuated his own productions in Hollywood. The result was neither a success nor a masterpiece, but nevertheless one of the most experimental movies of the French pre-*nouvelle vague* period, as well as a significant link to postmodern cinema.

That this film has been entirely underestimated is proved by the fact that even the most supportive critics and biographers have dismissed *Les Carnets du Major Thompson* in comparison to Sturges's Hollywood films. Diane Jacobs refers to it as "by no means a Preston Sturges picture" and James Ursini says he misses "the whole milieu [Sturges] created in his American films — the stock company of comic book characters who nevertheless radiated their own peculiar humanity, the frantic race for success, the naturalistic American dialogue, and the congestion and speed.

Very little of this remains in this sadly 'foreign' film. Like Sturges himself during the period, it is a listless and tired work."[13]

Such interpretations make perfect sense only if we use the classical Hollywood paradigm as a term of comparison, instead of accepting the discrepancies, the pastiche, and the dissonant concoction of different narrative registers as signs of an aesthetics that, in significant ways, anticipates the later traits of postmodern cinema. For, in reality, *Les Carnets du Major Thompson* is an unusual hybrid of classic comedy and journalistic reportage. It alternates Sturges's accounts of Thompson's domestic life with his wife Martine with Thompson's own descriptions of French customs: a way to deconstruct the traditional comedy of manners that anticipates not only the narration techniques developed by the *nouvelle vague* (as in the usage of voice-over by Truffaut and Resnais), but also the French and Italian comedies of the 1960s, centered on a similar mix of dramatic and descriptive sequences, slapstick and satire (from Jacques Tati to Louis De Funès and from Alberto Sordi to Vittorio Gassman and the "omnibus" movies).

In *Les Carnets du Major Thompson*, Sturges delegates most of the narration to Thompson, whose voice-over opens the movie introducing Paris and its inhabitants in a quick montage of streets, people, and situations that ends with a presentation of the main characters: Thompson's extremely French wife Martine, the very British governess Miss Fryth, his half-French, half-British son Marc, and the very French Monsieur Taupin (Major Thompson's friend and the film's embodiment of Everything French).

In this way, the movie's opening not only fulfills the classical requirement of establishing time, locale, and action, but it also molds the concoction of different narrative techniques that Sturges will use in the rest of the movie. *Les Carnets du Major Thompson,* in fact, assigns classical dialogue to its *characters* (usually in the form of fast-paced discussions between Thompson and his wife), and employs the narratage technique for *types* such as Monsieur Taupin (in the non-dramatic chronicles of the French habits that Thompson dictates to his secretary in the form of a journal).

Sturges uses narratage to describe all sorts of stereotypical French types (bureaucrats, motorists, train passengers, restaurant managers) and their habits (the language of gestures, the practice of hand-shaking, the constant suspicion and mistrust towards everything, the obsession with time, the complaints against public service, the womanizing attitude). The casting of Noël-Noël as the silent Monsieur Taupin, who faces the most

banal daily circumstances with a mix of Keaton-esque ingenuity and irritating selfishness modeled on Ben Turpin, also anticipates characters and situations from Jacques Tati's movies — and bears an impressive physical resemblance to Jean-Pierre Zola, the actor who plays Monsieur Arpel in *Mon Oncle* (*My Uncle*) (1958). Taupin's bureaucratic nightmare trying to get an ID at a Parisian register office, for example, is a typical Tati-like game of interaction with modernity, where technology does not fulfill the goals for

Top: Monsieur Arpel (Jean-Pierre Zola), a modern Monsieur Taupin, in Jacques Tati's *Mon Oncle. Bottom:* Monsieur Taupin (Nöel-Nöel), the embodiment of everything French in *Les Carnets du Major Thompson.*

which it was created, and instead of simplifying the communication between customers and employees, turns the whole process into an alienating experience — exactly like in *Mon Oncle* and in *Playtime* (1967).

Top: An alienating experience for Monsieur and Madame Arpel (Jean-Pierre Zola and Adrienne Servantie) in Jacques Tati's *Mon Oncle. Bottom:* Monsieur Taupin's (Nöel-Nöel) alienating experience in *Les Carnets du Major Thompson.*

Thompson's flashback about his life with his first British wife witnesses narratage applied with the most exhilarating effect. Inspired by a *Figaro* column called "Martine and Ursula," the sequence is a surreal piece of silent cinema, filled with grotesque visual gags. Thompson's recollection of his first encounter with Ursula during a fox hunt turns satire into a slapstick comedy in which horses eat hats and flowers, women get drunk, and the effects of intoxication become the pretext for physical gags (Ursula begins crossing her eyes, falls off her horse, and drags Thompson down in the water). Ursula's lack of style and refinement is carried on in a conjugal scene in which the two characters chase each other round the dining room, breaking vases and ornaments in the process. In this sequence, as in the following one, involving Ursula's mother giving her some last-minute instructions on her wedding night, Sturges has Thompson's voice-over dub all the characters, with an hilarious effect for the women.

Portrait of the Artist

By contrast to Sturges's sporadic usage of narratage in Hollywood, in *Les Carnets du Major Thompson* this technique is at the core of the film's structure, and it is overtly displayed through a constant opposition between recounting versus performing, miming versus acting, indirect versus direct speech, or — to use a terminology devised by the narratologists in the years to come — "telling" versus "showing."

Once again, behind the entertaining value of the movie lies a postmodern meta-linguistic awareness that Sturges displays by connecting the two registers through framing scenes of Thompson dictating his "script" to a secretary — a representation of the act of narration that not only underlines the role of the internal narrator, but also reminds us of Sturges's own career as a writer, in an extra-textual reference to the figure of the implied author.

In this context, it is very relevant that Sturges's first idea for the movie was a brand new story "about an author who creates a fictitious character ... who subsequently appears."[14] At the end, reports James Curtis, "it came out that he was a war hero who had lost his memory fighting for France, and the French author admitted that he had taken his notebooks — which he hadn't of course — and gave this man who had no identity an authentic identity."[15] Halfway between *Hail the Conquering Hero* and a Pirandello play (for instance, *Come tu mi vuoi* [*As You Desire Me*] [1929], centered on a very similar case of mistaken identity, and *Sei personaggi in cerca d'autore* [*Six Characters in Search of an Author*] [1921], about six characters who have not been fully brought to life and are in need of an identity), this approach added a relevant meta-linguistic touch to the project, whose traces are still visible in the final script — the more faithful adaptation of Daninos's book required by Gaumont. In the final movie, in fact, Sturges dedicates several sequences to depicting Thompson's acts of narration-dictation to his secretary, his discussions with the publisher, and his discontent over the characters he has "created," with implications very similar to the ones in *Sullivan's Travels*: Like Sullivan, Thompson has to fight against an environment of pragmatic people who constantly threaten his project and work. In both movies, the only person who seems to understand the two characters is a beautiful young woman ("The Girl" in *Sullivan* and the secretary in *Les Carnets*).[16] More important, both the fictional American filmmaker and the fictional French writer end up abandoning their quest for social analysis — Sullivan recognizes the importance of laughter, while Thompson repudiates the shallow stereotypes he has conjured up in his diary. But if young Sullivan could still afford to learn from his mistakes, discard his screenplay, and start all over again, old Thompson has neither the power nor the strength to throw his work away and start to write a new book.

Perfectly aware of his condition, Thompson concludes: "I'm damned. I'm no longer an Englishman, and I will never be quite a Frenchmen." And like Preston Sturges admitting, at the end of his career, that he "was in no position to refuse work,"[17] Thompson yields to the publisher's pressures and agrees, at the end of the movie, to publish a book he is unhappy with. It is this struggle between the narrator and its narratives that turns *Les Carnets du Major Thompson* into Sturges's ultimate meta-movie: an aesthetic testament of a postmodern screenwriter.

Conclusion

In his analysis of film style and mode of production in the Classical Hollywood Cinema, David Bordwell comes to the conclusion that "in Hollywood cinema, there are no subversive films, only subversive movements. For social and economic reasons, no Hollywood film can provide a distinct and coherent alternative to the classical model."[1]

Certainly Sturges's Hollywood films are no exception: Not only they do not represent an alternative to the institutional mode of representation, but they also perfectly match the characteristics of that "distinct mode [of production], cinematic style and industrial conditions of existence" that Bordwell identifies at the roots of any movie produced in Hollywood between 1915 and 1960.[2]

Nevertheless, Sturges was able to achieve, as an insider, unusual results which scrutinize the rules of the classical paradigm and expose them in a way that is unusual and prescient.

If Sturges lacked the theoretical consciousness that future filmmakers such as Woody Allen and the Coen Brothers would show in their work, writings, and interviews, nonetheless his "practical" concerns about the audience's reactions show an undeniable awareness regarding the differences between his work and a classically constructed film text. "It was actually the enormous risks I took with my pictures, skating right up to the edge of non-acceptance, that paid off so handsomely," writes Sturges in his memoirs, referring to the pastiche of romantic comedy and slapstick he applied to *The Lady Eve*. "It paid off. Audiences, including the critics, surrendered to the fun, and the picture made a lot of money for the studio."[3]

Sturges's work clearly reveals the restless mind of a great experimenter, an artist who was as intuitively aware of the rules and structures of the

Classical Hollywood Cinema as the narratologists who would define them several decades later; a screenwriter who managed to depict his characters with the traits of figures of textual communication; a director able to introduce meta-linguistic elements behind the most innocuous gags, and to mix together genres, norms, narrative and stylistic archetypes; a "Hollywood" personality who managed to talk about the industry itself by creating one of the most explicit Hollywood meta-films ever conceived in those days (*Sullivan's Travels*).

Reinforcing Bordwell's statement, moreover, is the fact that Sturges's potentially subversive tendency to deconstruction would explode in all its anti-classicism (in *Les Carnets du Major Thompson*) only *after* Sturges himself moved outside the golden gates of the Hollywood system.

However, such an outbreak of this type would have been impossible if Sturges had not previously laid down the seeds of a radically new approach to the practice of filmmaking. In this way, the relativism over all values and judgments which emerges in Sturges's most classical comedies was accompanied by a recurrent tendency to deconstruct the classical text in different ways (the contamination of Hollywood genres and styles already visible in his films of the early 1930s, the anti-classical management of timelines in *The Great Moment* and *The Power and the Glory*, the peculiar usage of hypothetical narratives in *Unfaithfully Yours*, and the extensive meta-linguistic approach that emerges in several films and TV projects). Taken together, these things did threaten the institutional mode of representation, as perhaps was dimly sensed by the studio executives who intervened over the structure of *The Great Moment* and bombarded Sturges on almost every single movie with censorious notes and memos.

This way, whether in form of a draft, screenplay, project, or a finally released movie, Sturges's work challenged the Classical Hollywood paradigm in a variety of ways, and — as a result — operated as a major precursor for several directors of recent decades.

Appendix A.
Interview with Sandy Sturges

Alessandro Pirolini: How did you and Preston Sturges meet?
Sandy Sturges: I entered his restaurant the Players to warn him about the sparks spitting out of a neon sign outside the building. Have you been by the Players, have you seen it?

No, I actually thought that the building had been razed. Is it still there?
Oh yes! It's at 8225 Sunset Boulevard. It's still a restaurant, of course, but the configuration has been somewhat changed. For instance, it used to have an outdoors restaurant, with a porch where you could eat. But that's gone.

And does it still have all the elevators and mechanisms that Preston had designed?
Oh yes, as far as I know. There's no reason to take them out.

A few people know that his career was equally divided between his movies and his inventions...
... And the article he was the most happy about was the one that appeared in *Popular Mechanics*, describing the mechanics of the elevator-floors for the restaurant. You know, the restaurant was built on these four elevators which made perfect seating ... one higher than the next for the people behind the seat well; and at the end of the play they would all go sink to one level, and make a beautiful dance floor.

The building has been there for a long time.
Oh yes, because before Preston had it, first it was the home of Chester Conklin. Then it was sold, and it became the Hollywood Wedding Chapel, but when Preston bought it, the chapel wasn't active any more. He dug under the hill to build the lower part of the restaurant.

So, I was on my way home, because I lived up the hills from the Players. After the Chateau Marmont, then the Players' property starts, and the first street that you come to, I lived up that street. So, going up that street, I saw this neon sign sparking, and I thought that there was going to be a fire. I came in rushing,

"Fire, fire, you have to call the fire department!" Preston came out to have a look at it, and he said there was no problem. But I didn't know he was the owner of the restaurant, I thought he worked there: They were building the theater at the time, and he was dressed in his hang-around clothes, helping to carry lumber in there, and all kinds of stuff. So I had no idea. Then he introduced himself, and said his name was Preston Sturges. And you know that little hesitation that the people give so that you have time to say: "Oooh! You don't mean..."

He was waiting for some reaction...

Well, it was an infinitesimal little pause, giving me an opportunity to be overcome. But I wasn't, because I had never heard of him. You know, in those days, when you went to the movies, when they were showing the credits for writers and directors, that's when you got popcorn!

So, I introduced myself and he asked me if I cared to see how the theater was coming along. He brought me in to see the theater. And this not on the street level, but up the street level. If you go there, you'll drive up the street and there's an entrance further up, and that was the entrance to the theater.

And then he offered you a part in one of his plays, *Room Service*.

That was after we were married, because when Preston opened the theater, his intention was not to be a presenter of plays. His intention was to have attractions to bring in the customers, and the customers would spend money. "Theater in which you eat is the oldest form of theater," he used to say. During a period of time, in the Forties, before I knew him, the Players had been the greatest place in the world to eat: You could see everybody there, get great food, all during the war ... and then of course it fell out of favor, as everything does in Hollywood (you know, then there's a new Greek restaurant you've got to go to...), so the idea of a theater was to build it to bring in customers. And the original idea was to open it with five one-act plays. What happened was that in one of the plays called *Hello Out There!*, one of the actresses, Cathy O'Donnell (the wife of Bob Wyler, William's brother), got an opportunity to do a film in London. She had signed, as everybody else, for the run of the play contract, but she came to Preston and begged him to let her go to London to take this wonderful opportunity. And Preston said: "No problem. Sandy will do your part!" The reason he thought I could do the part is because I knew everybody's part, like a member of the orchestra — the orchestra pit was under the stage, and the musicians would sit there, waiting for the end of the play. When the play was over, the orchestra pit would rise.

Was that your first performance?

No, before that, in high school I had played the soldier: I came in, said something (I had one line), and then I fell dead!

So, *Hello Out There!* was your first professional role.

Yes.

And then you got married on the stage of the Players, right?

Yes. Preston had arranged everything. Eddie Bracken was in *Room Service*, and of course Preston knew it from before, when they had made those two films together, *The Miracle of Morgan's Creek* and *Hail the Conquering Hero*. So he was the best man. He gave me away. And what happened was ... after the play was over, Preston went up to the stage, and he told everybody that if they wish to, they would be welcome to stay, but they would have a little ceremony. So, about half the people stayed, not realizing what kind of a ceremony it was going to be.

So he didn't want any kind of publicity, he didn't invite any reporters?
No. Nobody knew until it happened — except the guests who had been invited particularly for the wedding, of course.

There's something incredibly fascinating about this event: a strong connection between his work and his private life, art and existence. Were these two aspects so strongly connected in Preston?
Inextricably connected. There wasn't a private life and a work life. That was his life.

How did he work?
Actually, he had a huge problem in getting himself down to the business of writing. He had no problem writing, but the problem was to start. First we'd have dinner at the Players (because we ate there practically every night), then we'd hang out and have some chitchat with friends, then the Players would close, maybe we'd have a drink before we went home. Finally, when finally he would get home, he would start to work. He would find any kind of excuse not to do it, but he knew he had to do it, so eventually he would get himself there and do it. The way he worked (at least when I was around) was very interesting: I would get behind the typewriter, and he would walk up and down and dictate. Dictating, he would assume the part of the person that he was dictating. So, if he were playing a girl, for instance, and she would start to cry and have a cracked voice, he would dictate it with a crack in his voice and so forth. If the person were angry or furious, he would be dictating it that way. In other terms, he would "act" it. I learned very early that I had to pay attention, because, at first, when he was dictating to the machine and I was taking it down, I had a book on my lap that I would read while he'd be thinking of a line, or what to do next. Then one day he asked me: "What have you got down there?" and I said: "My book." He said: "*A book?*" He was horrified!

Would he "act" his characters also when he was on the set?
Oh yes, it was the same thing. He would tell the actors exactly and precisely how to say the line, how to deliver it ... and every gesture to go with it. The only other time I've ever heard of that kind of directing (of course I don't know much about directing at all) was an interview that someone did with Claire Bloom. She said that Charlie Chaplin directed in the same way. It had to be absolutely just as he directed it: as he said the line, as softly or as loudly as his voice came through. If you've seen the documentary on Preston, *The Rise and Fall of an American Dreamer* [1999], there's an interview with Betty Hutton, where she talks about how Preston directed her.

Did you see him direct?
Only in France, on the set of *Les Carnets du Major Thompson*. The funny

thing about *Les Carnets* was that Gaumont hired him because the story was about an English major married to a French wife, and the observation of the Englishman about French idiosyncrasies. So, they hired Preston because we were in London at the time, and they thought he was an Englishman. Preston shot the movie in two languages. He shot the scene in English and then he'd shoot it again in French, right then and there. It was particularly ... I was going to say "hard to do," but it wasn't hard for him, as he knew exactly what he was doing. You know, you had to be very adept to get the picture in on time and on budget, particularly when you were shooting actually two films, one in English and one in French, at the same time.

Do you remember any difference between the English and the French version?

I've never seen the version in English. I saw the French version because we were living in Paris at the time, so we went to the opening night, and of course it was all in French. Preston spoke perfect French, you know ... he lived much of his boyhood there, until he grew up — from the time he was eight to the time he was fifteen. That's where he lived...

... With his mother and Isadora Duncan.

Well, his mother and Isadora Duncan were bosom buddies. All Isadora had to do was to make a scene: "Oh, Mary, I have to go, please come!" And Mary would go, and forget the baby! She would find somebody to drop the baby off with.

Of course, in her mind, he was always "the baby." When she married her last husband (but also with the previous one), she kept complaining about how much she missed her baby, and so her husband said: "Let's bring the baby over." So, one night Preston arrived in the middle of the night from America, he went to the hotel where his mother was and went to the desk, where he asked for her. The desk clerk said: "You know, it's past midnight. I wouldn't think of calling somebody." And Preston replied: "Well, excuse me, but I'm her son, I'm sure she'll be happy to see me." He said: "No, no, no. You must have the wrong lady. She can't possibly have a son your size." Finally he talked the guy into taking him up to the room, knock on the door, and of course his mother was thrilled, and she started screaming: "Oh my baby, my baby!" and kissed him. Then she introduced him to this absolutely astonished husband: "This is the baby!"

What is interesting is that this story (like most of the stories that appear in the autobiography *Preston Sturges by Preston Sturges*) sounds like a sequence from one of his comedies.

I know, that's why in one of the [book] reviews they said that his life was funny and even more funny than his movies.

He had such an incredible intense life, packed with events, that I was expecting a much longer biography....

Yes, and the things he accomplished. When I look back, I don't know how he did what he did, because he had his film business, writing, the restaurant, the engineering company, and he was always inventing, beside that.

Many of his inventions appeared in his movies; for example in *The Palm Beach Story...*

Oh yes, where he's going to build a suspended airport over the city.

You did an incredible job of adapting and editing Preston's memoirs and notes into the book *Preston Sturges by Preston Sturges*. Was it difficult? What was your main goal behind that?

I used what he had written in his autobiography, pulled stuff out of letters, notes, memos that he had written. I didn't use my memory at all, as I just wanted to show exactly how he saw his own life. The main problem was that if, for example, he mentioned Chicago, he would come up with two or three stories about that part of his life in Chicago, which then reminded him of other stories ... so that you hardly ever got to the thread of his real life. He had started his autobiography before he died, and got up to, I believe, age 11...

Among the documents that you donated to the UCLA Library I found a memo from 1944 called "The Events Leading Up to My Death," which is the same title of the autobiography that he was writing before he died.

Sandy Sturges

That's right. Once he conceived that title, he stuck with it. The 1944 memo is just a sort of a beginning. Nothing in any depth whatsoever. Just a few pages.

To go back to *Les Carnets du Major Thompson,* his first non–American production, was it difficult for him to work in an environment so different from the one he was used to?

One of the difficulties he had on the film was that Martine Carole said she spoke perfect English, and Jack Buchanan said he spoke perfect French. And so when Preston started shooting the scene at the breakfast table, and they're talking about the little boy, Martine says her line. Silence! "Cut." And Preston asks: "Jack, do you know your line?" And he replies: "Of course, of course!" So, they'd start over. Jack responds, and now it's Martine's turn... Total silence! It turned out that neither one of them would recognize their cues in a different language. So Preston had Martine sitting in Jack's lap for that part of the scene. And when the characters were having a discussion, Jack would talk to Martine, and when he was finished talking he would give her a poke — and that was her cue. Then she would give Jack a poke in his back—and that was his cue. They knew their lines perfectly, they just didn't know *when* to say them!

And if you see the movie now, you can feel, sometimes, that Martine Carole is repeating a well-rehearsed series of sounds...

The trouble, for the audience, is when someone has an accent: If you miss the first two words, you don't understand anything else they say.

Now, one of the difficulties was the fact that Preston was used to the American studio system. You know: wardrobe department, art department, sound, everything you need is right there. So, one day he was shooting a scene with Martine Carole, and she got a run in her stocking, so Preston said: "Call wardrobe and get another pair of stockings up here." So, in about ten minutes this little old lady comes, with a needle and a thread in her collar, and she says she is wardrobe. Preston (who, of course, spoke perfect French) says: "Madame, we need another pair of stockings," and she replies: "But I don't have them." And it turned out that she *was* wardrobe, but she didn't *have* any wardrobe. So Preston and she walked around the set looking for somebody with the same color of stockings. And they had to borrow the stockings from that person, put them on Martine, and took them off Martine when the scene was finished.

Another time he was doing a scene where an actor was mounting a train, and Preston wanted the dolly to go up with him. And there was not such a thing! Basically, the studio was just a building with stages in it. They didn't have all these departments. And do you know how Preston solved that problem? He had them pick up manhole covers ... you know, those big holes in the street where people climb down under to go and fix things. So what he did was have some manhole covers taken off these holes and have them slowly move the camera on a little stand. He would always have to be that kind of innovative.

Do you remember that scene in the picture where he's talking to Thompson's British wife, Ursula ... the hunting scene? Well, the hunting scene had been planned, and they were supposed to meet at the Bois de Boulogne. So, all the extras arrived, everything's there except ... guess what? No hounds! What went wrong, who knows? So Preston immediately re-wrote the scene without the hounds and he just covered it with dialogue. He was very, very good at that: If something wasn't there he did it in another way.

I found an article about *Les Carnets* at the UCLA Library, where he said that he asked Gaumont to organize a preview, but the producers' reply was: "We don't believe in that!"

Yes, they thought it was just a waste of time and money, because that was the picture, and what was the point of having a preview. They have previews in America, so that you can see how the audience reacts, and if there's a particular part of the film that doesn't go over or if it appears that the audience doesn't understand something, you can fix it before you really put it in release.

And Preston obviously believed in that, as I found some records of previews he had organized in Hollywood, that relied on a complex system to measure the intensity of the laughter.

Right, "the laugh meter." But he didn't invent it. It was invented by his secretary Gillette, Edwin Gillette. Preston found it very useful, because you could lengthen the scene if it was really going well, shorten it if the audience didn't get the joke and take it out.

The records I found seem to suggest that he almost didn't need it after all, as the laugh meter always indicated pretty high scores.
Yes, there were always lots of good laughs, but it never failed to have a few cards with comments saying: "This film stinks."

Now when I said that, unlike the Hollywood studios, in France they didn't have all these departments, it doesn't mean that they didn't have talent.

No, just the lack of equipment and organization.
Right. So, the people who would work at the studio knew how to do their job, but they didn't have a department behind them. For instance, there wasn't a prop department. If you've been to an American prop department, you know that there's so much stuff there ... unbelievable amounts of it, and for the things that you don't have, they have absolute first class carpenters who make it. Now, in France they didn't have all that stuff. They had talented people, and if they needed a carpenter they would go out and rent a carpenter, but he didn't have a whole department behind him.

He probably missed Hollywood and the days at the Paramount studios.
Well, he didn't talk about the past very often. And he certainly didn't sit around and say: "Oh dear, how things have gone so badly for me," because he always thought that the day after tomorrow everything would change. You know that story of the pencil and paper that he mentions at the end of the book: "More than once over the years I had told Sandy that if worse came to worst, that if we lost *every*thing and found ourselves without a roof over our heads sitting on the curbstone at Franklin and Vista, we would not be without resources. From a car passing to the east, I would borrow a pad of paper; from a car passing west, I would borrow a pencil. By evening I would have written a story and we would be back in business. I always believed this."

But it's hard even now and, of course, it was practically impossible at that time, for me to imagine what it was like to be the number one guy in Hollywood. Number one! People used to fight to get seated at his lunch table. Before leaving Paramount he would come in and everybody would look up and say: "Hi, Mr. Sturges..." Lots of people coming around, shaking hands, during lunch. But when it was known that he was leaving, and having a disagreement with the head of the studio, suddenly there wasn't anybody there. Nobody stopped by the table, not even the people he thought of as friends. That was a hard lesson. He had a hard time getting to be a director, but once that happened, they just practically gave him the studio. Then, all of a sudden it just doesn't mean anything.

Do you think he did recognize the importance of the studio system?
I don't think he saw that it was all that important, or he wouldn't have left. And then he went with Hughes and their company, and after Howard Hughes he went over to Fox, and at Fox he was the third highest paid man in the United States.

How did he decide to start a business with Howard Hughes?

Well, he knew him before, as Hughes used to come to the Players, and would hold the orchestra after hours (paying them as a private person). They both liked each other, because they were both inventors, in essence, both interested in flying and, of course, films. They conceived the idea of a picture company where Hughes would provide the money, and Preston would make the pictures. And instead of taking the salary that he was taking at the time, he would work for something like a tenth of the salary, because he was also an owner of the picture company.

Why you think it didn't work out in the end?

Well, the two of them said: "We're going to do it!" Then of course the lawyers had to go to work. When I was taking entertainment law, one of the things that the professor said was: "If you've got a deal, don't hire the lawyers, because each one will try to get the best deal for his own client, and quite often they get so down to the basics that their deal falls apart." Now, that's not why that deal fell apart, but it took them months and months to put the CalPix agreement together. In the meantime, Howard Hughes and Preston were working. Preston was writing *The Sin of Harold Diddlebock,* and that wound up. It took a long time to make that picture, because Preston, as a co-owner of the studio, was suddenly responsible for all kinds of things he had no talent for, or no real interest in — budgets, etc. You know how very complicated running a studio is. He was there to make pictures, not really to run a studio, but that became also part of his job. He hired people that he knew, but of course none of the people he hired had been in a company, starting from scratch.

And then what happened?

The problem was that Harold Lloyd would have one idea of how the scene would go, and Preston would have another. Harold Lloyd thought that the script was too talky, and that it should have more silent movie kind of stuff in it. So, they compromised by Preston saying: "Ok, we'll do it both ways: We'll shoot it your way, we'll shoot it my way." And that extended the length of time it took to make the film. And, of course, Preston would always pick his way, like what else... That picture wound up, and they began to make another one. Preston purchased the book *Colomba,* by Prosper Mérimée, which for the film they were calling *Vendetta* [released in 1950]. Preston had already done the script, he had already started production. I don't know how far through the picture they were, but one morning at seven o'clock he got a telephone call. It was from Howard and he said: "Preston, we're through!" Now that was part of their deal, it was not part of the contracts that the lawyers were drawing up. The deal between Howard and Preston was that if either one of them wanted out, it was over. All they had to do was to say so. So, at seven o'clock one morning Preston got a call saying that it was over. Now, there were already two or three hundred extras already on the set prepared to arrive that day, and that was a shock. But that was their deal, so Preston had nothing to complain about on that.

Did Howard Hughes give him any reasons?

We never knew why. He just said, "We're finished." Some time later (this is when I knew him), we were having dinner at the Players, and we were joined by Bill Cagney, Jimmy Cagney's brother, and that happened to come up. Preston had invented a gimbel, a candlestick holder that they use on yachts: It keeps the candle steady when it's rocky out there. Preston had invented that, and had them for sale. Well, Bill Cagney told this story that Howard Hughes had been over to his house, where there was a gimbel. Howard Hughes saw it, gave it a little push, and it started to rock. And he said: "Where did you get this? From Preston?" And Bill Cagney replies: "Yes." And Howard says: "I got one of those too. Mine cost me $5,000,000!"

Another time we found out that the reason why Howard did it was probably that he thought that Preston had no regard for Howard's money, and that he spent it just like it hardly mattered. We came to that conclusion, because when they were shooting *Vendetta* they did a bunch of scenes on horseback, and Preston asked the wrangler how much it would cost if he rode the horses during lunch period. And the guy said: "Oh, Mr. Sturges, don't be foolish! For you?" So, Preston assumed that it was not going to cost anything. So every day, during lunchtime, Preston would ride the horse. And it turned out that the wrangler and his company were charging CalPix, the production company, tons of money, for the use of the horses. Of course, Hughes never said a thing about it. All he said was: "We are finished."

I guess it was probably then that Preston realized the importance of the studio system...

He later wrote that Paramount had been his home. He thought of himself as having grown up at Paramount. He knew everybody, everybody knew him, everybody liked him. And it was a nice place to work, with those conditions.

Was it the same at Fox?

At Fox he was received by Zanuck. Zanuck wanted him to come over and do a film. [Zanuck] had liked his work for years and years and was thrilled to get him. He thought they would really have something fantastic going on. As I said before, he became the third highest paid man in the United States, while he was at Fox. I think he was making $12,500 a week. They did *Unfaithfully Yours,* and that went very, very well. Of course, there were memos, requests, changes, etc. (as they are all the time). When the picture was finished and ready to be released, Rex Harrison, who was the male star, was dating Carole Landis (Rex Harrison was married, but he was also dating this blonde actress), and she wanted him to leave his wife. Of course, he wasn't going to do that, and when she finally realized that, she committed suicide [on July 5, 1948]. So, instead of having the great splash opening that they had intended to have, the studio decided to slip the picture under the door, because it was a huge scandal. Harrison was the one who found her body, 'cause he was going to her house.

Among the documents at the UCLA Library I found some papers regarding *Unfaithfully Yours,* saying that someone sued Preston over the main idea of the movie, saying that he allegedly heard a similar story at a party.

Yes.

However, he had worked on that idea since the early 1930s, with the title *The Unfinished Symphony*. How did he react to that?

He didn't care. You have to realize that in Hollywood, no matter what kind of a picture you make or when you make it, there's always sixteen people saying: "Ah, ah! That's my idea." It's just part of being in Hollywood. The same thing happened with songwriters. Six people step out saying: "Oh I wrote that song sixteen years ago. I sang it to my wife!"

After *Unfaithfully Yours*, he did *The Beautiful Blonde from Bashful Bend*, a very unusual movie for him, in a way.

He did that as a favor to Zanuck, but didn't like that. Then he did a lot of rewriting and stuff, but it's not a picture he wanted to do, and it didn't turn out all that well. One of the strange things about that picture: Betty Grable was the girl famous for her legs, and all through the picture she wore long skirts!

It was at that point, at the end of his Hollywood career, that you met him. What was your family life like?

In the place where we lived in Paris he had his office in that sort of half basement ... you know, where the windows would come chest-high, if you're standing up, and if you look up to look out on the street, you can see people walking by. That's where he had his office, and when he was dictating to the secretary that Gaumont provided, for instance, he would work down there, but he would also make stuff for the house, with little Preston, at the same time. They made a beautiful lamp together. He did all kinds of things with the baby while he was dictating. Little Preston was three and a half or four years old then. The nice thing about it was that, if he went downstairs to go to his office and do some work, and he would come back upstairs, little Preston would run over, as if his father had been out of sight for several years, and leap and say: "Up! Up!" And Preston would pick him up. And if he went to the bathroom and read a book while he was in there, he'd still be received the same way. He used to drive us to the park every day, the park Monceau. He didn't drive us every day, but he picked us up every day, because sometimes we just walked over there.

How did he view aging?

In a letter written in 1957, a few days after he attained age 59, he said he was getting to look too much like Dr. Schweitzer, and that he no longer wondered what young ladies would say when he extended an invitation ... merely what reason they would give for not accepting. However in 1933, long before aging was a current consideration for him, he wrote: "Time in the general acceptance of the word does not exist. It is a road upon which we walk, always in the present. To our ancestors we are not yet born; to our descendants we are already dead. Yet all of us, the ancestors, the descendants, and we, ourselves, are marching down the same road, each as real or as unreal as the other."

Was he very sentimental, romantic?

Very romantic, very romantic! And when he was writing romantic scenes, for instance, it would just be as if they were happening to him in that instant. As a writer he played both sides of that duel. But he also had a vicious temper.

I read about that.

He did, but after having a temper fit, he was over with it. He didn't carry grudges around, and say: "Remember when you did this? Remember when you did that?" Ever.

Did his personality change with the years?

No, he very much lived in the present. I can't really speak for the time before I knew it, except by what he said in the things he wrote. But I think that at the end of the book when he's talking about what a man approaching sixties starts to think, and the lessons that he's learned in life ... it was said in a way that nothing's changed. He was still the same impulsive person he was when he was twenty.

What do you think gave him the most happiness?

That's an interesting question. I know he was extremely happy with the baby, and if his work was going well he was very happy. He was a happy person. The most happiness, I would say, when I knew him, was his relationship with little Preston and then Tom-Tom when he got born.

In *The Rise and Fall of an American Dreamer,* one of the people interviewed said that Preston paid the price for being an American dreamer. Do you agree with the idea that he had to pay the price?

Well, paying the price, at least to me, means that you recognize what the price is going to be and you say: "Okay, I'll go for it." But if you're paying a price you don't know you're paying, that's quite another thing.

In the same documentary, Frances Ramsden also says that he ran away from culture. What do you think?

I think that's true, because when he was a kid, his mother dragged him to every concert, every opera, and then put him to bed in the afternoon, to have a nap, so he could be up late and see these shows. So, while the other kids were going out to play, he had to lie down and take naps, which already set him against it. And that stayed with him for the rest of his life. For example, during the time that I was with him in Paris, José Yturbi came over. He was a classical pianist who also made a few films as an actor (and therefore he was taken less seriously by his contemporaries). He went to Paris to do a concert, and he invited Preston and me to it. It was an evening of *études,* and Preston just couldn't ... I mean, he was very polite, he sat through tapping his fingers — you know when you want to get out of there. He had that look that says: "When is this going to be over?"

However, his restlessness for that type of music didn't prevent him from performing a quite interesting choice of classic pieces in *Unfaithfully Yours.*

What he was trying to do was to find music to suit what the character had in mind. And he happened to know and like those pieces. It was just the forced cultural feeding (I guess you can call it that way), that his mother did with him when he was small. You just mentioned the word "opera" and he'd already be shivering ... which didn't prevent his enjoying it, but it wasn't something we sought out exactly. He and I never ever went to a single opera, and we practically never went to the movies.

What do you think is the biggest misconception about him?

Mostly what I read (and I don't read everything in the world) are references like: "If Sturges had made this film, it would have been 100 percent better." So, I don't know what the perception of him is. For example, if you're not a movie fan, you wouldn't have heard of him. I remember Preston's friend Priscilla Bonner had lunch with somebody, some years ago, and she mentioned Preston. She might have mentioned John Doe, for all the response she got, and then she asked the person if they had not heard of him, and they said: "No!" And she came to me horrified: "Can you believe it?" I said: "Priscilla, who do you suppose won the Nobel Prize for chemistry last year?" She says: "I have no idea!" "Likewise," I said, "there are people in the world who have no idea what goes on in the movies."

What was his relationship with money?

Money was for spending, 'cause he made and lost a couple of fortunes during his lifetime. I don't think he ever saved a penny during all the time I knew him. And I don't mean that he was out buying cars and velvet dresses, or anything like that. You know he just used the money as it came along. Of course we didn't have a lot of money.

How about his relationship with success. How did he define success? Did he consider himself a success?

Success was if his work was well received, and not by critics, by the public. And he always thought, every single time, no matter what he was writing, that this was the best thing he had ever written.

So, he didn't care much about the critics' reactions?

Oh no, he was very interested in their reactions too. And Bosley Crowther, the *New York Times* critic ... well, they began a career-long correspondence. He was delighted to see the critics' reactions, especially if they got exactly what he was doing.

In his movies, Preston always avoided any discourse on religion or politics, even in the early phase of his career — in times when it was fashionable to be a leftist. But he didn't seem to care for that.

Not in the least. He was just not interested. And don't forget that he was brought up in a way, for instance, with his mother embracing one religion, and then another, and then another ... and different husbands and lovers.... So he was quite accustomed to know nothing being steady. You know, people who have strong opinions on political situations usually don't have the history that he had, where he realized that it doesn't really mean that much, because you've seen how it changes.

It's interesting how such attitudes shows up in his movies too, even during World War II, when the studios were asking Hollywood directors to glorify the war.

Yes, and he actually was against wars.

And he managed to do all that without getting in trouble with the Hays Office.

That takes a man like Preston. Billy Wilder too was good at that.

Even watching *The Miracle of Morgan's Creek* today, for example, you cannot but wonder how he managed to get around the censors.

The critic James Agee said that Preston had raped the Hays office in its sleep by getting *Miracle* done. What Preston said he did was: "Obey strictly the letter of the law ... and totally ignore the spirit." If you look up the production notes and stuff on *Miracle* at the library, there was a ton of stuff (memos, notes, letters): "We can't do this, we can't do that, we can't do the other thing." So he was smart not to change the intent, the spirit.

You mentioned Billy Wilder. What did he think of other contemporary directors?

I never heard him mention anybody. The only person he showed any interest in their future was not a film person. It was a French politician: Pierre Mendès-France. He said he was an interesting man and it would be interesting to see where his career took him.

I think we saw Minnelli's *An American in Paris* (1951) together, but I can't really remember any other movies that we actually went to. The thing is that when you make a film, that's the only thing that matters, you don't even think about anything else. I remember when we were doing *Les Carnets du Major Thompson* in Paris, that was all we wrote and talked about. So much so that when the Hungarian Revolution tried to start in 1956 and Eisenhower didn't help, it was like: "What, what, what? What's going on?" You know, we'd never heard of all this stuff, 'cause it just couldn't impinge on the moment in time when we were, and all the other people connected with the film. The film was really the whole world, and then these things would come in from outside, and always with surprise.

But he was friends with many directors.

Well, he was great pals with Willy Wyler. They became friends in 1934, when Willy was directing *The Good Fairy*. Preston had written that script and was on the set most of the time, when Willy was directing it. They became buddies, and they stayed buddies for the rest of Preston's life.

And in the Fifties, Wyler asked him to fix the screenplay for *Roman Holiday*.

Yes, Willy asked him to read it through and see if he could make it a little sharper from place to place, but since it was Preston, of course, he started to write the whole screenplay all over from scratch.

So, he did re-write the entire movie?

Yes, but Willy did not use that rewritten script. He did use some few things that Preston had written in the new script.

Do you remember what he used?

I'd have to really think hard. I don't remember offhand.

I'm asking because there's one specific sequence in that movie that, to me, seems very Preston Sturges-like. It's one long silent gag very similar to the ones that we find in *The Palm Beach Story* and *Sullivan's Travels*—a chase in the narrow Roman streets that ends in a traffic jam, and everybody is taken

to the police station. The whole sequence is a long series of silent gags punctuated by music.

I don't know whether that was Preston's or not. It could be. In fact, I think
the script that Preston did write is in the collection, so that you could read it and
see if there's anything left.

**How about his relationship with other directors? For instance, he explicitly
mentions Lubitsch in the dialogue of *Sullivan's Travels*.**

Oh yes, and Veronica Lake says, "Who's Lubitsch?" Well, Preston really
admired Lubitsch. So much so that in the first picture that he wrote and directed,
The Great McGinty, he wanted to have a dedication to Lubitsch. But the studio
said: "Please, you know we don't do dedications in film." But he much admired
Lubitsch's work. And they, of course, were friends.

How about Capra?

I don't know if he even knew Capra. Of course he knew about him, but I
don't know if they knew each other, because Capra was over at Columbia.

**I was curious about that because, to me, we have Sturges, Lubitsch, René Clair
on one side (that is, directors who were able to talk about everything, including politics, in a very subtle, indirect way), and on the other hand we have
Capra...**

Yes, Capra didn't mind giving you a lecture, but he also did it with such sweet-
ness. It's not like going to a film, I'm really getting lectured.

Well, one of the things that's different is the fact that of all the men who
made the movies before Preston and during his time, not a single one of them had
ever heard of a film school. There wasn't such a thing. They learned on their feet.
Like Griffith, who invented all kinds of things to do with the camera. Now you
go to a film school and they teach you all those things, but it's not the same as
needing something and inventing it for yourself.

There's a place in Paris called the Cinémathèque Française where they pre-
serve and show old movies. When we were living there, they would run Preston's
movies, and he would always be invited to speak, and he would always accept.
They would run the film, and then he would be on stage, afterwards, so that people could ask him questions. These were true "students of films," I mean, they
studied every nuance, every little movement of a finger. One of the questions I
particularly remember was about *Hail the Conquering Hero.* There's a scene in that
movie where the Marines have dragged the main character off the train, and he's
all dressed in his new uniform, with medals hanging all over, and they're pulling
and pushing him forward, and you see his feet off the ground, because they're actually really impelling him forward with their own push. Well, one of the questions
from the students was a long speech on why Preston had shot that showing mostly
the feet and the fence behind them (sometimes, of course, the questions were
much longer than the answers). Preston said that he hated to disappoint them, or
anybody else of the same opinion, but the reason they shot it that way is that they
had finished the film, realized that they needed a little additional movement in
there. Rather than reconstructing the entire set, they just did the fence and the

feet. And you know what the response to that was from the questioner? "Ah, monsieur, you joke with us!"

Did he spend time with Jean Renoir, René Clair or Jacques Tati, when he was in Paris?

Well, we used to see a lot of René Clair in Paris, at a club. You know, Preston knew him from before: Clair had come to Hollywood to make *I Married a Witch* [1942], and he was going to have a René Clair Productions, and Preston was the producer, and so Preston said to take his name off his film as producer. And René said: "You know, that's really too much." And Preston said: "Well, you can't have a René Clair production produced by somebody else." Of course they do it all the time now, but Preston wrote a lot of that one too.

I don't know if he knew Tati or Renoir. He certainly knew them by reputation. In general, when he was going to make a film with a particular person in mind, either a particular actor that he had in mind, or that the casting office had come up with, he would run all the films they had on them, while he was writing.

Do you receive many requests for interviews, especially from young directors?

No, because there are so many books out on that stuff. Mostly what I hear is from the students, or professor, because if anybody is interested in his work as an actor or director, they only have to look at his films.

You know that the Coen brothers made a movie called *O Brother, Where Art Thou?*

Oh yes, straight out of *Sullivan's Travels*, but it's not a remake of Preston's movie. It's the film that Sully, Preston's character, wanted to make. I didn't see it.

Did they contact you or ask you or say anything about their artistic relation with the cinema of Preston Sturges?

The Coen brothers just love Preston and everything he ever did. I didn't talk to them, but my son Tom has talked to them, several times.

The fact that so many scholars and directors are still interested in Preston's work really proves that he really was ahead of his time.

I don't really know what you mean by "ahead of his time." Can you give me an example?

Well, what I mean is that now, directors like Woody Allen and Robert Zemeckis quote previous movies and even use them in their own ones. Clips of Orson Welles's *The Lady from Shanghai* [1948], for example, appear in Woody Allen's *Manhattan Murder Mystery* [1993]; Zemeckis manipulated *Birth of a Nation* in *Forrest Gump*, and there's even a movie called *Dead Men Don't Wear Plaid* made of bits and pieces of old film noirs. Now, they call this "postmodern pastiche," but Preston was already doing all this in 1947, with *The Sin of Harold Diddlebock*, where he incorporated footage from a silent movie by Harold Lloyd and had it interact with new footage and a new story.

Well, first of all he was lucky enough to have Harold Lloyd to be there to shoot new scenes. Preston used Harold Lloyd's *The Freshman*, particularly the last reel, the one that shows Harold Lloyd making this fantastic touchdown, and being a hero. What Preston was really trying to show was, here's a guy who's the hero of the world, and what happens to him? The first thing that happens ... he goes to see the man who told him: "Come and see me, I've got a job for you." Then he doesn't even remember him. "Ah yes ... baseball... No, no ... it was hockey...." He doesn't remember him at all. And only three weeks have passed. And then he gives him his job, he's expected to be a fantastic success on the job, but nothing happens. Harold thinks so himself, and never goes anywhere. And when it's time to retire, he's still doing exactly what he did when he came in...

That seems to suggest a vision of the job market and the economic system quite pessimistic, especially in the first part of the movie.

I don't think he was thinking of the whole economic system, he was thinking of a particular person, who's led to believe that because he's done one great thing when he is young, is going to have a brilliant future. But running a ball down the field doesn't make you a businessman. I think it's about one's expectations as a kid, in a way — and of course, also about the fact that Harold Lloyd takes all those platitudes so seriously.

What's your favorite Preston Sturges movie?

That he wrote? It's *Easy Living*. I love that movie. Have you seen it?

Yes, a remarkable screenplay.

Plus it's so funny and so utterly unreal, even if it's entirely believable. Among the films that he wrote and directed, I have a hard time picking a favorite. I love *The Lady Eve*, for instance, and *The Miracle of Morgan's Creek*. I can't think of one I don't like. The only one that I didn't enjoy very much was *The Great Moment*.

It's probably one of the less entertaining, but the structure of the story, its chronology, and the way he played with it are, once again, incredibly ahead of his times.

Well, the life of Dr. Morton was difficult to tell: He's a person whose life, once he invented the anesthesia and let the secret go ... nothing much could have happened. Some fan wrote to complain about the fact that it was not as exciting as he'd expected. Preston replied by saying that he did the best he could with the man and the way he lived his life, and trying to tell the story so that it would last long enough. What are your favorite movies?

The one that makes me laugh the most is probably *The Miracle of Morgan's Creek*.

And that also makes me cry the most! You know Eddie Bracken is so hopelessly in love with the girl, and loves her so much (he takes cooking classes, just to be in the same class she's in). It's very touching.

But my favorite movie is definitely *Unfaithfully Yours*.

That's a great film.

I find fascinating the way the same story is told three times.

Yes, but... Do you have a copy of my book? In that, he mentions *Unfaithfully Yours* and the fact that a very few people caught on to what he was doing. For instance, many critics complained that Linda Darnell appeared very wooden in parts of it, but what Preston was trying to do was actually very precise: You know when you're planning a scene, for instance if you're going to propose to a girl, and you rehearse it in your mind (how you're going to ask her, what you're going to say, etc.), and while you're doing that you also provide answers for her. For example you say: "Darling, will you marry me?" and she'll probably say: "What do you mean?" Or "I'll think about it." So you provide the answers in your mind for her, and respond to those answers. The same happens in *Unfaithfully Yours,* where Rex Harrison imagines the scene that is going to happen: His wife says only the lines that *he* imagines she would say, and she responds exactly the way his mind thinks she would respond. Of course, she came out as still as a dummy, because she was allowed to say only what was in his mind. Very few people got that.

Preston also thought that the reason at the time, that it was not such a success is because in the end, of course, nothing happens...

Which is another interesting and modern aspect, compared to other movies made in Hollywood in the same era.

Another original thing that was also remarked upon, at the time, is the scene when Rex Harrison leads the orchestra, and in order to get into his mind, they get a close-up on his face, which is tighter and tighter and tighter until you go right into the pupil of his eye. That was remarkable at the time.

Do you think he was aware of his own innovations?

Preston never had the intention of being innovative in order to break a record. If there was something he had to do, he'd find a way to do it, as in *Les Carnets du Major Thompson.*

One of the most difficult to find movies by Preston Sturges is *Diamond Jim,* which is another story of a tycoon who commits suicide, like in *The Power and the Glory.*

Yes. It opens on a man [Edward Arnold] who's going to buy a suit as he wants to appear wealthy and rich. So he asks the man who's selling him the suit what would make him look like a millionaire, and the man answers: "A diamond stud." And he replies: "I'll have one!"

Diamond Jim was actually a real person. Preston said that he had actually seen him, dining with both of the Dolly Sisters (who at the time were very famous, always dating millionaires ... that's in the days, of course, before there was income tax). His problem was that he ate too much and drank too much, and knew it was bad for him. So, when his heart gets broken again, he just sits down and orders the biggest meal that ever, ever had been eaten by a human. In other words, he's saying: "Let's go!" And one assumes he dies after that meal. It's a good picture.

Did any of Preston's sons follow in his footsteps?

Well, Preston is a writer, and Tom-Tom is in the music business. He's executive vice-president for the Universal Music Publishing Group.

And his father was in the music business as well.

Oh yes, he started as a songwriter, and the first restaurant he opened, Snyder's, was opened for songwriters, and he considered himself one of them.

Did he write many songs?

Oh, he wrote songs all the time, when he did a picture. He was writing a picture in 1952 for Paramount called *Look Ma, I'm Dancing*, which was not produced. The studio hired him to write it for Betty Hutton, and it had been on Broadway. He did a great script. They loved it, but Betty Hutton wouldn't do it, unless they made her husband direct it. And the studio just said: "Forget it!" But he wrote songs for that. Every picture he wrote, he wrote songs for. And I think it's in the DVD extras of *Sullivan's Travels* that you'll hear him sing. You won't see him, but you'll hear him sing some of the songs he did write.

How about painting?

He could paint, and he did wonderful caricatures, but, as he said, caricature is an evanescent art, because unless you know the people who are being caricatured in the drawing, the whole fun of it is gone. You don't recognize the talent it took to change that person into a caricature. For instance, in Paris there was an artist called Sem, before our times, who did some fantastic caricatures, and he was world-famous at the time, but a couple of decades passed and nobody knew who these people were, and so they didn't recognize the brilliance of his caricature. Preston took painting lessons himself, music lessons, I mean, everything that you can think of ... violin lessons ... there's a couple of shots of him playing the violin on the set of *Unfaithfully Yours*.

I remember seeing a beautiful caricature of you and Faulkner.

Oh yes, I have it. That's at the end of the French DVD of *Unfaithfully Yours*, in the extras. They did include some caricatures of me and William Faulkner that Preston had drawn. He did it on the back of a menu.

What did he think of television?

He thought it was a fantastic invention, just incredible, especially because it was so ... instantly available. He thought that if candy makers and people like that didn't get hold of it, it might be a powerful force in the world. Of course the candy makers did get hold of it, with the commercials. In a note [dated 1949] he wrote: "As of this moment I am tremendously enthusiastic about television. Not about what I have seen on these sulfurous little screens, but about what I see in my head, what I know can be done with the technical equipment now available. Unless television gets into the hands of the same real estate men and candy butchers who inherited sound film from the movies, it will discharge the obligation that talking film failed to do and will diffuse to the smallest hamlets in the furthest part of the world the treasures of literature and of music. I hope this will happen."[1]

He had a few projects in mind that were being seriously discussed at the time he died. One was titled *It Happened Exactly Here*. So that you go to a particular part of the sidewalk in Paris, and that's exactly where Joan of Arc was burnt at the stake [see note 60, chapter 3].

So the project was to show different sites where historical events had happened?

Yes, a comparison between what it looks like now and what it must have looked like then, and what happened there. Very interesting because, of course you walk the streets and the last thing you're thinking about is Joan of Arc. Another project was about plays he always wanted to see again, but that weren't been done any more.

Do you remember any TV appearances?

Well, on local TV when we had the theater, when the Players first opened, he was interviewed on screen for a couple of different stations. I never saw the results, but we got feedback. I was expecting our first baby then.

And then you went back to Hollywood with the kids to pick up a script, an old script that Preston had written before, and that some producer had shown a new interest in, right?

Yes, only we never got back. We were really out of money. When I got to the house I found the script — as I knew about where to look for. But by the time it got to Paris (in less than a week), the guy had no more interest in it than feathers on a fish. That was, I think, the hardest part, because so many things would be on the verge of happening, even going so far where they would put money in escrow, sign contracts, and all that stuff, and then change their minds. Of course, he had the basis for several lawsuits with that kind of thing happening, but he was not going to waste his time messing around in court. And it wasn't that he didn't find work. People, in Europe, would come to him, and several times you'd be right there: "We got it, it's done." But it wasn't. It was very heartbreaking, actually. And then in America he had the reputation for being hard to handle and too expensive.

Why do you think he had a hard time finding a job?

He did say something rather interesting, and that is: "When people want you, or when people don't want you, in either case you never know exactly why." But even David Wark Griffith, who practically invented movies, couldn't get work. Who knows why...

Yes, the case of Griffith is definitely similar to that of Preston Sturges. One wonders if the revolution introduced by sound, which put Griffith out of work, could be compared to the coming of television, which affected the Hollywood system in an even more radical way.

That's when the studio system kind of fell apart, with the threat of television. The studios got very nervous about that. For instance, they let all their contract players go, so that when they wanted to make a movie they couldn't call, for instance, Clark Gable and say: "Let's make this movie." He was now an independent artist, so he had to be wooed, salaried, and all kinds of stuff that the studios didn't have to do before. Before they had you under contract and you did what you were told to do, but then, as a means to save money, they cut off all those contracts, and then they found it was much, much more expensive hiring people one by one. I'm talking about actors, of course, not talking about departments.

In any case, Preston never let himself go. Even his late articles and the last pages of his autobiography show a strong optimism.

That doesn't mean that if something happened, he didn't get depressed about it. But he always thought he could write his way out of trouble. I think 1958 was the worst year that he had. Because that year he didn't have any work. Not that he didn't try. As I said before, he would sign contracts with people, stuff like that, and then the guy would just say: "Well, I'm not going to make the picture. Let's tear up the contract." He had several reasons that he could have sued different people, for breaking their promises. But as he said, "What's the point?"

Do you think that he would be able to make his movies in the climate of today?

I don't know why not. He did have his so-called stock company, and those were actors under contract to Paramount. But, when I see his films, when they run on TV, they could have been made ... last week. So, I can't see that there'd be any much reason for not making them.

How would he like to be thought of now?

The only time he ever mentioned about it was that he'd like to be remembered as an honorable man.

Appendix B.
Les Carnets
du Major Thompson:
Unpublished Documents

Les Carnets du Major Thompson
(Notes by Preston Sturges on the difference between the English and French versions.)

My view is that the English version should commence with a narrative sequence, to establish from the very beginning what the picture's about. Not everyone has read the book, or even heard about it, and to start the film with the breakfast scene — much more heavily played in the English version than in the French, as is from which there is no recovery afterwards.

The continuity I visualize is as set out below —

I do not know yet whether it will be possible to realize the plan in full, but I am reassembling the picture with this continuity at the back of my mind:

1. Start with a series of travel agency posters advertising France. These posters mix in with stock shots of the parts of France they advertise, the more beautiful the better, and the *commentary* says in effect that it is the ambition of everyone in England to cross twenty miles of salt water and once in a lifetime to visit France. We now see a picture of Major THOMPSON himself. It must be a fairly extended picture so as to enable him in commentary to introduce himself as an Englishman who visited France many years ago and who has been there ever since, much to his surprise, for he still finds it difficult to understand the behavior of those strange people, the French — a crowded compartment in a train for instance —

2. After a shot of a train approaching camera, dissolve to the Train Narrative sequence, exactly as it is, even with dialogue in French if it is impossible to render it in English.

It would be good to end this narrative sequence with a scene of a train receding into the distance.

3. Dissolve to the Major in a taxicab thinking things over. The taxi draws up at the curb, the Major gets out, pays the taxi and looks up. Cut to the Fusillard notice board. Over these scenes the commentary states that after many such experiences as the one we have just witnessed, the Major thought that there might be some advantage in visiting a publisher.

4. Dissolve to the scene in the publisher's office. Mr. FUSILLARD agrees in the end to provide facilities for the Major to write his comments. The scene ends with Mr. FUSILLARD saying: "[T]he beginning requirements for all literary inspiration is a pretty woman."

5. Dissolve to a C.S. of Martine in negligee awaiting the return of the major. The commentary could say: "with which I was already thankfully provided in the person of Martine, my wife!"

Continue with the scene of the Major's return home to find Miss FFYFTH waiting for him in the trophy room. Omit all references to India in this sequence, and end on Martine exclaiming "Really, darling, the English!"

6. Dissolve to the C.U. of the Major at the breakfast table completely hidden by the *Times*. This scene may now have some sense in reference to Miss FFYFTH since we have seen her. The scene finishes when the Major is saying: "It's exactly because I *am* a foreigner, darling, and see everything about me with clearer eyes than someone who has looked at it all his life, that I am better qualified to guide the destiny of this charming little half–French boy — who has the good fortune to have his other half–English!"

Cut to a C.U. of the Major, who continues in this sense: "As an Englishman I belong to a prudent, far-seeing race, qualities which I must admit I can scarcely find in the country where I have made my home." As he speaks there is a long dissolve to the keys of the typewriter, which in turn dissolve to —

7. The Narrative of the French on the roads, beginning with the Major himself driving on the wrong side. At the end of this narrative, again dissolve to the keys of the typewriter and then come to the secretary, as she finishes. —

8. This is the first time we have seen the secretary, she looks up and smiles at the Major, who asks if it is funny. The secretary replies that it is not only funny, but deep, in the sense of depth.

9. Now dissolve to Martine reading the manuscript, *but no reading from it*. This scene develops into Miss FFYFTH's display of military drill, which should, but does not, have a violent reaction from Martine. Therefore follow at once with:

10. The scene in which Martine objects strongly to Miss FFYFTH's interpretations of history. More arguments between the Major and Martine over Anglo-French incompatibilities, ending with Martine going out and slamming the door.

11. This brings us to the narrative of French bureaucracy: "France is the only country I know of in which, if you add ten citizens to ten other citizens, you have not made an addition ... you have made a division."

12. The narrative ends in Fusillard's office, with Fusillard indignant. The Major calls for no Anglophobia.

13. The Major returns home to find Miss FFYFTH and Marc doing exercises.

"Rule Britannia"— but Martine is not in the flat. He has dinner alone. It has been prepared by Miss FFYFTH and he cannot eat it. He prepares to dine elsewhere and encounters Martine at the front door. They wake it up and go out to dine together.

14. The Major and Martine in a restaurant. He starts talking about his earlier romance with Ursula.

15. Narrative of the Major's romance with Ursula.

16. Return to the restaurant. The Major and Martine kiss.

17. The following morning. The Major has his breakfast brought to him in bed. Meanwhile means must be found to interpolate Miss FFYFTH and Marc at their exercises, to act as a visual reminder that Miss FFYFTH is very much in the present, and to add force to Martine's indignation when she speaks about Miss FFYFTH's interpretation of NAPOLEONIC History.

18. In Fusillard's office, the argument continues over the subject of history. This leads to —

19. The narrative of distrustful French: the oysters sequence, the exact time sequence. The catacombs sequence —

20. Back to the Major and Fusillard in the publisher's office. The Major shakes hands with Fusillard on leaving.—

21. The Major comes home and discovers that Martine has been selling the furniture. Martine tries to cajole him into getting rid of Miss FFYFTH, but he refuses and goes out in a fit of pique.

22. Short montage of revelry, to be devised.

23. The Major returns home, tipsy. He falls out of this hammock and then there is another reconciliation.

24. The narrative of the shake-hands.

25. At the end of the shake-hand narrative, the Major shakes hands with the secretary in Fusillard's office.

26. The Major returns home to find his two maidservants dressed to leave. I would like to open this sequence with an insert of a door on which has been pinned a note which reads — Exercises in progress, keep out! FFYFTH (signed). One hears "Rule Britannia" going on, and then the Major comes home. In the end the two maidservants leave and when Martine tells the Major that Miss FFYFTH has offered to do the cooking, he is horrified.

27. Dissolve to a close-up of a fizzing glass of bicarbonate. The Major then starts his narrative on sex.

28. The narrative on sex.

29. M. FUSILLARD tells the Major that he is published. The Major laments that he is neither English nor French.

30. Short narrative of the Major being neither English nor French.

31. C.U. of the Major looking supremely depressed, with his bowler hat not at all at the right angle.

32. The Major returns home to find the flat empty. Then follows the telephone conversation between Martine and the Major.

33. The scene in the restaurant, with the Major crying at the end "Vive la France."

34. For a final shot —?

In the foregoing arrangement I have tried to make the narrative sequences grow out of what happens to the Major in his home.

12 MARS 1956

Les Carnets du Major Thompson
(Article by Preston Sturges)

"Where do we preview?" I asked my French producer one day as we neared the end of the shooting.

"Where do we what?" he answered. We were speaking in French naturally, a language I learned as a boy.

"Preview," I said, "you know: when you try the picture out on the dog, le chien, and see where he laughs. Or *if* he laughs."

"Why should le chien laugh?" said my producer, then suddenly: "Wait a minute, *un moment*. I know what you are talking about: You are talking about a prévue!"

"That's it," I said, "that's what I was trying to say. Where do we do it?"

"We don't believe in that," said my producer.

I pause here briefly for personal identification.

My name is Preston Sturges and I used to make pictures out in the Golden West, in a town called Hollywood, until the Big Wind blew up and a number of us wandered on. Now I was in Paris shooting *Les Carnets du Major Thompson*, a best-selling French book about the idiosyncrasies of the French, as seen through the eyes of a retired English Major. As the book was written by a Frenchman, his compatriots got a very fair shake in the comparisons with their hereditary enemies: the English. It was really a series of essays, and when it was first proposed to me by Gaumont, the largest of the French pictures companies, I had voiced considerable doubt as to its suitability for the screen.

"It ain't got no sex," I said, feeling they would expect me to talk like this after a stretch in Hollywood. That it would give them confidence. That they would realize that I was "à la page."

"It's very funny," said Gaumont, "Everybody in France is laughing at it!"

"I know that," I said, "and they are laughing at themselves, which is a very healthy sign. It indicates the French are an intelligent, high-class race. But you must remember that all these people who are laughing are people who can read. Not everybody who goes to the movies can read. You must think of that too!"

"Everybody in France can read!" said Gaumont.

"I'll take your word for it," I said, "but we must also think of the rest of the world! Not everybody in the rest of the world can read."

"We don't make pictures for barbarians!" said my French friends. "Kindly remember that France, the intellectual center of the world ... the seat of erudition and the torchbearer of civilization, was already an extremely cultured nation ... while our neighbors across the Channel, who give themselves such airs, were still painting their faces with blue mud ... and nesting in the trees."

"You are referring to the English," I said.

"The truth is the truth," said my producers apologetically, "perfidious Albion!"

"I see," I said. "Were you thinking of selling this picture over there? I mean, to perfidious Albion?"

"We never sell *anything* over there!" said my French friends. "When we start a film and try to guess beforehand what the different countries might possibly bring in, behind England all we put is a question mark!"

"What do you put behind America?" I asked.

"We don't even write them down on the paper," said my friends. "Cowboys! They don't speak French, but they refuse to look at dubbed pictures! Even when they are so beautifully dubbed that you can hardly tell it is not the original actors speaking ... except once in a while!"

"They aren't mouthing the same words," I said.

"If you want to look at pictures through a magnifying glass," said my friends, "stay home and collect stamps."

"I was thinking of making the picture in two languages," I said, "English and French. In fact if I make this picture at all, I think it will be in two languages. I would not care to put in all the time and effort it is going to take to turn this book into a picture, and then show it in France only!"

"There is also Belgium," said my French friends, "and don't forget Switzerland."

"I won't," I said, "I went to school there."

"Canada is also a very large market," said the producers, "the *French* part, naturally. The rest is so illiterate!"

"I didn't realize it was so big," I said. I had visited Quebec because my mother was born there.

"Then there is North Africa," said my friends, "not to mention Madagascar and several of the Antilles!"

"Look," I said, "during my years in this industry I have quite often read the world-wide box-office reports of pictures I had a piece of. I have a fair idea of where the money comes from, and whereas I agree completely with you that anyone who does not speak fluent French is not only an analphabet, but a louse, I still wouldn't care to make a picture that didn't have a chance in the English-speaking countries."

"But could one *make* an Anglo-American picture out of this subject?" asked the producer.

"If one could make a picture out of it all," I said, "one could do it just as well in English as in French. The fascination about this subject is that it opens up great vistas. If I can make a picture out of this, I plan also to make a picture out of the Dictionary of the Academy, Fanny Farmer's Cook Book and Doctor Phyffe's Twenty Thousand Words Often Mispronounced."

"You are being humorous," said my friends, "you doubt the subject."

"By itself: I do," I said, "although I am enchanted with the idea of making an *adult* subject. Few have been offered me. If you will agree with me, however, that even an adult likes to be amused once in a while, give me a hell of a cast, let me add a story of sorts with jokes, a little sex and maybe some suspense; then sprinkle it all with a few pratfalls, I think I can give you back something.

"What is it Le Pratfall?" asked my puzzled friends.

"You know," I replied, "tomber... Bang! Sur le derrière... Boom!"

"Ah," said my friends, "Le gag!"

"That's right," I said, "Le gag sur le Prat!"

"This is enjoyed in your countries?" asked my friends sadly.

"Relished," I replied.

"Slightly childish," said my friends.

"You never said a truer thing," I replied. "You have to be young in heart."

"But what," asked one of the gentlemen, "is Le Gag sur le Prat to do in this adultish picture?"

"It's the sugar," I said. "You know, like they put on pills."

Now the two pictures were nearly finished. The producers had really come through, charmingly and generously, with everything I had asked. I had had two complete and loyal crews, and I didn't lose more than thirty-five or forty pounds running between the stage to give them set-ups. Giving up my lunch and dinner also saved a little time, and by working in the cutting room every night till midnight, I hadn't fallen too far behind the assembly. Also, they had really given me a hell of a cast: Martine Carole, the toast of Europe, ravishingly pretty, funny, and a ripe peach of a girl in every department; Jack Buchanan, the best dressed man in the world, the English star of stars and a hilarious comedian; and finally Noël-Noël, the great French mime, probably one of the funniest men on earth. The fact that they were not all exactly bilingual and that I did not change one single actor for either version, added to the fun. I was pretty sure I had the stuff in the can and I had a mountain of cans. What I needed was a preview: to verify my quantities ... to check what the highbrows call the rhythm.

"What do you mean you don't believe in them?" I said, as my hair slowly rose on my head. "This is a comedy! A *funny* comedy! Nobody ever put out a comedy without a preview ... without *several* previews."

"We tried one once," said my producer, "and it was a disaster! Nobody laughed from beginning to end, we cut out everything that nobody had laughed at, and when we were finished there was nothing left but the Main Title, with music, and the final trademark. We had to put everything back just the way it was. It was a complete waste of time."

"I see," I said, mopping my head. "How did the picture do?"

"I told you," said my producer, "a disaster! We have never tried the *prévue* since."

"Well, sir, that just goes to show you," I said, not knowing what else to say. "Over where I used to work, they still consider the preview about as indispensable as the compass on a ship. Why a friend of mine, called Billy Wilder, previewed *The Seven Year Itch* seventeen times! They were thinking of calling it *The Seventeen Year Itch*."

"Probably an eccentric," said my producer.

"He's that too," I said, "but his pictures make quite a lot of money. You ever hear of him?"

"No," said my producer, "but tell me: do all of you in England use this method?"

"Not being English," I said, "I know very little about their methods, but I *believe* they preview over there."

"What do you mean you're not English!" said my producer, stunned. "It was because you were English that we engaged you to *make* this picture in the first place!"

"I'm awfully sorry to disappoint you," I said, "I was born in Chicago and it's pretty late to do anything about it now! I could buy a suit that was a little tight in the armholes if you like, and tuck my handkerchief up my sleeve, but I don't think it would fool anybody."

"But you came to lunch with me the first time in a Rolls-Royce," said my producer accusingly.

"That's right," I said, "and you ate ravioli! But I didn't draw any conclusions from it."

"This is a shock," said my producer.

"You'll just have to live with it," I said, "as I'll have to live with the one you just handed me! I mean about opening this comedy cold, without any kind of preview, without knowing where I'm too long or too short, or where a small unintentional laugh ruins the big one you'd counted on, or any other of the ten thousand things you ought to find out beforehand! How big is this theater we're opening cold in?"

"We are not opening in *one* theater," said my producer sternly. "We are opening in *five* theaters."

"All at once?" I yammered.

"Naturally," said my producer, "how else?"

"But cold," I said, mopping my head. The idea made me hot.

"Whatever you call it," said my producer.

"How many seats?" I asked in a small voice, trying to estimate the size of the catastrophe.

"Eleven thousand, three hundred and twenty six," said my producer.

"In each theater?" I asked, willing by now to believe anything.

"No, no," laughed my producer, "for the whole five. Then the next day we open in Lyons in *three* theaters, with four thousand two hundred and ninety eight seats, then the day after that..."

"You don't have to go any further," I said, wishing for once that I were British, so that I'd have some of that celebrated calm to fall back on. "And all I can tell you is this: You don't believe in previews, and you are possibly entirely right about them, but you are about to hold the *biggest* one that's ever been held in this racket since the Frères Lumière invented the Cinématographe and Edison came through with the Kinetoscope ... I believe in 1894! Because all this French version, that you're going to show all over Europe and Madagascar and North Africa and the Antilles, is going to do, is serve as a preview for the English and American versions we put out afterwards! You talk about seventeen previews! You're going to have seventeen THOUSAND previews!"

My producer looked at me glumly for so long I thought I had made my point. Finally, his eyes pleading like a water spaniel's, he broke the silence.

"You're SURE you're not English?" he said, but there was no hope in his voice.

A tear rolled down my cheek, but I could not find words. The moment was too sad.

P.S. Truth compels the author most reluctantly to admit that the picture did extraordinarily well all over Europe and Madagascar, even breaking a few house records, without benefit of any preview whatsoever.

P.S.

Appendix C.
Television Projects

The Preston Sturges Show

In describing this show which exists, so far, only in my imagination, I would like to begin with the setting, which I believe to be extremely important, because, whereas ideas and inventions will determine the format, the architectural setting will determine the form. It so happens that I have constructed recently a small and quite handsome theater with certain very practical back stage devices. Among these are overhead track, movable in two directions, which permit the extremely rapid transportation of relatively heavy places of scenery and the pre-arrangement of twelve of fifteen settings entirely adequate for the type of television scenes I envisage.

The auditorium itself, which I have already described as handsome, is separated from the stage by two curtains: a travelling curtain and a raising curtain. The letter lends itself very well to the application of a trademark or identification of some sort.

Immediately in front of the footlights there is an orchestra pit extending under the stage which looks full with six men but can accommodate up to twenty-five in descending gradations. Besides its footlights, the theater has two banks of twenty-four spots each, permanently located and all necessary dimming devices. The stage is furthermore equipped with a large variable mirror for efficient stereopticon or rear process projection.

The orchestra seats, which are readily removable and supported on four elevators, are surrounded by boxes. The latter only would be filled by spectators during a television show, at least as I see it now, and are conveniently located next to a bar.

The show would start with a drawing of the exterior of the Players at night. Activity in the form of shadows would be seen past the windows and out of these same windows would come music and laughter. As many times as required we would push into a close shot of a door which, opening magically, would reveal a

153

necessary credit. We now dissolve to a cue of people presenting tickets at the door. A saturnine gentleman of fifty is taking the tickets muttering, "Good evening... Come right in... I hope you will like the show... Yes, Madam, the seats are *quite* comfortable... That depends entirely on what you smoke, sir ... one or two of the weeds are forbidden... Madam? No, this is *not* the Jack Benny show... Well, I'm disappointed that you're disappointed... No, that's about five miles down Sunset Boulevard and turn sharp to the left ... you can't miss it, it's opposite a hamburger stand... No, Madam, this is *The Preston Sturges Show*... I'm *quite* positive, Madam... Would you care to see my driving license?... Well, now that you're here why don't you come in anyway... What? Oh, no! Not a nickel, Madam ... it's all paid for by the U.S. Soup Company ... you pay for it in the soup ... every time you find a soup marked USS ... I mean every time you find a U and two S's in your alphabet soup ... remember you are feeding the family that feeds the nation ... et cetera, et cetera." Now a man in uniform taps the saturnine gentleman on the shoulder and says, "All ready with the show, Mr. S." "How is it going to be," says Mr. S. "Terrific," says the man in uniform, "the house is packed ... all the lights is working nice ... the musicians is all tuned up ... all you gotta do is get our there and crack a few jokes and you'll have them eating out of your hand." "If you just wouldn't be so blasted cheerful every week..." says Mr. S. "...That is what depresses me." "Don't be nervous," says the gentleman in uniform, "remember the coward dies a thousand deaths ... the valiant dies but once." "Do you believe in reincarnation?" says Mr. S. "I do not," says the gentleman in uniform firmly. "Then once is plenty," says Mr. S.

DISSOLVE TO trademark on the main curtain. CAMERA number 2.

We hear very lovely music ... and the camera pans down to the back of the orchestra leader, then pans or cuts to various members of the orchestra as they indulge in brilliancies.

CUT TO CAMERA number 1

The apron behind the curtain. The music continues, of course, although is slightly muffled. Mr. S. appears from the stage door, rather nervously checks the props on his desk, still more nervously consults his watch, shakes it, then checks it with another — or emergency — watch. After this he sits at this desk and practices a few smiles. Suddenly remembering something he slides over the top of his desk, knocking down only a few things that have to be picked up, then goes to the curtain of the small proscenium six feet behind the first proscenium and sticks his head through the curtain.

CUT TO CAMERA number 3

This catches Mr. S.'s head sticking through the curtains. Nervously he says, "All ready?" CAMERA pans to the can-can girls dressing and making up at a wheeled dressing table. One of the girls says, "We're always ready ... you know that ... like the Marine Corps ... Semper Fidelis."

Mr. S. who is visible in the mirror now says, "No Latin, please ... you're supposed to be can-can girls!" "Can we help it if we're all Ph.D.'s?" says another very pretty girl adjusting her stockings. "Shut up, will you?" says Mr. S. in the mirror. "You let out stuff like that and our sponsor will divorce us." "Who *is* our sponsor, by the way?" says another can-can girl. "Have we got one?" "Sufficient unto the day is the evil thereof," says the reflection of Mr. S. "Ask me no questions and I'll tell you no lies."

CUT TO CAMERA number 1

Mr. S. from the rear. Across the back of his coat is the sponsor's slogan. Mr. S. turns into CAMERA and says "Have we got a sponsor!" Now he looks at his watch, vaults over the desk again, knocking down the props which have once more to be picked up, he arranges himself once more, tries a few more smiles, examines his teeth in a mirror then answers a phone. "Of course I'm ready ... if those musicians will ever stop playing... All right, see what you can do." He hangs up the telephone. "What a life! And what do you get for it? A fortune!"

CUT TO CAMERA number 2

The orchestra finishes the overture, there is applause and the leader takes a bow. CAMERA number 3 which has now come around picks up spectators applauding in a panning SHOT. CAMERA number 1 which has also come around picks up some extra heavy applause from the maitre d'hotel, some waiters and a bartender.

CUT TO CAMERA number 2

That picks up the orchestra leader who turns and starts the signature piece of the show. The CAMERA tilts up on the trademark and follows it up to the ceiling as the curtain rises. Now it comes down again on to the velvet parting curtain.

CUT TO CAMERA number 1

which has turned to pick up an arc spot in the back of the theater. As the arc sputters and iris opens letting the beam out...

CUT TO CAMERA number 2

which picks up the circle of light on the curtain. The curtain opens revealing Mr. S. in the light beam. He bows and says, "Good evening, ladies and gentlemen, near and far." At the applause he says, "Thank you very much" and raises his hand for silence. The applause dies in all parts of the house except one corner to which Mr. S. now directs a baleful look.

CUT TO CAMERA number 3

which picks up the maitre d'hotel, the waiters and the bartender.

CUT TO CAMERA number 2

on Mr. S. It has moved in closer. Mr. S. says to this group, "Thank you for your loyalty... One ham and cheese on rye ... right after the show."

CUT TO CAMERA number 3

The maitre d'hotel, the waiters and the bartender. The maitre d'hotel whips out a pad and says, "With pickles?" Mr. S's voice replies, "Naturally, with pickles." The bartender says, "Anything to wash it down with?"

CUT TO CAMERA number 2

on Mr. S. who says, "Never end your sentences with a preposition ... and kindly remember we're on television ... and I'd better remember it myself. Welcome to the Players Theater, ladies and gentlemen, in the heart of Hollywood which is the heart of America according to our local Chamber of Commerce. What great works, what new philosophies, what enduring novels, tragedies, comedies have not come out of this modern Athens ... I will not even attempt to enumerate. We have also per square mile more cat and dog hospitals and newfangled religions than any other city in the world ... but this is certainly not what I came out here to talk about... Now if I could just remember *what* I came out here to talk about... I'd be delighted to talk about it." The bartender's voice hollers, "Television." "Tell e what?" says Mr. S.

CUT TO CAMERA number 3

on the bartender, cocktail shaker in hand. He says, "Television ... you were supposed to talk about television."

CUT TO CAMERA number 3

on Mr. S. who says, "That's right, thank you very much, Herman. We will take as our text for tonight: Television! What is it? Do we like it? Will it endure? To tackle first things first: until such time as a successful method is devised enabling the viewers of television and other air shows to pay directly for what they receive ... as you pay for a bushel of corn or even for a television set ... the indirect form of payment will continue and you will pay ... as you are paying now ... through the nose ... I mean through the purchase of those wonderful products our sponsors sell you for a high price ... and which cost them so little they can afford to waste money on sending shows like this out into the infinite ether. Incidentally, one of the beauties of television is the fact that it travels on straight rays ... they leave ... and go out and pass right over the horizon and disappear. They never come back as opposed to the rays which carry radio programs ... which sometimes conform to the curvature of the earth and wind up going around and around it ... forever ... which brings up the dreadful possibility of some amateur in the year 3000 picking up Fibber McGee and Molly... Can you imagine how those jokes would sound after they've been going around 2000 now." At this Mr. S. picks up a round disc labeled "Laughter" and holds it up by the handle. After a moment he turns it backwards and the audience reads: "Thank you." After this he continues: "Anyway the lovely word sponsor suggests [the] even lovelier one 'commercial' ... so that is what we come to next. What beautiful memories does the word 'commercial' not evoke! I can think of quite a *few* it does not evoke!

For this reason I made a small inquiry into the subject of commercials for television to see if I could help a little and if I can't ... well ... I can always go back to what I was doing before I was doing this ... if I could just remember what it was. Now one of the disadvantages of radio commercials which was that they had to be spoken ... which was bad ... then re-spoken ... which was worse ... or sung ... which was *much* worse. Now let us imagine that our sponsor is the We Never Sleep Collection Agency whose motto is 'We'll get them in the end.' I would solve this problem in the following way..." Mr. S. gives a signal to the orchestra leader and starts for his desk. On the way he points to the other side of the stage where to the lovely music of the can-can there appears on CAMERA 3 the six beautiful can-can girls. They dance, kick and disport themselves gracefully and at the end of the number turn the back of their little panties toward the spectators. CAMERA number 1 picks up the two girls bearing the words "We'll get." CAMERA number 2 picks up two girls who divide the words "them in." CAMERA number 3 picks up the last two girls who bear the words "the end."

CUT TO CAMERA number 1

which picks up Mr. S. at his desk. He picks up a circular sign reading "Applause" and turns it around to "Thank you." After this CAMERAS 2 and 3 permit the pretty girls to take bows and CAMERA 1 brings us back to Mr. S. who says, "You'll see them again ... you don't think I'm going to waste them on a collection agency. Now of course this commercial I've just shown you might be a little daring for a manufacturer of religious paraphernalia or even for a good undertaker ... but it has infinite possibilities ... with a set-up like that the variations are endless. You can just picture 'One hot dish with each cool meal'... 'They satisfy'... 'The pause that refreshes'... 'Eventually, why not now?'... 'Ask the man who owns one' ... and so forth and so forth]. Then of course there is the perfectly frank, or direct, approach of simply making a commercial a commercial ... just stopping whatever is going on dead in these tracks and socking it to them. This is how it is done in radio and I will endeavor to show you how the same method would work in television." Mr. S. moves toward his desk and hollers, "Let 'er go, Gallagher!" The CAMERA pans back to the center of the small proscenium. The curtains part, revealing the front room of a shabby house. On stage are an old paralytic in a wheelchair, called Gramps, a shrew of sixty and their granddaughter, a beautiful young girl. The latter is weeping

THE SHREW

... coming home at all hours of the night... giving us a bad name with the neighbors...

THE GIRL

I didn't.

THE SHREW

... bringing a stroke on your poor grandfather...

THE GIRL
(weeping)

I didn't ... I didn't.

THE SHREW

... and now *this* ... the final infamy!

THE GIRL
(sobbing)

It wasn't my fault! It wasn't! It wasn't!

THE SHREW

I suppose it was *his* fault.

THE GIRL

It wasn't anybody's fault ... it was just ... just

THE FIRST ANNOUNCER
(coming on brightly)

We will now pause briefly for Channel Identification.

THE SECOND ANNOUNCER
(coming on from the other side and speaking in a very bass voice)

You are enjoying Channel Six, ladies and gentlemen, the Drama Channel ...
happiness with a tear. We will now pause briefly for our celebrated chimes.

A grip now hurries on stage with a large set of chimes on wheels. On this he
does a run.

THE THIRD ANNOUNCER
(hurrying on stage)

And a good, good evening, ladies and gentlemen. We now pause briefly for
a few well chosen words from our sponsor without whom this marvelous show
would never reach you.

Another grip hurries on stage wheeling a frame which supports a large Chinese gong. Now a gentleman in a dinner jacket comes on and whacks the gong.
During all this THE SHREW holds her approximate position, the YOUNG GIRL
continues to look miserable and GRAMPS incessantly shakes his head from side to
side, this being another disease he is afflicted with.

THE FOURTH ANNOUNCER
(hurrying on stage)

The top of the evening to you, ladies and gentlemen ... I bring you greetings from REXLAXO, Nature's relaxant ... spelled R-E-X-L-A-X-O ... and Oh!

how good you feel in the morning ... how clear your eye ... how firm your voice after a foaming beaker of sparkling REXLAXO, Nature's relaxant ... spelled R-E-X-L-A-X-O. Do you suffer from gas?... Bilious attacks ... dizziness ... flatulence ... flat feet ... obesity ... back ache ... front ache ... muscular pains, arthritis, neuritis, phlebitis osmosis, neurosis or halitosis?... Ah, you do! I thought so ... but you don't have to ... Merely dissolve six big, fat REXLAXO... Nature's relaxant ... spelled R-E-X-L-A-X-O ... tablets in a quart of hot spring water and toss it off! *Then* see how you feel! Hear the words of pretty little Mrs. Amandine L. DeBosquet of 369 Genessee Street, Purple City, Nebraska. Just hear this unsolicited and totally unrehearsed testimonial.

MRS. DeBOSQUET
(hurrying on stage. She is a frumpy misshapen fat woman
of fifty-five with an adenoidal voice)

I was sufferin' sumpin turrible. Every time I stood up I felt like sittin' down and every time I sat down I felt like ... well, I don't know should I say this on the air...

THE FOURTH ANNOUNCER
(hastily)

This is entirely unsolicited.

MRS. DeBOSQUET

All my friends said I was sufferin' from fratulence.

THE FOURTH ANNOUNCER

This is entirely unrehearsed.

MRS. DeBOSQUET

Nobody even come to see me any more and I felt just turrible ... thenone day I heard about ELASCO...

THE FOURTH ANNOUNCER
(waspishly)

*REX*LASCO
(then furiously)

REX*LAX*O ... I mean RELAXO.

THE THIRD ANNOUNCER

*REX*LASCO.

MRS. DeBOSQUET
(to the fourth announcer)

It ain't so easy...

THE FOURTH ANNOUNCER

This is entirely unsolicited.

MRS. DeBOSQUET

.... then one day a friend give me a bit tube of RELAXNO...

THE THIRD ANNOUNCER

REXNAXO.

THE FOURTH ANNOUNCER

This is entirely unrehearsed.

MRS. DeBOSQUET

... the big economy size...

THE FOURTH ANNOUNCER
(raising a finger)

Unsolicited.

MRS. DeBOSQUET

... It still cost plenty.

THE THIRD ANNOUNCER

Unrehearsed.

MRS. DeBOSQUET

I happen to have a wash boiler fulla clothes on the stove at the time...
The third and the fourth announcer exchange a look.

MRS. DeBOSQUET

I dropped the whole tube of RELAXNOT into it...

(the fourth Announcer opens his mouth to
say something then thinks better of it)

... and the clothes come out whiter than they ever done before.

THE FOURTH ANNOUNCER

This is entirely unrehearsed

THE THIRD ANNOUNCER

We will now pause for Channel Identification.
The grip hits the Chinese gong and the curtain closes.
    Mr. S. moves to stage center and says, "This is just to give you an idea..." At
the applause he pulls a small "I Thank You" plaque from his pocket and holds it

up by the handle, then continues, "Of course this is just one of the facets of television, which being new has more facets than a millionaire's bathroom..." He pauses at the silence, then repeats, "than a millionaire's bathroom." Then as a solitary laugh comes from the audience, "Thank you, Herman."

CUT TO CAMERA number 3

which picks up Herman the bartender who says: "Any time."

CUT TO CAMERA number 1

which picks up Mr. S. who says, "Thank you. Another thing which differentiates television from radio is the fact that in television the cast, that is the actors, have to look more or less what they sound like. This, of course, is not the case in radio where the sound of the voice alone built the hero to his proper size, gave the heroine her beauty and the villain his menace. I don't know whether you were ever privileged to see an important radio show going out over the air, but I stood in line for several hours one day and then saw something approximately as follows ... I want you to listen first to this torrid love scene ... I will show you its point of emanation afterwards." Through the microphone we hear a melodious male voice which says...

After all, Clementine, let us face facts. Although I am young ... younger than I would care to remind you of ... I am not unacquainted with the shabbier sides of that condition which, for lack of a better word, we call Life. I knew when I married you that I was gambling with my happiness ... that your beauty was too devastating to be what I might call, for lack of better word, Safe. For three years now ... three long years I have overlooked familiarities which, for lack of a better word, might almost be called *Over*-familiarities ... but now with the advent of Christ into our lives I feel the time has come to call a spade, for lack of a better word ... a Spade.

Now a deeper male voice says:

Don't you think, my dear Charles, that you are indulging in slight hyperbole?

The curtain parts and standing in front of two microphones, reading their parts from type-written sheets clipped to laundry boards we see Charles, bald-headed, forty-five, portly and five feet one; the beautiful lady parked behind a pair of chic spectacles from which protrudes the nose of a parrot; and last but not least in front of his own little microphone, the possessor of the extremely deep voice: Chris, a midget.

This scene continues along obvious lines after which the curtain closes and Mr. S. resumes his lecture.

Letter to John Hertz

November 14, 1951
John Hertz, Jr.

Buchanan & Company
1501 Broadway, New York, N. Y.

Dear John,

About a year and a half ago I was in a store that sells television sets. I saw two things ... and I saw the light. The first thing I saw was the hair on the back of a man's hand. He was giving a drawing lesson. The second thing was a panning shot across some dress models, winding up on the cloak-and-suiter himself, who didn't know he was in the shot and was scratching his pants. It was the movement of the camera and the quite excellent lighting that impressed me. I hurried out of the shop know that I could tell any story on television.

I knew all about the screen size arguments already, because Karl Freund had taught me seventeen years ago that motion picture film need be sharp enough only to stand a 2.5 enlargement, i.e. a blowup $1\frac{7}{8}$ inches, because that is the size of the average motion picture screen if measured between the fingers at reading distance: fourteen inches. In other words a television screen approximately two inches high, fourteen inches from the eyes, is the same size as the screen in the Rivoli theater from an average seat.

As I said, I hurried out of the shop and in a great burst of enthusiasm called up a few television people I knew at ABC. They were pleased about my enthusiasm, invited me to see some of the shows in the flesh, took me into the control room, allowed me to talk to the engineer in charge, said they would love to have me in television and hoped that some day there would be enough money in it to tempt me to join the fold. I said I didn't care about the money but that I had so damn many debts I had to keep earning as much as I could. We parted.

I continued to think about television. I appeared on a few shows including Klaus Lansberg's *City at Night*, which came to the Players, and was surprised to start receiving offers to MC quiz shows, to replace a comic pretending to be a director, to put together a variety show and appear on it, etc., etc. I was less surprised at a great number of offers to write and direct a first or pilot film for practically nothing ... with promises of great riches to follow. But I was interested in television.

I continued to think about it and I have that kind of mind which returns constantly to unsolved problems. I watched television when I could, listened to the arguments about live shows vs. the filmed variety, was told that only close shots are any good and immediately thereafter saw wonderful chases on horseback with heroes leaping on to trains, heard that flat, dull lighting was the only kind that didn't shake the tower down and then tried to reconcile this with well lighted pictures made without thought of television ... I continued to think about television. I saw a hundred comedians' jokes burned up in half an hour by one comedian. I met a man who was reducing the world's masterpieces to thirteen minute shorts. I told him television should be slow because it was aimed at small, leisurely groups, taking their ease, not large, rude, impatient crowds. He said television should be faster. (I saw a show the other night played at what I had said was the right tempo. It has taken the Coast by storm and is receiving national publicity.)

I saw the efforts of people trying to do in five days what takes six months in a motion picture studio. I talked with haggard writers trying to do a half hour show a week. I said I was a fast writer but I couldn't do seventeen *Miracle of Morgan's Creek* in a year ... that I had written *Strictly Dishonorable* in six days but that I hadn't written fifty-one other plays that year. I talked with a man who said there would be nothing left to show except sporting events by the 1952 election. I said the longest continuing and most widespread entertainment in the history of mankind had come out of one book and one book only, namely, the Bible.

I continued to think about television ... and all at once, the other night, a lot of thoughts came together and jelled: a film format I invented twenty years ago, a lot of ways to cut cost, some beliefs about keeping up quality and dignity, my opinions about proper pace, and a lot of other things. I knew that I had found one of the things I was looking for: a continuing show of the finest dramatic quality, designed exclusively for television, that would never run out of material or, for that matter, have the slightest difficulty in finding it, that would take all of my time and could also, quite easily, pay me a satisfactory wage. I immediately telephoned you.

John, I am absolutely certain that I have hit upon an idea of incalculable value, but I don't know how to go about selling it without endangering my intrinsic rights. Offering it through the channels of the usual talent agencies would give too many people access to the idea at this point, although I would undoubtedly use my present representative when I had made a substantial contract. I am, therefore, my dear friend, imposing on your kindness once more to ask you to do me a favor. Will you, with no thought of remuneration to yourself, except with gratitude you may engender in the person you approach for having brought him the idea, endeavor to bring me in contact with the head of some broadcasting chain who might have enough regard for my past performances to consider availing himself of my services for the creation of this new idea?

Affectionately yours,
PRESTON STURGES

They Still Live

This is an idea for a panel show, based upon the thoroughly logical but seldom thought of fact that our lives are ruled by those who went before us ... in other words, by the dead. The name of the show stems from the theory then that since these men still rule us and their words and philosophies and laws are part of our everyday life, in a sense, THEY STILL LIVE.

Thus a man might be executed today for the violation of a law originating in the Code Napoleon, adopted by the thirty-eight Congress, ratified by the then Senate, upheld by Supreme Court Justice, Oliver Wendell Holmes (I may be a little off on my dates) and signed by Abraham Lincoln. He might have been unsuccessfully defended by quotations from Blackstone, cases of long defunct personages would have been mentioned at the trial and the prayer what might have been said over his body was probably written two thousand years ago.

After this depressing preamble I hasten to state that the show itself would be quite gay. Two identical panel arrangements would be set up for the purpose of dissolving in the members of the panel after the introduction and at the request of the Moderator. This latter would start the show alone, empty seats on either side of him, possibly with the reading of a letter from a lady in Wilkes-Barre, Pennsylvania, requesting advice on how to keep her husband home at night. The Moderator would pretend to remember that Voltaire had something to say about that, at the striking of a gong, a reasonable facsimile of Voltaire in the habiliments of his time, would materialize at the desk of the Moderator's right. After being apprised of the question, Voltaire would quote from himself a suitable and authentic passage. The Moderator might then ask if Shakespeare had not an opposing opinion, and, after a disparaging opinion of Shakespeare from Voltaire, Shakespeare would be summoned, would materialize, exchange rudeness lively with Voltaire, then quote from himself. The Moderator might now summon Socrates and finally the show would continue with a full panel of arguing celebrities [on the margin, Sturges adds "Madame de Sevigny"]. Their dialogue would be invented ... their quotations authentic.

This would not be a difficult show to do ... requiring a few books of quotations and a scholar who spent his time down at the Public Library. It would be instructive, however, of very high quality and much good humor. I believe the viewers would feel they had actually seen the great people of the past. The salaries of the actors and the rental of the costumes would not be exorbitant.

You Be Witness

This show is based on the undeniable fact that most people are unable to recall, with any degree of accuracy, any given event they may witness. Proof of this fact can best be illustrated in the almost daily occurrences in courtrooms, when honest, well meaning people are called upon to reconstruct some scenes and then give such conflicting testimony. To err is only human — but in this show a simulated scene of violence will be enacted, three (or more) persons selected from the audience will witness a scene then they will be questioned on the witness stand by a man who will conduct his interrogation in a manner not unlike regular courtroom procedure. Each witness will be graded on his O.Q. (observation quotient). The televiewer may enter into this test by keeping his own score to determine his O.Q. and compare his own mental alertness with the contestants. This adds to the enjoyment of the program. The witness-contestants may or may not be awarded some sort of gratuity for their mental alertness in earning the best score of the program.

To impress the audience and the contestants with the responsibility a witness has when he gives testimony in a trial, the opening scene takes place in a courtroom. (long shot) A young woman is being called by the court clerk to come to the witness stand. A close shot reveals her to be rather attractive and a bit frightened and confused. With the camera on her, the voice of the prosecuting attorney (o.s.) begins — NOW MISS LANE WILL YOU TELL TO THE BEST OF

YOUR ABILITY EXACTLY WHAT HAPPENED ON THE NIGHT OF JUNE 14 AT APPROXIMATELY NINE etc. Dissolve to — contestants and the interrogator of the show *You Be Witness*. The witnesses are introduced to the audience. The interrogator gives a brief talk on the responsibility of a witness in giving correct testimony. He cites some cases where accused persons have been convicted on incorrect testimony. After explaining to the witnesses to observe closely a scene which will be enacted for them, the curtains part and a quickly enacted scene of violence transpires. One by one the witnesses are grilled. A blackboard in the background keeps a tally of the correctness of the testimony. After two or possibly three different scenes have been presented the scores are compared and the winner receives his reward. To end the show in a lighter vein, the interrogator suggests that the witnesses now assume that they are the jury and he gives a brief synopsis of a law case that actually happened, one that is quite ridiculous in content and asks each one exactly how he would judge the case. After each passes judgment, he comes forth with the ridiculous judgments which was actually handed down in the case.

[Follows a handwritten screenplay]

Appendix D.
"Writing and Directing"

I see that I am down here to say something about writing and directing motion pictures ... well, the first thing I would like to say is that it's very nice ... it's nice because it's so restful, the directing, I mean ... it gives you a chance to stop writing for awhile ... the wonderful thing about a stage hit is that you don't have to write another one until the first one runs out ... only sometimes you have to write quite a few in between ... which gets very tiresome ... one time I didn't have to write anything for two years ... after that I was so used to loafing I just couldn't get going again, so I came out here and went to work for a picture company. After they fired me I *had* to get to work again, so I went home and wrote a piece called *The Power and the Glory* ... the title sold it ... they say I stole it from Orson Welles but that isn't true ... I stole it from Conrad. I spent six weeks on the set while we were shooting that ... at my own expense ... helping to stage the dialogue and as sort of general handy-man ... what you would call "speculative directing" ... and right then and there I decided that directing was my dish. The director, a very good one, by the way, William K. Howard, had a bice [sic] chair in front of the camera, had a property man to take care of his hat and coat, told everybody what to do and had a nice time generally. I stood on a step-ladder in the back and from where I looked I didn't see anything going on that was so hard you would call it impossible.

You say to your cameraman, "How about using a thirty-five here, Jimmy?" and he says, "Well, I was thinking of using a three-inch on that." So you say, "Well ... there's something to that," and then the wardrobe lady comes over and says, "Do you want her to wear the taupe with the fur buttons or the razzberry [sic] gussets with the frogging [sic] down the back?" and you say, "Well ... a little of each." And the art director comes over and says, "I see a high mansard roof here supported on a facade of Ionic columns on Corinthian pediments," and you say, "Aha ... very nice." And then you say to the actors, "Where does the scene feel best to you?" ... and they'll always manage to get the scene well in the camera ... usually facing the right way. So I decided I was going to become a director. There wasn't a moment to lose. I started putting the pressure on everybody I knew and it wasn't nine years till somebody said, "All right ... go ahead ... you win."

Of course, when I said directing is easy, I meant it's easy for the writer-director, because he did all his directing when he wrote his screenplay. It may be very hard for a regular director. He probably has to read it the night before and do a little homework. The writer-director never has to read anything ... which gives him the bulge. Of course, there are some disadvantages too ... there comes the awful day, when you have to write a new one ... and you can't pull any hocus-pocus either. You can't say, "Boy, what that fathead did to my scene" ... and when you get to direct it, you can't say, "Boy, was that cheesy until I took it in hand." You forfeit the two best alibis in the business ... but it has its good points: all the policemen on the lot get to know you by name ... the same ones who wanted to throw you out of a suspicious character when you just wrote here ... and the extra girls get to know you and smile at you in the commissary ... and anybody you have for lunch, it's always about business, of course ... it's very pleasant ... I could go on like this for quite a while, but you have lots of other speakers here and I'm not apt to say anything very important. Thank you.

Filmography

Screenplays and Dialogue by Preston Sturges

The Big Pond (1930)

Producer: Monta Bell. *Director:* Hobart Henley. *Scenario:* Robert Presnell, Garrett Fort, based on the play by George Middleton, A. E. Thomas. *Dialogue:* Preston Sturges. *Photography:* George Folsey. *Editor:* Emma Hill. *Sound:* Ernest Zatorsky. *Musical Arranger:* John W. Green. *Studio:* Paramount Long Island Studio. *Production and Distribution:* Paramount. *Release Date:* May 1930. *Running Time:* 72 minutes. *Cast:* Maurice Chavalier (Pierre Mirande), Claudette Colbert (Barbara Billings), George Barbier (Mr. Billings), Marion Ballou (Mrs. Billings), Andree Corday (Toinette), Frank Lyon (Ronnie), Nat Pendleton (Pat O'Day), Elaine Koch (Jeanie).

Fast and Loose (1930)

Director: Fred Newmeyer. *Dialogue Director:* Bertram Harrison. *Screenplay:* Doris Anderson, Jack Kirkland, based on the play *The Best People* by David Gray, Avery Hopwood. *Dialogue:* Preston Sturges. *Photography:* William Steiner. *Sound:* C. A. Tuthill. *Studio:* Paramount Long Island Studio. *Production and Distribution:* Paramount. *Release Date:* November 1930. *Running Time:* 70 minutes. *Cast:* Frank Morgan (Bronson Lenox), Miriam Hopkins (Marion Lenox), Carole Lombard (Alice O'Neil), Charles Starrett (Henry Morgan), Henry Wadsworth (Bertie Lenox), Winifred Harris (Carrie Lenox), Herbert Yost (George Grafton), David Hutcheson (Lord Rockingham), Ilka Chase (Millie Montgomery), Herschel Mayall (Judge Summers)

They Just Had to Get Married (1932)

Director: Edward Ludwig. *Assistant Director:* Eddie Snyder. *Screenplay:* Gladys Lehman, H. M. Walker, Preston Sturges (uncredited), based on a play by Cyril Harcourt. *Additional Dialogue:* Clarence Marks. *Photography:* Edward Snyder.

169

Editor: Ted Kent. *Sound:* Gilbert Kurland. *Makeup:* Jack P. Pierce. *Production and Distribution:* Universal. *Release Date:* January 1933. *Running Time:* 69 minutes. *Cast:* Slim Summerville (Sam Sutton), ZaSu Pitts (Molly), Roland Young (Hume), Verree Teasdale (Lola Montrose), Fifi D'Orsay (Marie), C. Aubrey Smith (Hampton), Robert Greig (Radcliff), David Landau (Montrose), Elizabeth Patterson (Lizzie), Wallis Clark (Fairchilds), Vivian Oakland (Mrs. Fairchilds), Cora Sue Collins (Rosalie Fairchilds), David Leo Tollotson (Wilmont Fairchilds), William Burress (Bradford), Louise Mackintosh (Mrs. Bradford), Bertram Marburgh (Langley), James Donlan (Clerk), Henry Armetta (Tony), Virginia Howell (Mrs. Langley).

The Power and the Glory (1933)

Producer: Jesse L. Lasky. *Director:* William K. Howard. *Assistant Director:* Horace Hough. *Screenplay:* Preston Sturges. *Photography:* James Wong Howe. *Editor:* Paul Weatherwax. *Art Director:* Max Parker. *Musical Score:* J. S. Zamencik, Peter Brunelli. *Musical Director:* Louis De Francesco. *Sound:* A. W. Protzman. *Costumes:* Rita Kaufman. *Production and Distribution:* Fox. *Release Date:* August 1933. *Running Time:* 76 minutes. *Cast:* Spencer Tracy (Tom Garner), Colleen Moore (Sally), Ralph Morgan (Henry), Helen Vinson (Eve), Clifford Jones (Tom Garner, Jr.), Henry Kolker (Mr. Borden), Sarah Padden (Henry's Wife), Billy O'Brien (Young Tom), Cullen Johnston (Young Henry), J. Farrell MacDonald (Mulligan), Robert Warwick (Edward).

Thirty Day Princess (1934)

Producer: B. P. Schulberg. *Director:* Marion Gering. *Assistant Director:* Art Jacobson. *Screenplay:* Preston Sturges, Frank Partos. *Adaptation:* Sam Hellman, Edwin Justus Mayer, based on the story by Clarence Budington Kelland. *Photography:* Leon Shamroy. *Editor:* June Loring. *Art Director:* Hans Dreier. *Sound:* J. A. Goodrich. *Production and Distribution:* Paramount. *Release Date:* May 1934. *Running Time:* 74 minutes. *Cast:* Sylvia Sidney (Princess Catterina/Nancy Lane), Cary Grant (Porter Madison III), Edward Arnold (Richard Gresham), Henry Stephenson (King Anatol), Vince Barnett (Count), Edgar Norton (Baron), Robert McWade (Managing Editor), George Baxter (Spottswood), Ray Walker (Mr. Kirk), Lucien Littlefield (Parker), Marguerite Namara (Lady-in-Waiting), Eleanor Wesselhoeft (Mrs. Schmidt), Frederick Sullivan (Doctor at Gresham's), Robert E. Homans (First Detective), William Augustin (Second Detective), Edgar Dearing (Policeman), Bruce Warren (Spottswood's Friend), William Arnold (City Editor), Dick Rush (Sergeant of Police), J. Merrill Holmes (Radio Man), Thomas Monk (Gresham's Butler).

We Live Again (1934)

Producer: Samuel Goldwyn. *Director:* Rouben Mamoulian. *Assistant Director:* Robert Lee. *Screenplay:* Thornton Wilder, Preston Sturges (uncredited). *Adapta-*

tion: Maxwell Anderson, Leonard Praskins, based on the novel *Resurrection* by Leo Tolstoy. *Photography:* Gregg Toland. *Editor:* Otho Lovering. *Art Director:* Richard Day. *Production Designer:* Sergei Sudeikin. *Musical Score:* Alfred Newman. *Sound:* Frank Maher. *Costumes:* Omar Kiam. *Studio:* United Artists. *Production:* Samuel Goldwyn. *Distribution:* United Artists. *Release Date:* October 1934. *Running Time:* 85 minutes. *Cast:* Anna Sten (Katusha Maslova), Fredric March (Prince Dmitri Nekhlyudov), Jane Baxter (Missy Kortchagin), C. Aubrey Smith (Prince Kortchagin), Ethel Griffies (Aunt Marie), Gwendolyn Logan (Aunt Sophia), Jessie Ralph (Matrona Pavlovna), Sam Jaffe (Simonson), Cecil Cunningham (Theodosia), Jessie Arnold (Korablova), Fritzi Ridgeway (The Red Head), Morgan Wallace (The Colonel), Davison Clark (Tikhon), Leonid Kinskey (Kartinkin), Dale Fuller (Botchkova), Michael Visaroff (Judge), Edgar Norton (Judge).

Imitation of Life (1934)

Producer: Carl Laemmle, Jr. *Director:* John M. Stahl. *Assistant Director:* Scotty Beal. *Screenplay:* William Hurlbut. *Adaptation*: Preston Sturges, based on the novel by Fannie Hurst. *Photography:* Merritt Gerstad. *Editors:* Phil Cahn, Maurice Wright. *Art Director:* Charles D. Hall. *Musical Score:* Heinz Roemheld (uncredited). *Sound:* Gilbert Kurland. *Makeup:* Jack P. Pierce. *Production and Distribution:* Universal. *Release Date:* November 1934. *Running Time:* 106 minutes. *Cast:* Claudette Colbert (Beatrice Pullman), Warren William (Stephen Archer), Ned Sparks (Elmer), Louise Beavers (Aunt Delilah), Baby Jane (Jessie Pullman, age 3), Marilyn Knowlden (Jessie Pullman, age 8), Rochelle Hudson (Jessie Pullman, age 18), Seble Hendricks (Peola Johnson, age 4), Dorothy Black (Peola Johnson, age 9), Fredi Washington (Peola Johnson, age 19), Alan Hale (Martin), Clarence Hummel Wilson (Landlord), Henry Armetta (Painter), Henry Kolker (Doctor Preston), Wyndham Standing (Butler), Alice Ardell (French Maid), Franklin Pangborn (Mr. Carven), Paul Porcasi (Restaurant Manager), Walter Walker (Hugh), Noel Frances (Mrs. Eden), Tyler Brooke (Tipsy Man).

The Good Fairy (1934)

Associate Producer: Henry Henigson. *Director:* William Wyler. *Assistant Director:* Archie Buchanan. *Screenplay:* Preston Sturges, based on the play by Ferenc Molnár. *Photography:* Norbert Brodine. *Editor:* Daniel Mandell. *Art Director:* Charles D. Hall. *Musical Score:* David Klatzkin (uncredited), Heinz Roemheld (uncredited). *Sound:* Joe Lapis. *Makeup:* Jack P. Pierce. *Production and Distribution:* Universal. *Release Date:* January 1935. *Running Time:* 98 minutes. *Cast:* Margaret Sullavan (Luisa Ginglebusher), Herbert Marshall (Dr. Max Sporum), Frank Morgan (Konrad), Reginald Owen (Detlaff), Alan Hale (Schlapkohl), Beulah Bondi (Dr. Schultz), Eric Blore (Dr. Motz), Hugh O'Connell (Telephone Man), Cesar Romero (Joe), Luis Alberni (The Barber), Torben Meyer (Head Waiter), Al Bridge (Doorman), Frank Moran (Moving Man), Matt McHugh (Moving Man).

Diamond Jim (1935)

Producer: Edmund Grainger. *Director:* A. Edward Sutherland. *Assistant Director:* Joseph McDonough. *Screenplay:* Preston Sturges. *Adaptation:* Harry Clork, Doris Malloy, based on the book by Parker Morell. *Photography:* George Robinson. *Editor:* Daniel Mandell. *Art Director:* Charles D. Hall. *Musical Score:* Franz Waxman, Ferde Grofé. *Musical Director:* C. Bakaleinikoff. *Sound:* Gilbert Kurland. *Makeup:* Jack P. Pierce. *Production and Distribution:* Universal. *Release Date:* August 1935. *Running Time:* 90 minutes. *Cast:* Edward Arnold (Diamond Jim Brady), Binnie Barnes (Lillian Ruseell), Jean Arthur (Jane Matthews/Emma), Cesar Romero (Jerry Richardson), Eric Blore (Sampson Fox), Hugh O'Connell (Horsley), George Sidney (Pawnbroker), William Demarest (Harry Hill), Robert McWade (A. E. Moore), Bill Hoolahahn (John L. Sullivan), Baby Wyman (Brady as a child), George Ernest (Brady as a boy), Robert Emmett O'Connor (Brady's Father), Helen Brown (Brady's Mother), Mabel Colcord (Brady's Aunt), Fred Kelsey (Secretary), Charles Sellon (Station Agent), Purnell Pratt (Physician), Tully Marshall (Minister), Al Bridge (Poker Player).

Next Time We Love (1935)

Producer: Paul Kohner. *Director:* Edward H. Griffith. *Assistant Director:* Ralph Slosser. *Screenplay:* Melville Baker, Preston Sturges (uncredited), based on the story "Say Goodbye Again" by Ursula Parrott. *Photography:* Joseph Valentine. *Editor:* Ted Kent. *Art Director:* Charles D. Hall. *Musical Score:* Franz Waxman. *Sound:* Gilbert Kurland. *Makeup:* Jack P. Pierce. *Production and Distribution:* Universal. *Release Date:* January 1936. *Running Time:* 87 minutes. *Cast:* Margaret Sullavan (Cicely Tyler), James Stewart (Christopher Tyler), Ray Milland (Tommy Abbott), Grant Mitchell (Michael Jennings), Anna Demetrio (Madame Donato), Robert McWade (Frank Carteret), Ronnie Cosbey (Kit), Florence Roberts (Mrs. Talbor), Christian Rub (Otto), Charles Fallon (Professor Dindet), Nat Carr (Assistant Stage Manager), Gottlieb Huber (Swiss Porter), Hattie McDaniel (Hanna), Leonid Kinskey (Designer), John King (Juvenile), Nan Grey (Ingénue).

Love Before Breakfast (1935)

Producer: Edmund Grainger. *Director:* Walter Lang. *Assistant Director:* Phil Karlsson. *Screenplay:* Herbert Fields, Preston Sturges (uncredited), based on the novel *Spinster Dinner* by Faith Baldwin. *Additional Dialogue:* Gertrude Purcell. *Photography:* Ted Tetzlaff. *Editor:* Maurice Wright. *Art Director:* Albert D'Agostino. *Musical Score:* Franz Waxman. *Sound:* Charles Carroll. *Makeup:* Jack P. Pierce. *Production and Distribution:* Universal. *Release Date:* March 1936. *Running Time:* 90 minutes. *Cast:* Carole Lombard (Kay Colby), Preston Foster (Scott Miller), Janet Beecher (Mrs. Colby), Cesar Romero (Bill Wadsworth), Betty Lawford (Contessa Campanella), Douglas Blackley (College Boy), Don Briggs (Stuart Farnum), Bert Roach (Fat Man), André Beranger (Charles), Richard Carle (Brinkerhoff), Forrester Harvey (Steward), Joyce Compton (Southern Girl), John King (Friend), Nan Grey (Telephone Girl), E. E. Clive (Captain).

Hotel Haywire (1937)

Producer: Paul Jones, Henry Henigson (uncredited). *Director:* George Archainbaud. *Assistant Director:* Stanley Goldsmith. *Screenplay:* Preston Sturges, Lillie Hayward (uncredited). *Photography:* Henry Sharp. *Editor:* Arthur Schmidt. *Art Director:* Hans Dreier. *Non-original music:* John Leipold (uncredited). *Musical Director:* Boris Morros. *Makeup:* Wally Westmore. *Production and Distribution:* Paramount. *Release Date:* June 1937. *Running Time:* 66 minutes. *Cast:* Leo Carrillo (Dr. Zodiac Z. Zippe), Lynne Overman (Dr. Parkhouse), Mary Carlisle (Phyllis), Benny Baker (Bertie Sterns), Spring Byington (Mrs. Parkhouse), George Barbier (I. Ketts), Porter Hall (Judge Newhall), Collette Lyons (Genevieve Stern), John Patterson (Frank Ketts), Lucien Littlefield (Elmer), Chester Conklin (O'Shea), Terry Ray (Switchboard Operator), Nick Lukats (Reception Clerk), Josephine Whittell (Mrs. Newhall), Guy Usher (Reilly), Teddy Hart (O. Levy), Franklin Pangborn (Fuller Brush Salesman).

Easy Living (1937)

Producer: Arthur Hornblow, Jr. *Director:* Mitchell Leisen. *Assistant Director:* Edgar Anderson. *Screenplay:* Preston Sturges, based on a story by Vera Caspary. *Photography:* Ted Tetzlaff. *Editor:* Doane Harrison. *Art Director:* Hans Dreier. *Musical Score:* Frederick Hollander (uncredited), Milan Roder (uncredited). *Musical Director:* Boris Morros. *Makeup:* Wally Westmore. *Production and Distribution:* Paramount. *Release Date:* July 1937. *Running Time:* 88 minutes. *Cast:* Jean Arthur (Mary Smith), Edward Arnold (J.B. Ball), Ray Milland (John Ball, Jr.). Luis Alberni (Mr. Louis Louis), Mary Nash (Mrs. Ball), Franklin Pangborn (Van Buren), Barlowe Borland (Mr. Gurney), William Demarest (Wallace Whistling), Andrew Tombes (E.F. Hulgar), Esther Dale (Lillian), Harlan Briggs (Office Manager), William B. Davidson (Mr. Hyde), Nora Cecil (Miss Swerf), Robert Greig (Butler), Vernon Dent, Edwin Stanley, Richard Barbee (Partners), Arthur Hoyt (Jeweler), Gertrude Astor (Saleswoman).

College Swing (1938)

Associate Producer: Lewis Gensler. *Director:* Raoul Walsh. *Assistant Director:* Rollie Asher. *Dance Director:* LeRoy Prinz. *Screenplay:* Walter DeLeon, Francis Martin, Preston Sturges (uncredited). *Adaptation:* Frederick Hazlitt Brennan, based on an idea by Ted Lesser. *Photography:* Victor Milner. *Editor:* LeRoy Stone. *Art Director:* Hans Dreier. *Musical Score:* Gordon Jenkins (uncredited), John Leipold (uncredited), Victor Young (uncredited). *Songs:* Hoagy Carmichael, Burton Lane, Frank Loesser, Manning Sherwin. *Musical Director:* Boris Morros. *Sound:* Harold Lewis, Howard Wilson. *Makeup:* Wally Westmore. *Production and Distribution:* Paramount. *Release Date:* April 1938. *Running Time:* 86 minutes. *Cast:* George Burns (George Jonas), Gracie Allen (Gracie Alden), Martha Raye (Mabel), Bob Hope (Bud Brady), Edward Everett Horton (Hubert Dash), Florence George (Ginna Ashburn), Ben Blue (Ben Volt), Betty Grable (Betty), Jackie Coogan (Jackie),

John Payne (Martin Bates), Cecil Cunningham (Dean Sleet), Robert Cummings (Radio Announcer), Skinnay Ennis (Skinnay), Slate Brothers (Themselves), Jerry Colonna (Prof. Yascha Koloski), Jerry Bergen (Prof. Jasper Chinn), Tully Marshall (Grandpa Alden), Edward J. LeSaint (Dr. Storm), Bob Mitchell and St. Brandan's Choristers (Themselves).

Port of Seven Seas (1938)

Producer: Henry Henigson, Carl Laemmle, Jr. (uncredited). *Director:* James Whale. *Assistant Director:* Joseph McDonough. *Screenplay:* Preston Sturges, Ernest Vajda (uncredited), based on the *Fanny* trilogy by Marcel Pagnol. *Photography:* Karl Freund. *Editor:* Frederick Y. Smith. *Montage Effects:* Slavko Vorkapich. *Art Director:* Cedric Gibbons. *Musical Score:* Franz Waxman. *Sound Recording:* Douglas Shearer. *Makeup:* Jack Dawn. *Production and Distribution:* Metro-Goldwyn-Mayer. *Release Date:* July 1938. *Running Time:* 81 minutes. *Cast:* Wallace Berry (César), Frank Morgan (Panisse), Maureen O'Sullivan (Madelon), John Beal (Marius), Jessie Ralph (Honorine), Cora Witherspoon (Claudine), Etienne Girardot (Bruneau), E. Allyn Warren (Captain Escartefigue), Robert Spindola (Boy), Doris Lloyd (Customer).

If I Were King (1938)

Producer: Frank Lloyd. *Associate Producer:* Lou Smith. *Director:* Frank Lloyd. *Assistant Director:* William Tummel. *Screenplay:* Preston Sturges, based on the play by Justin Huntly. *Photography:* Theodore Sparkuhl. *Special Effects Photography:* Gordon Jennings. *Editor:* Hugh Bennett. *Art Director:* Hans Dreier. *Musical Score:* Richard Hageman. *Musical Director:* Boris Morros. *Sound:* Harold C. Lewis, John Cope. *Makeup:* Wally Westmore. *Production and Distribution:* Paramount. *Release Date:* November 1938. *Running Time:* 100 minutes. *Cast:* Ronald Colman (François Villon), Basil Rathbone (Louis XI), Frances Dee (Katherine de Vaucelles), Ellen Drew (Huguette), C.V. France (Father Villon), Henry Wilcoxon (Captain of the Watch), Heather Thatcher (The Queen), Stanley Ridges (René de Montigny), Bruce Lester (Noel le Jolys), Walter Kingsford (Tristal l'Hermite), Alma Lloyd (Colette), Sidney Toler (Robin Turgis), Colin Tapley (Jehan le Loup), Ralph Forbes (Oliver le Dain), John Miljan (Thibaut d'Aussigny), William Haade (Guy Tabarie), Adrian Morris (Colin de Cayeuix), Montagu Love (General Dudon), Lester Matthews (General Saliere), William Farnum (General Barbezier), Paul Harvey (Burgundian Herald), Barry McCollum (Watchman).

Never Say Die (1939)

Producer: Paul Jones. *Director:* Elliott Nugent. *Assistant Director:* Harold Schwartz. *Screenplay:* Don Harman, Frank Butler, Preston Sturges, based on the play by William H. Post. *Photography:* Leo Tover. *Editor:* James Smith. *Art Director:* Hans Dreier. *Musical Score:* Charles Bradshaw (uncredited), John Leipold (uncredited), Milan Roder (uncredited), Leo Shuken (uncredited). *Songs:* Ralph Rainger, Leo

Robin. *Musical Director:* Boris Morros. *Sound:* Philip Wisdom, Walter Oberst. *Makeup:* Wally Westmore. *Production and Distribution:* Paramount. *Release Date:* April 1939. *Running Time:* 82 minutes. *Cast:* Martha Raye (Mickey Hawkins), Bob Hope (John Kidley), Ernest Cossart (Jeepers), Paul Harvey (Jasper Hawkins), Andy Devine (Henry Munch), Sig Rumann (Poppa Ingleborg), Alan Mowbray (Prince Smirnow), Gale Sondergaard (Juno), Frances Arms (Mama Ingleborg), Ivan Simpson (Kretsky), Monty Woolley (Dr. Schmidt), Foy Van Dolson (Kretsky's Bodyguard), Donald Haines (Julius), Gustav von Seyffertitz (Chemist).

Remember the Night (1939)

Producer: Mitchell Leisen, Albert Lewin (uncredited). *Director:* Mitchell Leisen. *Assistant Director:* Hal Walker. *Screenplay:* Preston Sturges. *Photography:* Ted Tetzlaff. *Editor:* Doane Harrison. *Art Director:* Hans Dreier. *Musical Score:* Frederick Hollander. *Makeup:* Wally Westmore. *Production and Distribution:* Paramount. *Release Date:* January 1940. *Running Time:* 94 minutes. *Cast:* Barbara Stanwyck (Lee Leander), Fred MacMurray (John Sargent), Beulah Bondi (Mrs. Sargent), Elizabeth Patterson (Aunt Emma), Willard Robertson (Frances X. O'Leary), Sterling Holloway (Willie), Charles Waldron (Judge — New York), Paul Guilfoyle (District Attorney), Charley Arnt (Tom), John Wray (Hank), Thomas W. Ross (Mr. Emory), Snowflake (Rufus), Tom Kennedy ("Fat" Mike), Georgia Caine (Lee's Mother), Virginia Brissac (Mrs. Emory), Spencert Charters (Judge — Rummage Sale).

Roman Holiday (1953)

Producer and Director: William Wyler. *Screenplay:* Dalton Trumbo. Ian McLellan Hunter, John Dighton, Preston Sturges (uncredited) *Photography:* Franz Planer, Henry Alékan. *Editor:* Robert Swink. *Art Directors:* Hal Pereira, Walter Tyler. *Musical Score:* Georges Auric. *Makeup:* Alberto De Rossi, Wally Westmore. *Production and Distribution:* Paramount. *Release Date:* August 1953. *Running Time:* 118 minutes. *Cast:* Gregory Peck (Joe Bradley), Audrey Hepburn (Princess Ann), Eddie Albert (Irving Radovich), Hartley Power (Mr. Hennessy), Harcourt Williams (Ambassador), Margaret Rawlings (Countess Vereberg), Tullio Carminati (Gen. Provno), Paolo Carlini (Mario Delani — hairdresser), Claudio Ermelli (Giovanni — landlord), Paola Borboni (Charwoman), Alfredo Rizzo (Cab Driver), Laura Solari (Secretary), Gorella Gori (Shoe Seller), Heinz Hindrich (Dr. Bonnachoven), John Horne (Master of Ceremonies)

Films Written and Directed by Preston Sturges

The Great McGinty (1940)

Associate Producer: Paul Jones. *Screenplay-Director:* Preston Sturges. *Assistant Director:* George Templeton. *Photography:* William Mellor. *Editor:* Hugh Bennett. *Art*

Director: Hans Dreier *Musical Score:* Frederick Hollander. *Sound:* Earl Hayman, Richard Olson. *Makeup:* Wally Westmore. *Production and Distribution:* Paramount. *Release Date:* August 1940. *Running Time:* 81 minutes. *Cast:* Brian Donlevy (Dan McGinty), Muriel Angelus (Catherine McGinty), Akim Tamiroff (The Boss), Allyn Joslyn (George), William Demarest (The Politician), Louis Jean Heydt (Thompson), Harry Rosenthal (Louie), Arthur Hoyt (Mayor Tillinghast), Libby Taylor (Bessie), Thurston Hall (Mr. Maxwell), Steffi Duna (The Girl), Esther Howard (Madame LaJolla), Frank Moran (Chauffeur), Mary Thomas (Catherine's Girl), Donnie Kerr (Catherine's Boy), Jimmy Conlin (The Lookout), Dewey Robinson (Benny Felgman), Jean Phillips (Manicurist), Lee Shumway (Cop), Pat West (Pappia), Byron Foulger (Secretary), Richard Carle (Dr. Jarvis), Charles Moore (McGinty's Valet), Emory Parnell (Policeman), Vic Potel (Cook), Harry Hayden (Watcher), Robert Warwick (Opposition Speaker).

Christmas in July (1940)

Associate Producer: Paul Jones. *Screenplay-Director:* Preston Sturges. *Assistant Director:* George Templeton. *Photography:* Victor Milner. *Editor:* Ellsworth Hoagland. *Art Director:* Hans Dreier. *Musical Score:* Werner R. Heymann (uncredited), John Leipold (uncredited), Leo Shuken (uncredited). *Musical Director:* Sigmund Krumgold. *Makeup:* Wally Westmore. *Production and Distribution:* Paramount. *Release Date:* November 1940. *Running Time:* 70 minutes. *Cast:* Dick Powell (Jimmy MacDonald), Ellen Drew (Betty Casey), Raymond Walburn (Dr. Maxford), Ernest Truex (Mr. Baxter), William Demarest (Bildocker), Alexander Carr (Schindel), Franklin Pangborn (The Announcer), Michael Morris (Tom), Rod Cameron (Dick), Harry Rosenthal (Harry), Georgia Caine (Mrs. MacDonald), Torben Meyer (Mr. Schmidt), Al Bridge (Mr. Hillbeiner), Byron Foulger (Mr. Jenkins), Lucille Ward (Mrs. Casey), Julius Tannen (Mr. Zimmerman), Ferike Boros (Mrs. Schwartz), Harry Hayden (Mr. Waterbury), Vic Potel (Furniture Salesman), Arthur Hoyt (Mild Gentleman), Robert Warwick (Large Gentleman), Jimmy Conlin (Thin, Sour Gentleman), Dewey Robinson (Large, Rough Gentleman), Arthur Stuart Hull (Cashier), Esther Michelson (Sophie's Mother), Frank Moran (Patrolman Murphy), Georges Renavent (Sign Painter), Preston Sturges (Man — Shoeshine Stand), Pat West (Man with Telephone), Kay Stewart, Jan Buckingham (Secretaries), Snowflake, Charles Moore (Porters).

The Lady Eve (1941)

Associate Producers: Paul Jones, Albert Lewin (uncredited). *Screenplay-Director:* Preston Sturges. *Assistant Director:* Mel Epstein. Based on the story "Two Bad Hats" by Monckton Hoffe. *Photography:* Victor Milner. *Editor:* Stuart Gilmore. *Art Director:* Hans Dreier. *Musical Score:* Sigmund Krumgold, Phil Boutelje (uncredited), Charles Bradshaw (uncredited), Gil Grau (uncredited), John Leipold (uncredited), Leo Shuken (uncredited). *Musical Director:* Sigmund Krumgold. *Sound:* Harry Lindgren, Don Johnson. *Makeup:* Wally Westmore. *Production and Distribution:* Paramount. *Release Date:* February 1941. *Running Time:* 97 minutes.

Cast: Barbara Stanwyck (Jean), Henry Fonda (Charles Pike), Charles Coburn ("Colonel" Harrington), Eugene Pallette (Mr. Pike), William Demarest (Muggsy), Eric Blore (Sir Alfred McGlennan-Keith), Melville Cooper (Gerald), Martha O'Driscoll (Martha), Janet Beecher (Mrs. Pike), Robert Greig (Burrows), Dora Clement (Gertrude), Luis Alberni (Pike's Chef), Frank Moran (Bartender), Evelyn Beresford, Arthur Stuart Hull (Guests at Party), Harry Rosenthal (Piano Tuner), Julius Tannen (Lawyer), Arthur Hoyt (Lawyer at Telephone), Jimmy Conlin, Al Bridge, Vic Potel (Stewards), Esther Michelson (Wife), Robert Dudley (Husband), Torben Meyer (Purser), Robert Warwick (Passenger).

New York Town (1941)

Producer: Anthony Veiller. *Director:* Charles Vidor, Preston Sturges (uncredited). *Assistant Director:* Stanley Goldsmith. *Screenplay:* Lewis Meltzer, Preston Sturges (uncredited), based on a story by Jo Swerling. *Photography:* Charles Schoenbaum. *Editor:* Doane Harrison. *Art Director:* Hans Dreier. *Musical Score:* Leo Shuken. *Musical Director:* Sigmund Krumgold. *Sound:* Hugo Grenzbach. *Makeup:* Wally Westmore. *Production and Distribution:* Paramount. *Release Date:* November 1941. *Running Time:* 94 minutes. *Cast:* Fred MacMurray (Victor Ballard), Mary Martin (Alexandra Curtis), Robert Preston (Paul Bryson, Jr.), Akim Tamiroff (Stefan Janowski), Lynne Overman (Sam), Eric Blore (Vivian), Cecil Kellaway (Shipboard Host), Fuzzy Knight (Gus Nelson), Oliver Prickett [Oliver Blake] (Bender), Ken Carpenter (Master of Ceremonies), Iris Adrian (Toots O'Day), Edward J. McNamara (Brody), Sam McDaniel (Henry), Philip Van Zandt (Peddler).

Sullivan's Travels (1941)

Associate Producer: Paul Jones. *Screenplay-Director:* Preston Sturges. *Assistant Director:* Holly Morse. *Photography:* John F. Seitz. *Special Effects Photography:* Farciot Edouart. *Editor:* Stuart Gilmore. *Art Director:* Hans Dreier. *Musical Score:* Leo Shuken, Charles Bradshaw. *Musical Director:* Sigmund Krumgold. *Sound:* Harry Mills, Walter Oberst. *Makeup:* Wally Westmore. *Production and Distribution:* Paramount. *Release Date:* January 1942. *Running Time:* 90 minutes. *Cast:* Joel McCrea (John L. Sullivan), Veronica Lake (The Girl), Robert Warwick (Mr. LeBrand), William Demarest (Mr. Jones), Franklin Pangborn (Mr. Casalsis), Porter Hall (Mr. Hadrian), Bryon Foulger (Mr. Valdelle), Margaret Hayes (Secretary), Robert Greig (Butler), Eric Blore (Valet), Torben Meyer (Doctor), Al Bridge (The Mister), Esther Howard (Miz Zeffie), Almira Sessions (Ursula), Frank Moran (Chauffeur), Georges Renavent (Bum), Vic Potel (Cameraman), Richard Webb (Radioman), Charles Moore (Chef), Jimmy Conlin (Trustee), Jimmie Dundee (Labor), Chick Collins (Capital), Harry Hayden (Mr. Carson), Roscoe Ates (Counterman — Owl Wagon), Arthur Hoyt (Preacher), Robert Dudley (One-Legged Man), Dewey Robinson (Sheriff), Jess Lee Brooks (Colored Preacher), Julius Tannen (Public Defender), Emory Parnell (Man at Railroad Shack), Edgar Dearing (Cop), Esther Michelson (Woman — Poor Street), Chester Conklin (Old Bum), Howard Mitchell (Railroad Clerk), Harry Rosenthal (The Trombenick), Jan Buckingham (Mrs. Sullivan), Pat West (Counterman — Roadside), J. Farrell MacDonald (Desk Sergeant), Perc Launders (Yard Man), Paul Jones (Dear Joseph), Preston Sturges (Director).

Safeguarding Military Information (1942)

Producer: Darryl F. Zanuck. *Screenplay-Director:* Preston Sturges. *Studio:* Paramount. *Production:* The Research Council of the Academy of Motion Picture Arts and Science. *Release Date:* August 1942. *Running Time:* 9 minutes. *Cast:* Eddie Bracken, Walter Huston.

The Palm Beach Story (1942)

Associate Producer: Paul Jones. *Screenplay-Director:* Preston Sturges. *Assistant Director:* Hal Walker. *Photography:* Victor Milner. *Editor:* Stuart Gilmore. *Art Director:* Hans Dreier. *Musical Score:* Victor Young. *Sound:* Harry Lindgren, Walter Oberst. *Makeup:* Wally Westmore. *Production and Distribution:* Paramount. *Release Date:* December 1942. *Running Time:* 88 minutes. *Cast:* Claudette Colbert (Gerry Jeffers), Joel McCrea (Tom Jeffers), Mary Astor (Princess), Rudy Vallee (John D. Hackensacker III), Sig Arno (Toto), Robert Warwick (Mr. Hinch), Arthur Stuart Hull (Mr. Osmond), Torben Meyer (Dr. Kluck), Jimmy Conlin (Mr. Asweld), Vic Potel (Mr. McKeewie), Robert Dudley (Wienie King), Franklin Pangborn (Manager), Arthur Hoyt (Pullman Conductor), Al Bridge (Conductor), Snowflake (Colored Bartender), Charles Moore (Colored Porter), Frank Moran (Brakeman), Harry Rosenthal (Orchestra Leader), Esther Howard (Wife of Wienie King), William Demarest, Jack Norton, Robert Greig, Roscoe Ates, Dewey Robinson, Chester Conklin, Sheldon Jett (Ale & Quail Club), Harry Hayden (Prospect), Esther Michelson (Nearsighted Woman), Edward J. McNamara (Officer in Penn Station), Mantan Moreland (Waiter in Diner), Julius Tannen (Proprietor of Store), Byron Foulger (Jewelry Salesman), Frank Faylen (Taxi Driver), J. Farrell MacDonald (O'Donnell).

The Miracle of Morgan's Creek (1944)

Screenplay-Producer-Director: Preston Sturges. *Assistant Director:* Edmund Bernoudy. *Photography:* John F. Seitz. *Editor:* Stuart Gilmore. *Art Director:* Hans Dreier. *Musical Score:* Leo Shuken. *Sound:* Hugo Grenzbach. *Makeup:* Wally Westmore. *Production and Distribution:* Paramount. *Release Date:* January 1944. *Running Time:* 99 minutes. *Cast:* Eddie Bracken (Norval Jones), Betty Hutton (Trudy Kockenlocker), Diana Lynn (Emmy Kockenlocker), William Demarest (Constable Kockenlocker), Porter Hall (Justice of the Peace), Emory Parnell (Mr. Tuerck), Al Bridge (Mr. Johnson), Julius Tannen (Mr. Rafferty). Vic Potel (Newspaper Editor), Brian Donlevy (Governor McGinty), Akim Tamiroff (The Boss), Almira Sessions (Wife of Justice of the Peace), Esther Howard (Sally), J. Farrell MacDonald (Sheriff), Frank Moran (First MP), Connie Tompkins (Cecilia), Georgia Caine (Mrs. Johnson), Torben Meyer (Doctor), George Melford (U.S. Marhsall), Jimmy Conlin (The Mayor), Harry Rosenthal (Mr. Schwartz), Chester Conklin (Pete),

Byron Foulger (McGinty's Secretary), Arthur Hoyt (McGinty's Secretary), Robert Dudley (Man), Jack Norton (Man Opening Champagne), Bobby Watson (Hitler), Joe Devlin (Mussolini), Nora Cecil (Head Nurse), Jan Buckingham, Judith Lowry (Nurses), Freddie Steel (Soldier).

Hail the Conquering Hero (1944)

Screenplay-Producer-Director: Preston Sturges. *Assistant Director:* Harvey Foster. *Photography:* John F. Seitz. *Editor:* Stuart Gilmore. *Art Director:* Hans Dreier. *Musical Score:* Werner Heyman. Song "Home to the Arms of Mother" by Preston Sturges. *Musical Director:* Sigmund Krumgold. *Sound:* Wallace Nogle. *Makeup:* Wally Westmore. *Production and Distribution:* Paramount. *Release Date:* August 1944. *Running Time:* 101 minutes. *Cast:* Eddie Bracken (Woodrow Truesmith), Ella Raines (Libby), William Demarest (Sergeant), Bill Edwards (Forrest Noble), Raymond Walburn (Mayor Noble), Jimmy Dundee (Corporal), Georgia Caine (Mrs. Truesmith), Al Bridge (Political Boss), James Damore (Jonesy), Freddie Steel (Bugsy), Stephen Gregory (Bill), Len Hendry (Juke), Esther Howard (Mrs. Noble), Elizabeth Patterson (Libby's Aunt), Jimmy Conlin (Judge Dennis), Arthur Hoyt (the Reverend Upperman), Harry Hayden (Dr. Bisell), Franklin Pangborn (Chairman of Committee), Vic Potel (Progressive Band Leader), Torben Meyer (Mr. Schultz), Jack Norton (Regular Band Leader), Chester Conklin (Western Union Man), Robert Warwick (Officer), Dewey Robinson (Conductor), Charles Moore (Porter).

The Great Moment (1944)

Screenplay-Producer-Director: Preston Sturges. *Assistant Director:* Edmund Bernoudy. Based on the book *Triumph Over Pain* by René Fülöp-Miller. *Photography:* Victor Milner. *Editor:* Stuart Gilmore. *Art Director:* Hans Dreier. *Musical Score:* Victor Young. *Sound:* Harry Lindgren, Walter Oberst. *Makeup:* Wally Westmore. *Production and Distribution:* Paramount. *Release Date:* November 1944. *Running Time:* 83 minutes. *Cast:* Joel McCrea (W.T.G. Morton), Betty Field (Elizabeth Morton), Harry Carey (Prof. Warren), William Demarest (Eben Frost), Louis Jean Heydt (Dr. Horace Wells), Julius Tannen (Dr. Jackson), Edwin Maxwell (Vice-President of Medical Society), Porter Hall (President Pierce), Franklin Pangborn (Dr. Heywood), Grady Sutton (Homer Quimby), Donivee Lee (Betty Morton), Harry Hayden (Judge Shipman), Torben Meyer (Dr. Dahlmeyer), Vic Potel (Dental Patient), Thurston Hall (Senator Borland), J. Farrell MacDonald (Priest), Robert Frandsen (Mr. Abbot), Robert Greig (Morton's Butler), Harry Rosenthal (Mr. Chamberlain), Frank Moran (Porter), Robert Dudley (Cashier), Dewey Robinson (Colonel Lawson), Al Bridge (Mr. Stone), Georgia Caine (Mrs. Whitman), Roscoe Ates (Sign Painter), Emory Parnell (Mr. Gruber), Arthur Stuart Hull (Mr. Whitman), Chester Conklin (Frightened Patient), Esther Howard (Streetwalker), Byron Foulger (Receptionist), Esther Michelson (Patient), Jimmy Conlin (Mr. Burnett), Arthur Hoyt (Presidential Secretary), Sig Arno (Whackpot), Donnie Kerr (Little Boy), Billy Sheffield (Morton's Little Boy), Janet Chapman (Morton's Little Girl), Tricia Moore (Morton's Little Girl — older).

The Sin of Harold Diddlebock (1947)

Screenplay-Producer-Director: Preston Sturges. *Assistant Director:* Barton Adams. *Photography:* Robert Pittack. *Editor:* Thomas Neff. *Special Effects Photography:* John P. Fulton. *Art Director:* Robert Usher. *Musical Score:* Werner Heymann. *Love Theme by:* Harry Rosenthal. *Makeup:* Ted Larsen, Wally Westmore (uncredited). *Studio:* Samuel Goldwyn Productions. *Production:* California Pictures. *Distribution:* United Artists. *Release Date:* February 1947. *Running Time:* 91 minutes. *Cast:* Harold Lloyd (Harold Diddlebock), Frances Ramsden (Miss Otis), Jimmy Conlin (Wormy), Raymond Walburn (E.J. Waggleberry), Edgar Kennedy (Bartender), Arline Judge (Manicurist), Franklin Pangborn (Formfit Franklin), Rudy Vallee (Banker), Lionel Stander (Max), Torben Meyer (Barber), Margaret Hamilton (Harold's Sister), Al Bridge (Circus Manager), Frank Moran (Mike), Robert Greig (Coachman), Vic Potel (Professor Potelle), Georgia Caine (Bearded Lady), Robert Dudley (Banker), Jack Norton (James Smoke), Arthur Hoyt (Banker Blackston), Gladys Forrest (Snake Charmer), Max Wagner (Doorman), Jackie (The Lion).

Unfaithfully Yours (1948)

Screenplay-Producer-Director: Preston Sturges. *Assistant Director:* Gaston Glass. *Photography:* Victor Milner. *Special Effects Photography:* Fred Sersen. *Editor:* Robert Fritch. *Art Director:* Lyle Wheeler. *Musical Score:* Gioacchino Rossini, Richard Wagner, Peter Ilyitch Tchaikovski. *Musical Director:* Alfred Newman. *Makeup:* Ben Nye. *Production and Distribution:* 20th Century–Fox. *Release Date:* November 1948. *Running Time:* 105 minutes. *Cast:* Rex Harrison (Sir Alfred De Carter), Linda Darnell (Daphne De Carter), Rudy Vallee (August Henshler), Barbara Lawrence (Barbara), Kurt Kreuger (Anthony), Lionel Stander (Hugo Standoff), Edgar Kennedy (Detective Sweeney), Al Bridge (House Detective), Julius Tannen (O'Brien, the Tailor), Torben Meyer (Dr. Schultz).

The Beautiful Blonde from Bashful Bend (1949)

Screenplay-Producer-Director: Preston Sturges. *Assistant Director:* William Eckhardt. Based on a story by Earl Felton. *Photography:* Harry Jackson (Technicolor). *Technicolor Consultants:* Natalie Kalmus, Leonard Doss. *Special Effects Photography:* Fred Sersen. *Editor:* Robert Fritch. *Art Director:* Lyle Wheeler. *Musical Score:* Cyril Mockridge. *Musical Director:* Alfred Newman. *Sound:* Eugene Grossman, Harry M. Leonard. *Makeup:* Ben Nye. *Production and Distribution:* 20th Century–Fox. *Release Date:* May 1949. *Running Time:* 79 minutes. *Cast:* Betty Grable (Freddie), Cesar Romero (Blackie), Rudy Vallee (Charles Hingleman), Olga San Juan (Conchita), Sterling Holloway (Basserman Boy), Hugh Herbert (Doctor), El Brendel (Mr. Jorgensen), Porter Hall (Judge O'Toole), Pati Behrs (Roulette), Margaret Hamilton (Mrs. O'Toole), Danny Jackson (Basserman Boy), Emory Parnell (Mr. Hingleman), Al Bridge (Sheriff), Chris-Pin Martin (Joe), J. Farrell MacDonald (Sheriff Sweetzer), Richard Hale (Mr. Basserman), Georgia Caine (Mrs. Hingleman), Esther Howard (Mrs. Smidlap), Harry Hayden (Conductor), Chester

Conklin (Messenger Boy), Mary Monica MacDonald (Freddie — age 6), Torben Meyer (Dr. Schultz), Dewey Robinson (Bartender), Richard Kean (Dr. Smidlap), Russell Simpson (Grandpa), Marie Windsor (French Floozy).

Les Carnets du Major Thompson (Original French Version, 1955); *The Diary of Major Thompson* (English Version, 1955); *The French, They Are a Funny Race* (American Version, 1957)

Producers: Alan Poire, Paul Wagner. *Screenplay-Director:* Preston Sturges. *Assistant Directors:* Pierre Kast, Francis Caillaud. Based on the book *The Notebooks of Major Thompson* by Pierre Daninos. *Photography:* Maurice Barry, Christian Matras, Jean Lallier. *Editor:* Raymond Lanny. *Art Director:* Serge Pimenoff. *Musical Score:* Georges Van Parys. *Sound:* Jene Rieul. *Makeup:* Jean-Jacques Chanteau. *Production:* S.N.E. Gaumont-Paul Wagner. *Distribution:* Gaumont (France), Continental Distributing (U.S.A.). *Release Date:* December 1955 (France and U.K.), May 1957 (U.S.A.). *Running Time:* 105 minutes (France), 82 minutes (U.S.A.). *Cast:* Jack Buchanan (Major Thompson), Martine Carole (Martine Thompson), Noël-Noël (M. Taupin), Totti Truman Taylor (Miss Ffyth), Catherine Boyl (Ursula), André Luguet (M. Fusillard), Geneviève Brunet (Mlle. Sylvette), Paulette Dubost (Mme. Taupin).

Other Collaborations

I Married a Witch (1942)

Producer: Preston Sturges. *Director:* René Clair. *Assistant Director:* Art Black. *Screenplay:* Robert Pirosh. Marc Connelly, Dalton Trumbo (uncredited), based on the novel *The Passionate Witch* by Thorne Smith, completed by Norman Matson. *Photography:* Ted Tetzlaff. *Special Effects Photography:* Gordon Jennings. *Editor:* Eda Warren. *Art Director:* Hans Dreier. *Musical Score:* Roy Webb. *Sound:* Harry Mills, Richard Olson. *Makeup:* Wally Westmore. *Studio:* Paramount. *Production:* Paramount. *Distribution:* United Artists. *Release Date:* November 1942. *Running Time:* 76 minutes. *Cast:* Fredric March (Wallace Wooley), Veronica Lake (Jennifer), Robert Benchley (Dr. Dudley White), Susan Hayward (Estelle Masterson), Cecil Kellaway (Daniel), Elizabeth Patterson (Margaret), Robert Warwick (J.B. Masterson), Eily Malyon (Tabitha), Robert Greig (Town Crier), Helen St. Rayner (Vocalist), Aldrich Bowker (Justice of the Peace), Emma Dunn (Wife), Viola Moore (Martha), Mary Field (Nancy), Nora Cecil (Harriet), Emory Parnell (Allen), Charles Moore (Rufus), Al Bridge (Prison Guard), Arthur Stuart Hull (Guest), Chester Conklin (Bartender), Reed Hadley (Young Man).

Vendetta (1946)

Producer: Howard Hughes, Preston Sturges (uncredited). *Director:* Mel Ferrer, Max Ophüls (uncredited), Preston Sturges (uncredited), Stuart Heisler (uncredited), Howard Hughes (uncredited). *Assistant Director:* Edward Mull. *Screenplay:* W.R. Burnett, Preston Sturges (uncredited). *Adaptation:* Peter O'Crotty, from the novel *Colomba* by Prosper Mérimée. *Photography:* Franz Planer, Al Gilks. *Editor:* Stuart Gilmore. *Art Director:* Robert Usher. *Musical Score:* Roy Webb. *Musical Director:* C. Bakaleinikoff. *Sound:* William Fox, Vinton Vernon. *Makeup:* Norbert Miles. *Studio:* Samuel Goldwyn. *Production:* California Pictures/Hughes Productions. *Distribution:* RKO-Radio. *Release Date:* December 1950. *Running Time:* 84 minutes. *Cast:* Faith Domergue (Colomba Della Rabbia), George Dolenz (Orso Della Rabbia), Hillary Brooke (Lydia Nevil), Nigel Bruce (Sir Thomas Nevil), Donald Buka (Padrino), Joseph Calleia (Mayor Barracini), Hugh Haas (Brando), Robert Warwick (Prefect).

Letters from My Windmill (1955) — American Version of Les Lettres de mon moulin (1954)

Producer: Jean Martinelli. *Director:* Marcel Pagnol. *Screenplay:* Marcel Pagnol, based on the stories "The Three Low Masses," "The Elixir of Father Gaucher," and "The Secret of Master Cornille" by Alphonse Daudet. *English subtitles:* Preston Sturges. *Photography:* Willy Faktorovitch. *Editor:* Monique Lacombe. *Art Director:* Robert Giordani. *Musical Score:* Henri Tomasi. *Sound:* Marcel Royné. *Makeup:* Paul Ralph. *Studio:* Marseille Studio. *Production:* Mediterranean Film Company. *Distribution:* Tohan Pictures. *Release Date:* December 1955. *Running Time:* 120 minutes (original French version: 160 minutes). *Cast:* Guy Alland (Frère Ulysse), Henri Arius (M. Decanis), Breals (Le Maire), Pierrette Bruno (Vivette), Henri Crémieux (Me Honarat Grapazzi), Roger Crouzet (Alphonse Daudet), Daxely (Le diable), Edouard Delmont (Maître Cornille), Michel Galabru, Yvonne Gamy (La vieille), Keller (Le marquis), Christian Lude (Père Sylvestre), Rellys (Le père Gaucher), Joseph Riozet (Père Hyacinthe), Fernand Sardou (M. Charnique), René Sarvil (Le chef), Jean Toscan (Père Virgil), Andrée Turcy (Marinette), Robert Vattier (Le père Abbé), Henri Vilbert (Dom Balaguère).

Plays

The Guinea Pig (1929)

Author-Producer: Preston Sturges. *Director:* Walter Greenough. *Settings:* William Bradley Studio. *Theater:* President, New York. *Opening:* January 7, 1929. *Cast:* Rhoda Cross (Miss Snitkin), Robert Robson (Seth Fellows), Alexander Carr (Sam Small), John Ferguson (Wilton Smith), Ruth Thomas (Helen Reading), John Vosburgh (Robert Fleming), Mary Carroll (Catherine Howard), Audree Corday (Natalie).

Strictly Dishonorable (1929)

Author: Preston Sturges. *Producer:* Brock Pemberton. *Directors:* Brock Pemberton, Antoinette Perry. *Settings:* Raymond Sovey. *Theater:* Avon, New York. *Opening:* September 18, 1929. *Cast:* John Altieri (Giovanni), Marius Rogati (Mario), William Ricciardi (Tomaso Antiovi), Carl *Error! Contact not defined.* (Judge Dempsey), Louis Jean Heydt (Henry Greene), Muriel Kirkland (Isabelle Parry), Tullio Carminati (Count Di Ruvo), Edward J. McNamara (Patrolman Mulligan).

Recapture (1930)

Author: Preston Sturges. *Producer:* A. H. Woods. *Director:* Don Mullally. *Settings:* P. Dodd Ackerman. *Theater:* Eltinge, New York. *Opening:* January 29, 1930. *Cast:* Cecilia Loftus (Mrs. Stuard Romney), Hugh Sinclair (the Rev. Outerbridge Smole), Gustave Rolland (Monsieur Remy), Glenda Farrell (Gwendoliere Williams), Joseph Roeder (Monsieur Edelweiss), Meyer Berenson (Auguste), Melvyn Douglas (Henry C. Martin), Ann Andrews (Patricia Tulliver Browne), Stuart Casey (Capt. Hubert Reynolds, D.S.O.), Louza Riane (Madame Pistache).

The Well of Romance (1930)

Libretto and Lyrics: Preston Sturges. *Music:* H. Maurice Jacquet. *Producer:* G.W. McGregor. *Director:* J. Harry Benrimo. *Settings:* Gates and Morange. *Theater:* Craig, New York. *Opening:* November 7, 1930. *Cast:* Laine Blaire (Ann Schiltzl), Tommy Monroe (Wenzel), Lina Abarbanell (Frau Schlitz), Elsa Paul (Gertrude), Mildred Newman (Mildred), Louise Joyce (Louise), Louis Sorin (The Grand Chancellor), Norma Terris (The Princess), Howard March (Poet), Louis Rupp (Lt. Schpitzelberger).

Child of Manhattan (1932)

Author: Preston Sturges. *Producer:* Peggy Fears. *Director:* Howard Lindsay. *Settings:* Jonel Jorgulesco. *Theater:* Fulton, New York. *Opening:* March 1, 1932. *Cast:* Helen Strickland (Miss Sophie Vanderkill), Joseph Roeder (Eggleston), Reginald Owen (Otto Paul Vanderkill), Ralph Sanford (Spyrene), Charles Cromer (Clifford), Judy Abbot (Flo), Dorothy Hall (Madeleine McGonegal), Mitzi Miller (Gertie), Jackson Halliday (Buddy McGonegal), Maude Odell (Mrs. McGonegal), Jacqueline Winston (Martha), Franz Bendtsen (Lucinda), Joan Hamilton (Constance).

Symphony Story (1932)

Author: Preston Sturges. Early play version of *Unfaithfully Yours.* Unproduced.

Make a Wish (1951)

Book: Preston Sturges, based on the play *The Good Fairy* by Ferenc Molnar, and on Sturges's screenplay *The Good Fairy. Music and Lyrics:* Hugh Martin. *Produc-*

ers: Harry Rigby, Jule Styne, Alexander H. Cohen. *Director:* John C. Wilson. *Settings:* Raoul Pene Du Bois. *Theater:* Winter Garden, New York. *Opening:* April 18, 1951. *Cast:* Eda Heinemann (Dr. Didier), Phil Leeds (Dr. Francel), Nanette Fabray (Janette), Harold Lang (Ricky), Helen Gallagher (Poupette), Howard Wendell (Policeman), Melville Cooper (Marius Frigo), Stephen Douglass (Paul Dumont), Mary Finney (The Madam), Le Roi Operti (Felix Labiche), Howard Wendell (Sales Manager).

Carnival in Flanders (1953)

Book: Preston Sturges, based on the screenplay *La Kermesse héroïque* by Charles Spaak, Jacques Feyder, Bernard Zimmer. *Music:* James Van Heusen. *Lyrics:* Johnny Burke. *Producers:* Paula Stone, Mike Sloane, Johnny Burke, James Van Heusen. *Director:* Preston Sturges. *Settings:* Oliver Smith. *Theater:* Century, New York. *Opening:* September 8, 1953. *Cast:* Pat Stanley (Siska), Kevin Scott (Jan Breughel), Paul Reed (Tailor), Paul Lipson (Butcher), Bobby Vail (Barber), Lee Goodman (Innkeeper), Roy Roberts (Mayor), Dolores Gray (Cornelia), Dolores Kempner (Martha), Matt Mattox (Courier).

A Cup of Coffee
(written in 1931; first production 1988)

Author: Preston Sturges. *Producer:* SoHo Rep. *Director:* Larry Carpenter. *Settings:* Mark Wendland. *Theater:* Greenwich House, New York. *Opening:* March 25, 1988. *Cast:* Willie Carpenter (Julius Smith), Robin Chadwick (Lomax Whortleberry), Nesbitt Blaisdell (J. Bloodgood Baxter), Richard L. Browne (Oliver Baxter), Ellen Mareneck (Tulip Jones), Gwyllum Evans (Ephraim Baxter), Michael Heintzman (James MacDonald).

Chapter Notes

Introduction

1. James Curtis, *Between Flops: A Biography of Preston Sturges* (New York: Harcourt, Brace, Jovanovich, 1982).

2. Donald Spoto, *Madcap: The Life of Preston Sturges* (Boston, Toronto, London: Little, Brown, 1990).

3. Diane Jacobs, *Christmas in July: The Life and Art of Preston Sturges* (Berkeley: University of California Press, 1992).

4. Andrew Dickos, *Intrepid Laughter: Preston Sturges and the Movies* (Metuchen: Scarecrow, 1985).

5. James Ursini, *The Fabulous Life and Times of Preston Sturges, An American Dreamer* (New York: Curtis Books, 1973).

6. Jay Rozgonyi, *Preston Sturges's Vision of America: Critical Analyses of Fourteen Films* (Jefferson, NC: McFarland, 1995).

7. Curtis, *Between Flops,* pp. 196–97.

8. Alexander King, "Preston Sturges," *Vogue* (August 15, 1944), p. 179.

9. In the early postwar years, a young generation of French film critics and intellectuals (including Eric Rohmer, François Truffaut, Claude Chabrol, and Jean-Luc Godard) revolutionized the perception of Hollywood cinema by studying the recurrence of themes and styles in the work of directors such as Alfred Hitchcock, Howard Hawks and John Ford, whom they labeled "auteurs." Such an approach was extended into English-language film criticism in the 1960s by American critic Andrew Sarris, and it has become a common term used to identify filmmakers who are able to demonstrate a recurrent poetics and aesthetics under the most different conditions of production.

10. Andrew Sarris, "The American Cinema," *Film Culture,* no. 28 (Spring 1963), p. 21.

11. André Bazin, "Preston Sturges," in Bazin, *The Cinema of Cruelty* (New York: Seaver Books, 1982), pp. 34.

12. David Bordwell, Janet Staiger, and Kristin Thompson, *The Classical Hollywood Cinema* (London: Routledge, 1985), p. 4.

13. Bazin, "Preston Sturges," p. 35.

14. Dickos, *Intrepid Laughter,* p. vii.

15. Alan Robbe-Grillet's novels, together with his call for a *nouveau roman* which would challenge established narrative canons such as the third-person narrative, chronological timelines and psychological motivation, began appearing in 1953, while Raymond Queneau's initial edition of *Exercises de style* was published in 1947. Sturges directed *Unfaithfully Yours* in 1947, but early drafts of the script date back to the early 1930s.

16. Bordwell, Staiger and Thompson, *The Classical Hollywood Cinema,* p. xiii.

17. In marketing, segmentation is the selection of groups of people who will be most receptive to a product.

18. Bordwell, Staiger and Thompson, *The Classical Hollywood Cinema,* pp. 12–23.

19. Frederic Jameson, "Postmodernism and Consumer Society," in Hal Foster (ed.), *Postmodern Culture* (London: Pluto Press, 1985), pp. 111, 116.

20. Maureen Turim, "Cinemas of Modernity and Postmodernity," in Ingeborg Hoesterey (ed.), *Zeitgeist in Babel: The Postmodernist Controversy* (Bloomington: Indiana University Press, 1991), p. 182.

21. In France the production company Film d'Art borrowed theatrical authors and stage directors from the *Comedie Française* while in Italy, Giovanni Pastrone was signing up poets such as Gabriele D'Annunzio and musicians like Ildebrando Pizzetti for the creation of the epic *Cabiria*— a movie that would

pave the way for a series of historical epics inspired by Greek and Latin literature and focused on the purely theatrical concept of *diva*. Such ennoblement of the film medium through the recycling of other media's illustrious tradition expanded rapidly all over the world, from D.W. Griffith's adaptations of Tennyson, Tolstoy and de Maupassant, to pre-revolutionary Russian movies which borrowed most of their plots from the prestigious novels of Dostoyevsky, Tolstoy and Pushkin.

22. Jameson, "Postmodernism," p. 125.
23. *Ibid,* p. 118.
24. Kenneth von Gunden, *Postmodern Auteurs* (Jefferson, NC: McFarland, 1991), p. 3.
25. Thomas Schatz, *The Genius of the System: Hollywood Filmmaking in the Studio Era* (New York: Henry Holt, 1996).

Chapter 1

1. Dickos, *Intrepid Laughter.*
2. Ursini, *The Fabulous Life.*
3. Pirolini, *Interview,* see Appendix A.
4. *Postmodernism,* in Wikipedia (http://en.wikipedia.org/wiki/Postmodernism), accessed November 20, 2004.
5. See Gianni Vattimo, *Le avventure della differenza. Che cosa significa pensare dopo Nietzsche e Heidegger* (Milan: Garzanti, 1980), and Gianni Vattimo, *Al di là del soggetto. Nietzsche, Heidegger e l'ermeneutica* (Milan: Feltrinelli, 1981).
6. S. Sturges (ed.), *Preston Sturges,* p. 289.
7. Transcribed from the documentary *The Rise and Fall of an American Dreamer* (1999).
8. Jacobs, *Christmas,* p. 361.
9. Sturges makes fun of a similar idea in the opening sequence of *Christmas in July.*
10. Pirolini, *Interview,* see Appendix A.
11. *Ibid.*
12. *Ibid.*
13. S. Sturges, *Preston Sturges,* p. 320.
14. Pirolini, *Interview,* see Appendix A.
15. Preston Sturges, letter to Elizabeth Dickinson (September 2, 1944), quoted in Jacobs, *Christmas,* p. 328.
16. S. Sturges, *Preston Sturges,* pp. 324–25.
17. Pirolini, *Interview,* see Appendix A.
18. *Ibid.*
19. S. Sturges, *Preston Sturges,* p. 337.

Chapter 2

1. *Postmodernism,* in Wikipedia (http://en.wikipedia.org/wiki/Postmodernism), accessed November 20, 2004.
2. Rozgonyi, *Preston Sturges,* p. 153.
3. *Ibid.,* p. 149.

4. *Ibid,* p. 159.
5. Transcribed from the dialogue of *The Sin of Harold Diddlebock.*
6. Preston Sturges, *Christmas in July* (screenplay), in Brian Henderson (ed.), *Five Screenplays by Preston Sturges* (Berkeley: University of California Press, 1985), p. 238.
7. Rozgonyi, *Preston Sturges,* p. 62.
8. Thomas Harrison, "Gianni and Gianni," unpublished article, University of California, Los Angeles, p. 2.
9. Jacobs, *Christmas,* p. 316.
10. Sturges, *Christmas in July,* p. 315.
11. Rozgonyi, *Preston Sturges,* pp. 86, 91, 94.
12. See Jacques Derrida, *Of Grammatology,* translated by Gayatri Chakravorty Spivak (Baltimore: Johns Hopkins University Press, 1974).
13. *Mr. Smith Goes to Washington* was released less than a year before *The Great McGinty.*
14. Brian Henderson, "*Christmas in July,*" in Henderson, *Five Screenplays,* p. 40.
15. Rozgonyi, *Preston Sturges,* p. 54.
16. *Ibid.,* p. 59.
17. Sturges, "*Down Went McGinty* (screenplay),*"* in Henderson, *Five Screenplays,* p. 50.
18. When the U.S. entered the war, the Bureau of Motion Pictures issued "The Government Information Manual for the Motion Pictures," which included advice on how movies should be written to "help to win the war." On this topic, see the extensive studies by Ivan Butler, *The War Film* (New York: Barnes, 1974); Bernard F. Dick, *The Star-Spangled Screen: The American World War II Film* (Lexington, KY: University Press of Kentucky, 1985); Robert Fyne, *The Hollywood Propaganda of World War II* (Metuchen, NJ: Scarecrow, 1994).
19. Pirolini, *Interview,* see Appendix A.
20. Jacobs, *Christmas,* p. 298
21. S. Sturges, *Preston Sturges,* p. 296.
22. Sturges, *The Miracle of Morgan's Creek* (screenplay), in Brian Henderson (ed.), *Four More Screenplays by Preston Sturges* (Berkeley: University of California Press, 1995), p. 632.
23. Dickos, *Intrepid Laughter,* p. 116.
24. *Ibid.,* p. 118.
25. Preston Sturges, letter to Elizabeth Dickinson (September 2, 1944), quoted in Jacobs, *Christmas,* p. 328.
26. Unpublished, undated note reproduced with the permission of Sandy Sturges.
27. Preston Sturges, letter to Walter Reade (August 12, 1957), quoted in Jacobs, *Christmas,* p. 421.
28. Curtis, *Between Flops,* p. 271.

29. Sturges, *Triumph Over Pain,* p. 399.
30. *Ibid.,* p. 366.
31. S. Sturges, *Preston Sturges,* p. 302.
32. A few frames from this lost sequence are published in Henderson, *Four More Screenplays,* pp. 355–56.
33. Pat McGilligan (ed.), *Six Screenplays by Robert Riskin* (Berkeley: University of California Press, 1997), p. 461.
34. *Ibid.,* p. 462.
35. Sturges, *The Little Marine* (screenplay), in Henderson, *Five Screenplays,* pp. 835–37.
36. Transcribed from the dialogue of *Mr. Smith Goes to Washington.*
37. John F. Mariani, "Interview with Frank Capra," *Focus on Film,* no. 27 (1977), pp. 46–47.
38. Rozgonyi, *Preston Sturges,* p. 128.
39. *Ibid,* p. 128, fn *.
40. Sturges, *The Little Marine,* p. 834.
41. Bazin, "Preston Sturges," p. 40.
42. Rozgonyi, *Preston Sturges,* p. 127.
43. Brian Henderson, "*Hail the Conquering Hero,*" in Henderson, *Five Screenplays,* pp. 696–97.
44. Dickos, *Intrepid Laughter,* p. 112.

Chapter 3

1. Jameson, "Postmodernism," p. 115.
2. Metalanguage is a language or vocabulary used to describe or analyze language.
3. Cristina Degli-Esposti, "Postmodernism(s)," in Cristina Degli-Esposti (ed.), *Postmodernism in the Cinema* (New York: Berghahn Books, 1998), p. 4.
4. Von Gunden, *Postmodern Auteurs,* p. 3.
5. The original book by René Fülöp-Miller, on which the movie is based, attributed this action to Dr. Morton's assistants and described what happened in a totally different manner.
6. See, for example, the sequence where we witness the people's reaction to the screams of one of Morton's patients. From the moving silhouettes on the transparent door of the office, we can tell that the waiting room is quickly emptying out.
7. Jacobs, *Christmas,* p. 296.
8. Rozgonyi, *Preston Sturges,* pp. 122–23.
9. Jacobs, *Christmas,* p. 67.
10. Some of the notes and drafts, and even parts of the original screenplay crossed out at producer Darryl F. Zanuck's insistence, clearly show the presence of farcical elements that were removed from the final movie. The "Porthaul flashback," for example (a removed scene where Sir Alfred recollects his first meeting with his future wife), began with Sir Al-

fred's arrive at Porthaul during a flood. Sir Alfred needs to reach the town in a duck hunter's boat. The scene is followed by a burlesque shot of "a fat, seventeen-year-old coloratura [who] is accompanied by her mother, also very fat... Before each high note, her face takes on a desperate expression." Sturges, *Unfaithfully Yours* (screenplay), in Henderson, *Four More Screenplays,* p. 931.
11. Darryl F. Zanuck, letter to Preston Sturges (February 27, 1948), quoted in Henderson, *Four More Screenplays,* p. 809.
12. See Mickey and John falling into a swimming pool in the same circumstances as Sullivan and The Girl in *Sullivan's Travels.*
13. Jacobs, *Christmas,* p. 179.
14. King, "Preston Sturges," p. 156.
15. Curtis, *Between Flops,* p. 163.
16. Jacobs, *Christmas,* p. 238.
17. Sturges had a silent movie in mind also for the sequence in which the convicts go to church and watch a movie. While eventually Sturges used Disney's cartoon *Playful Pluto* (1934), all script versions suggest that the movie be "a silent comedy, possibly Chaplin in *The Gold Rush,* possibly a Laurel and Hardy two-reeler." Preston Sturges, *Sullivan's Travels* (screenplay), in Henderson, *Five Screenplays,* p. 671.
18. Dickos, *Intrepid Laughter,* p. 69.
19. Brian Henderson, "Cartoon and Narrative in the Films of Frank Tashlin and Preston Sturges," in Andrew Horton (ed.), *Comedy/Cinema/Theory* (Berkeley: University of California Press, 1991), p. 163.
20. Ursini, *The Fabulous Life,* p. 77.
21. Stanley Cavell, *Pursuits of Happiness* (Cambridge: Harvard University Press, 1981), p. 47.
22. *Ibid.,* p. 48.
23. It is interesting to note that one of the Basserman boys in *The Beautiful Blonde from Bashful Bend* is played by Sterling Holloway, an actor who voiced dozens of Disney characters.
24. Henderson, "Cartoon and Narrative," p. 161.
25. *Ibid.,* p. 165.
26. Twelve-page unpublished draft dated October 22, 1947, located at the UCLA Library, Box 24, Collection 1114 (Preston Sturges Papers).
27. Transcribed from the dialogue of *Safeguarding Military Information.*
28. Sturges, *The Little Marine,* p. 723.
29. For a sophisticated comedy like *Ninotchka,* filmed only a few months before September 3, 1939, and released after the war had started, Ernst Lubitsch had to add a card

at the end of the opening credits, saying: "This picture takes place in Paris in those wonderful days when a siren was a brunette and not an alarm ... and if a Frenchman turned out the light it was not on account of an air raid!"

30. Steven D. Scott, "'Like a Box of Chocolates:' *Forrest Gump* and Postmodernism," *Literature Film Quarterly*, vol. 29, no. 1 (January 2001), p. 25.

31. Degli-Esposti, "Postmodernism(s)," p. 6.

32. Rozgonyi notices that "McGinty actually was not governor long enough to do any of the things he does in *Morgan's Creek*." Rozgonyi, *Preston Sturges*, p. 18, fn *.

33. Degli-Esposti, "Postmodernism(s)," p. 5.

34. Transcribed from the dialogue of *The Beautiful Blonde from Bashful Bend*.

35. Stanley Cavell's theory according to which the screwball comedy is a "comedy of remarriage" could not find a better example. Cavell, *Pursuits of Happiness*, pp. 1–42.

36. Preston Sturges, *The Palm Beach Story* (screenplay), in Henderson, *Four More Screenplays*, p. 239.

37. Jacobs, *Christmas*, p. 156.

38. Sturges, *Sullivan's Travels*, p. 541.

39. *Ibid.*, p. 683.

40. Ursini, *The Fabulous Life*, p. 96.

41. Jacobs, *Christmas*, p. 251.

42. Sturges, *Sullivan's Travels*, p. 542.

43. *Ibid.*, p. 603.

44. This line does not appear in the original screenplay, but it is included in the movie.

45. Sturges, *Sullivan's Travels*, p. 673.

46. Jacobs, *Christmas*, p. 166.

47. *Ibid.*, p. 166.

48. *Ibid.*

49. Revealingly, this is the only movie that Jay Rozgonyi does not analyze in his sociological study on Preston Sturges's *Vision of America*.

50. Narratology has come up with all sorts of terms to identify the abstract entity that conveys the cinematic narration, from *grand imagier* to invisible narrator, from enunciator to *foyer*, from implicit narrator to mega-narrator. See André Gaudreault, "Narrator et narrateur," *Iris*, no. 7, 1986.

51. Sturges, *Unfaithfully Yours*, in Henderson, *Four More Screenplays*, p. 892.

52. Henderson, "*Unfaithfully Yours*," in Henderson, *Four More Screenplays*, p. 764.

53. Bordwell notices that, in Classical Hollywood Cinema, the credits sequence is relatively open to non-narrational elements, and betrays a narrative self-awareness which re-

mains concealed until the end of the movie. Bordwell, Staiger, and Thompson, *The Classical Hollywood Cinema*, p. 25.

54. Degli-Esposti, "Postmodernism(s)," p. 12.

55. Pirolini, *Interview*, see Appendix A.

56. Sturges, letter to John Hertz (November 14, 1951), see Appendix C.

57. *Ibid.*

58. *Ibid.*

59. Preston Sturges, *They Still Live*, undated TV project, see Appendix C.

60. Joan of Arc was actually burned at the stake in the Rouen marketplace.

61. Pirolini, *Interview*, see Appendix A.

62. Preston Sturges, *You Be Witness*, undated TV project (circa 1950–51), see Appendix C.

63. Sturges, *They Still Live*, see Appendix C.

64. Sturges, *You Be Witness*, see Appendix C.

65. Transcribed from the dialogue of *Christmas in July*.

66. See Bordwell, Staiger and Thompson, *The Classical Hollywood Cinema*, passim.

67. Preston Sturges, *The Power and the Glory* (screenplay), in Andrew Horton, *Three More Screenplays by Preston Sturges* (Berkeley: University of California Press, 1998), p. 44.

68. Transcribed from the dialogue of *Citizen Kane*.

69. Sturges, *The Power and the Glory*, p. 45.

70. T.L. Gregory and E.H. Gombrich (eds.), *Illusion in Nature and Art* (London: Duckworth, 1973), pp. 54–95, 193–243.

71. Transcribed from the opening credits of *The Great McGinty*.

72. Brian Henderson, "*The Great McGinty*," in Henderson, *Five Screenplays*, p. 44.

73. *Triumph Over Pain* was conceived by Sturges in the same period of *The Power and the Glory* and *The Great McGinty*. He first proposed it in 1939, and he reworked the script until *The Great McGinty* was ready for shooting. Brian Henderson even suggests that Sturges might have planned it as his second film. Henderson, "*Triumph Over Pain*," in Henderson, *Four More Screenplays*, p. 242.

74. Transcribed from the dialogue of *The Lady Eve*.

75. Cavell, *Pursuits*, p. 65.

76. Preston Sturges, *The Lady Eve* (screenplay), in Henderson, *Five Screenplays*, pp. 364–65.

77. Transcribed from the dialogue of *The Lady Eve*.

78. *Ibid*, p. 509.

Chapter 4

1. Jameson, "Postmodernism," p. 113.
2. Bordwell, Staiger and Thompson, *The Classical Hollywood Cinema*, p. 42.
3. Examples of this tendency would include Jean-Luc Godard's fragmentary structure of *Pierrot Le Fou* and Alain Resnais's experiments with memory and narration in *Hiroshima Mon Amour* and *L'Année dernière à Marienbad*, such experiments being closely related to the coeval literary experiments of the *nouveau roman*.
4. Eleanor Hutton was Sturges's second wife and, according to Sturges, the principal source of inspiration for the story.
5. S. Sturges, *Preston Sturges*, p. 271. Sandy Sturges told me that she experienced the same result when editing Preston's memoirs.
6. Brian Henderson, "Tense, Mood, and Voice in Film (Notes After Genette)," *Film Quarterly*, vol. 36, no. 4 (Summer 1983), p. 6.
7. It should also be noted that Sturges's credit and fortune had already started to decline after the relative commercial failure of *Sullivan's Travels* and the tepid reviews of *The Palm Beach Story*.
8. Bordwell, Staiger and Thompson, *The Classical Hollywood Cinema*, p. 42.
9. Sturges, *Triumph Over Pain*, p. 366.
10. *Ibid*, p. 367.
11. Preston Sturges, letter to Captain Jud Allen (August 25, 1944), quoted in Jacobs, *Christmas*, p. 288.
12. Henderson, "*Triumph Over Pain*" in Henderson, *Four More Screenplays*, p. 330.
13. Sturges, *Triumph Over Pain*, in Henderson, *Four More Screenplays*, p. 375.
14. Sturges, *Unfaithfully Yours*, pp. 836–38.
15. Henderson, "*Unfaithfully Yours*," p. 775.
16. Sturges, *Unfaithfully Yours*, pp. 927–34.
17. Andrew Sarris, "Preston Sturges in the Thirties," *Film Comment*, vol. 6, no. 4 (Winter 1970–71), p. 67.

Chapter 5

1. This oft-repeated quotation cannot be verified.
2. Jacobs, *Christmas*, p. 306.
3. Brian Henderson, "*The Miracle of Morgan's Creek*," in Henderson, *Four More Screenplays*, p. 533.
4. *Ibid*, "*The Miracle of Morgan's Creek*," pp. 528–30.
5. *Ibid*, p. 535.
6. Propp showed how the narrative architecture of any classical Russian folktale is based on the combination of a limited number of character types and actions (narrative "functions"). Vladimir Propp, *Morphology of the Folktale* (1928), translated by Laurence Scott (Austin: University of Texas, 1968).
7. Unpublished note quoted in Jacobs, *Christmas*, p. 330.
8. Absentation, Interdiction, Violation, Reconnaissance, Delivery, Trickery, Complicity, Villainy/Lack, Mediation, Counteraction, Departure, Testing or Interrogation, Hero's reaction, Receipt of a magical agent, Guidance, Struggle, Marking, Victory, Liquidation, Return, Pursuit, Rescue, Unrecognized arrival, Unfounded claims, Difficult task, Solution, Recognition, Exposure, Transfiguration, Punishment, Wedding. *Ibid*, pp. 19–65.
9. Henderson, "*The Miracle of Morgan's Creek*," p. 540.
10. Sturges will use the same technique in *Les Carnets du Major Thompson*, to portray the pages of the diary that Major Thompson dictates to his secretary.
11. Sturges, *Unfaithfully Yours*, in Henderson, *Four More Screenplays*, p. 849.
12. *Ibid*, *Unfaithfully Yours*, p. 851.
13. *Ibid*, p. 862.
14. *Ibid*, p. 896.
15. Germi's movie also borrows from *Unfaithfully Yours* the usage of a sound recorder as part of the protagonist's plot to commit murder.
16. Sturges, *You Be Witness*, see Appendix C.
17. Another parallel example would be a postmodern movie such as Gus Van Sant's *Elephant* (2002), where the reproduction of multiple characters' viewpoints over the same events produces a repetition of the same actions, over and over again — an interesting combination of the technique used by Robbe-Grillet in *La jalousie* with Kurosawa's multiple focalization.
18. Summary published on the Polish Cinema Database (http://info.fuw.edu.pl/Filmy/), November 20, 2004.
19. Jacobs, *Christmas*, p. 376.
20. Henderson, "*Unfaithfully Yours*," in Henderson, *Four More Screenplays*, p. 771.
21. In the original screenplay, Sturges had Sir Alfred directed the orchestra to play a classical piece in boogie-woogie. Zanuck crossed out the five and a half pages concerned because "it has no story content and it is an extravagance we cannot afford." Sturges, *Unfaithfully Yours*, p. 807.
22. Sturges entitled the first draft *Unfinished Symphony*, and he worked on a play

version called *Symphony Story* that went unproduced.
23. Curtis, *Between Flops*, pp. 227–28.
24. Jacobs, *Christmas*, p. 370.

Chapter 6

1. Sarris, "The American Cinema," p. 21.
2. Gérard Genette, *Narrative Discourse:
An Essay in Method*, translated by Jane E.
Lewin (Ithaca: Cornell University Press,
1980), p. 35.
3. Bordwell, Staiger and Thompson, *The
Classical Hollywood Cinema*, p. 21.
4. The single-shot sequence or *plan-
séquence* is a long take (a shot that continues
for an unusually lengthy amount of time)
which covers an entire narrative sequence.
5. André Bazin, *Montage Interdit* (1953),
translated by Hugh Gray in *What Is Cinema?*
(Berkeley, Los Angeles, and London: UC
Press, 1967), vol. I, pp. 41–52.
6. The whole scene is virtually a one-shot
sequence interrupted by two close-ups showing the check that Sir Alfred is writing.
7. *The Power and the Glory*, pressbook, p.
5.
8. *Ibid*, p. 6.
9. *Ibid*, p. 5.
10. Alexandre Astruc, "La camera-stylo,"
in Peter Graham (ed.), *The New Wave* (New
York: Doubleday, 1968), pp. 18–20 (first publication: *Écran Français*, no. 144, 1948).

Chapter 7

1. S. Sturges, *Preston Sturges*, p. 299.
2. *The Power and the Glory*, pressbook, p.
5.

3. Jacobs, *Christmas*, pp. 390–91.
4. Ibid, *Christmas*, p. 420.
5. Preston Sturges, letter to Marcel Pagnol
(March 25, 1947), quoted in Jacobs, *Christmas*, p. 43.
6. Preston Sturges, "*Les Carnets du Major
Thompson*," unpublished article (January 14,
1957), see Appendix B.
7. S. Sturges, *Preston Sturges*, pp. 329–30.
8. Pirolini, *Interview*, see Appendix A.
9. Sturges, "*Les Carnets*," see Appendix B.
10. Ibid.
11. Pirolini, *Interview*, Appendix A.
12. Ibid.
13. Jacobs, *Christmas*, p. 423; Ursini, *Preston Sturges*, p. 207.
14. Preston Sturges, letter to Walter Reade
(August 12, 1957), quoted in Jacobs, *Christmas*, p. 421.
15. Curtis, *Between Flops*, p. 271.
16. This also sounds reminiscent, perhaps,
of Sturges's relationship with his 21-year-old
secretary Jeannie La Vell.
17. S. Sturges, *Preston Sturges*, p. 330.

Conclusion

1. Bordwell, Staiger, and Thompson, *The
Classical Hollywood Cinema*, p. 91.
2. Ibid, p. XIII.
3. S. Sturges, *Preston Sturges*, p. 294.

Appendix A

1. The note was sent to me by Sandy
Sturges a few days after our interview.

Bibliography

Primary Sources

Sturges, Preston. *Papers.* UCLA Collection #1114 (documents, notes, screenplays, and correspondence donated by Sandy Sturges to the University of California Los Angeles).

Books

Sturges, Sandy (ed.). *Preston Sturges by Preston Sturges* (New York: Simon & Schuster, 1990).

Articles

Sturges, Preston. "De quelques événements conduisant à ma mort." *Positif,* no. 281–282 (July-August 1984), pp. 9–11.

Published Screenplays

Sturges, Preston. *Down Went McGinty* (*The Great McGinty*). In Brian Henderson (ed.), *Five Screenplays by Preston Sturges* (Berkeley: University of California Press, 1985), pp. 49–83.
_____. *Easy Living.* In Andrew Horton (ed.), *Three More Screenplays by Preston Sturges* (Berkeley: University of California Press, 1998), pp. 155–313.
_____. *The Lady Eve.* In Brian Henderson (ed.), *Five Screenplays by Preston Sturges* (Berkeley: University of California Press, 1985), pp. 353–509.
_____. *The Little Marine* (*Hail the Conquering Hero*). In Brian Henderson (ed.), *Five Screenplays by Preston Sturges* (Berkeley: University of California Press, 1985), pp. 709–848.
_____. *The Miracle of Morgan's Creek.* In Brian Henderson (ed.), *Four More Screenplays by Preston Sturges* (Berkeley: University of California Press, 1995), pp. 593–754.
_____. *The New Yorkers* (*Christmas in July*). In Brian Henderson (ed.), *Five Screenplays by Preston Sturges* (Berkeley: University of California Press, 1985), pp. 209–32.
_____. *The Palm Beach Story.* In Brian Henderson (ed.), *Four More Screenplays by Preston Sturges* (Berkeley: University of California Press, 1995), pp. 83–240.
_____. *The Power and the Glory.* In Andrew Horton (ed.), *Three More Screenplays by Preston Sturges* (Berkeley: University of California Press, 1998), pp. 37–140.

_____. *Remember the Night.* In Andrew Horton (ed.), *Three More Screenplays by Pre-ston Sturges* (Berkeley: University of California Press, 1998), pp. 331–491.

_____. *Sullivan's Travels,* In Brian Henderson (ed.), *Five Screenplays by Preston Sturges* (Berkeley: University of California Press, 1985), pp. 535–683.

_____. *Triumph Over Pain (The Great Moment).* In Brian Henderson (ed.), *Four More Screenplays by Preston Sturges* (Berkeley: University of California Press, 1995), pp. 365–526.

_____. *Unfaithfully Yours.* In Brian Henderson (ed.), *Four More Screenplays by Preston Sturges* (Berkeley: University of California Press, 1995), pp. 823–975.

Secondary Sources

Books

Bordwell, David, Janet Staiger, and Kristin Thompson. *The Classical Hollywood Cin-ema: Film Style and Mode of Production to 1960* (London: Routledge, 1985).

Butler, Ivan. *The War Film* (New York: Barnes, 1974).

Cavell, Stanley. *Pursuits of Happiness: The Hollywood Comedy of Remarriage* (Cam-bridge, MA, and London: Harvard University Press, 1981).

Curtis, James. *Between Flops: A Biography of Preston Sturges* (New York: Harcourt, Brace, Jovanovich, 1982).

Cywinski, Ray. *Preston Sturges: A Guide to References and Resources* (Boston: G. K. Hall, 1984).

_____. *Satire & Side Shows* (Ann Arbor, MI: University Microfilms International, 1981).

Derrida, Jacques. *Of Grammatology,* translated by Gayatri Chakravorty Spivak (Bal-timore: Johns Hopkins University Press, 1974).

Dick, Bernard F. *The Star-Spangled Screen: The American World War II Film* (Lexing-ton: University Press of Kentucky, 1985)

Dickos, Andrew. *Intrepid Laughter: Preston Sturges and the Movies* (Metuchen, NJ: Scarecrow, 1985).

Fyne, Robert. *The Hollywood Propaganda of World War II* (Metuchen, NJ: Scarecrow, 1994).

Garrand, Timothy Paul. *The Comedy Screenwriting of Preston Sturges: An Analysis of Seven Paramount Auteurist Screenplays* (Ann Arbor, MI: University Microfilms International, 1984).

Genette, Gérard. *Narrative Discourse: An Essay in Method,* translated by Jane E. Lewin (Ithaca: Cornell University Press, 1980).

Gordon, James Rankin. *Comic Structures in the Films of Preston Sturges* (Ann Arbor, MI: University Microfilms International, 1980).

Gregory, T. L., and E.H. Gombrich (eds.). *Illusion in Nature and Art* (London: Duck-worth, 1973).

Harvey, James. *Romantic Comedy in Hollywood from Lubitsch to Sturges* (New York: Knopf, 1987), pp. 509–664.

Henderson, Brian (ed.). *Five Screenplays by Preston Sturges* (Berkeley: University of California Press, 1985). This volume contains the following essays by Brian Hen-derson: "*The Great McGinty,*" pp. 31–47; "*Christmas in July,*" pp. 185–207; "*The Lady Eve,*" pp. 323–51; "*Sullivan's Travels,*" pp. 511–34; "*Hail the Conquering Hero,*" pp. 685–707.

_____ (ed.). *Four More Screenplays by Preston Sturges* (Berkeley: University of Califor-nia Press, 1995). This volume contains the following essays by Brian Henderson:

"*The Palm Beach Story*," pp. 19–82; "*Triumph Over Pain/The Great Moment*" pp. 241–363; "*The Miracle of Morgan's Creek*," pp. 527–91; "*Unfaithfully Yours*," pp. 755–822.

Horton, Andrew (ed.). *Three More Screenplays by Preston Sturges* (Berkeley: University of California Press, 1998). This volume contains the following essays by Andrew Horton: "*The Power and the Glory*," pp. 21–35; "*Easy Living*," pp. 141–53; "*Remember the Night*," pp. 315–29.

Ivanov, Andrea Jean. *Sexual Parody in American Comedic Film and Literature, 1925–1948 (Mae West, James Thurber, Dorothy Parker, Preston Sturges)* (Ann Arbor, MI: University Microfilms International, 1994).

Jacobs, Diane. *Christmas in July: The Life and Art of Preston Sturges* (Berkeley: University of California Press, 1992).

McGilligan, Pat (ed.). *Six Screenplays by Robert Riskin* (Berkeley: University of California Press, 1997).

Propp, Vladimir. *Morphology of the Folktale* (1928), translated by Laurence Scott (Austin: University of Texas, 1968).

Rozgonyi, Jay. *Preston Sturges's Vision of America: Critical Analyses of Fourteen Films* (Jefferson, NC: McFarland, 1995).

Schatz, Thomas. *The Genius of the System: Hollywood Filmmaking in the Studio Era* (New York: Henry Holt, 1996).

Spoto, Donald. *Madcap: The Life of Preston Sturges* (Boston, Toronto, London: Little, Brown, 1990).

Ursini, James. *The Fabulous Life and Times of Preston Sturges, An American Dreamer* (New York: Curtis Books, 1973).

_____. *The Films of Preston Sturges, A Modern American Humorist,* microform (Los Angeles, CA: MA Dissertation, UCLA, 1971).

Vattimo, Gianni. *Al di là del soggetto. Nietzsche, Heidegger e l'ermeneutica* (Milan: Feltrinelli, 1981).

_____. *Le avventure della differenza. Che cosa significa pensare dopo Nietzsche e Heidegger* (Milan: Garzanti, 1980).

Von Gunden, Kenneth. *Postmodern Auteurs* (Jefferson, NC: McFarland, 1991).

Articles

Amiel, Vincent. "Hollywood et Lilliput." *Positif,* no. 349 (March 1990), pp. 32–33.

Astruc, Alexandre. "La camera-stylo." In Peter Graham (ed.), *The New Wave* (New York: Doubleday, 1968), pp. 18–20 (first publication: *Écran Français,* no. 144, 1948).

Barkan, Raymond. "L'ultimo Sturges." *Bianco e Nero,* no. 5 (May 1949), p. 94.

Bazin, André. "Preston Sturges." In Bazin, *The Cinema of Cruelty* (New York: Seaver Books, 1982), pp. 31–47 (first published in *L'Ecran Francais,* 1948).

Bazin, André. *Montage Interdit* (1953). Translated by Hugh Gray in *What Is Cinema?* (Berkeley, Los Angeles, and London: UC Press, 1967), vol. I, pp. 41–52.

Brown, Geoff. "Preston Sturges Inventor." *Sight and Sound,* vol. 55, no. 4 (Autumn 1986), pp. 272–77.

Busch, Noel F. "Preston Sturges." *Life* (January 7, 1946).

Caprara, Valerio. "La grande fuga di (Preston) Sturges." *Segnocinema,* no. 27 (1987), pp. 28–29.

Cluny, Claude Michel. "Les voyages de Sullivan." *Cinéma,* no. 173 (February 1973), pp. 115–16.

Codelli, Lorenzo. "De la génése du génie (notes sur Preston Sturges)." *Positif,* no. 281/282 (July-August 1984), pp. 12–19.

Corliss, Richard. "Preston Sturges." *Cinema,* vol. 7, no. 2 (Spring 1972), pp. 25–36.

_____. "Preston Sturges." In Corliss, *Talking Pictures: Screenwriters in the American Cinema 1927–1973* (New York: Overlook Press, 1974), pp. 25–61.

Cremonini, Giorgio. "*Infedelmente tua (Unfaithfully Yours)* di Preston Sturges." *Cineforum,* no. 272 (March 1988), pp. 59–63.

Cuenca, Carlos Fernández. "Preston Sturges, Creador maldito." *Film Ideal,* no. 212 (1969), pp. 100–10.

Curtis, James. "*The Great McGinty.*" *American Film,* vol. 7, no. 7 (May 1982), pp. 44–45, 50–52.

D'Arne, Wilson. "We Said This Would Happen." *Picturegoer,* vol. 11, no. 546 (January 24, 1942), p. 10.

De Baecque, Antoine. "Diabolicum Genericum." *Cahiers du cinéma,* no. 426 (December 1989), pp. 58–59.

Degli-Esposti, Cristina. "Postmodernism(s)." In Degli-Esposti (ed.), *Postmodernism in the Cinema* (New York: Berghahn Books, 1998), pp. 3–18.

Ericsson, Peter. "Preston Sturges." *Sequence,* no. 4 (Summer 1948), pp. 22–29.

Everschor, Franz. "Arsenal der Verführung. Die Filme des Preston Sturges." *Film-Dienst,* vol. 51, no. 19 (September 1998), pp. 34–37.

Eyles, Allen. "Hail Preston Sturges." *Films and Filming,* vol. 11, no. 11 (August 1965), p. 38.

Eyquem, Olivier, and Yann Tobin. "Fimographie de Preston Sturges." *Positif,* no. 281/282 (July-August 1984), pp. 24–29

Farber, Manny, and W.S. Poster. "Preston Sturges: Success in the Movies." *Film Culture,* no. 26 (Autumn 1962), pp. 9–16, written in 1954, then republished in Manny Farber, *Negative Space: Manny Farber on the Movies* (London: Studio Vista Ltd., 1971).

Fava, Claudio G. "Mister Sturges." *Rivista del Cinematografo,* vol. 49, no. 6 (June 1976), pp. 250–53.

Gaudreault, André. "Narrator et narrateur." *Iris,* no. 7, 1986.

Gow, Gordon. "Conversation with Preston Sturges." *Sight and Sound,* vol. 25, no. 4 (Spring 1956), pp. 182–83.

Harrison, Thomas. "Gianni and Gianni." Unpublished article, University of California, Los Angeles, p. 2.

Henderson, Brian. "Cartoon and Narrative in the Films of Frank Tashlin and Preston Sturges." In Andrew Horton, *Comedy/Cinema/Theory* (Berkeley: University of California Press, 1991), pp. 153–73.

_____. "Sturges at Work." *Film Quarterly,* vol. 39, no. 2 (Winter 1985-86), pp. 16–28.

_____. "Tense, Mood, and Voice in Film (Notes After Genette)." *Film Quarterly,* vol. 36, no. 4 (Summer 1983), pp. 4–17.

Houston, Penelope. "Preston Sturges." *Sight and Sound,* vol. 34, no. 3 (Summer 1965), pp. 130–34.

Interim, Louelle. "Preston le magnifique." *Cahiers du cinéma,* no. 347 (May 1983), pp. vii–viii.

Jameson, Frederic. "Postmodernism and Consumer Society." In Hal Foster (ed.), *Postmodern Culture* (London: Pluto Press, 1985), pp. 111–25.

Jones, Idwal. "Preston Sturges' Secrets." *Picturegoer,* vol. 12, no. 587 (August 21, 1943), p. 7.

Jones, Terry, Peter Farrelly, Clare Kilner, and Baz Luhrmann. "Preston Sturges Changed My Life..." *Sight and Sound,* vol. 10, no. 5 (May 2000), p. 20.

Jonsson, Eric. "Preston Sturges and the Theory of Decline." *Film Culture*, no. 26 (Autumn 1962), pp. 17-20.

Kast, Pierre. "Positivement votre." *Positif*, no. 281–282 (July-August 1984), pp. 3–8.

Kemp, Philip. "Ants in His Pants." *Sight and Sound*, vol. 10, no. 5 (May 2000), pp. 18–19.

King, Alexander. "Preston Sturges." *Vogue* (August 15, 1944), pp. 156–57, 176–80.

Kracauer, Siegfried. "Preston Sturges or Laughter Betrayed." *Films in Review*, vol. 1, no. 1 (February 1950), pp. 11–13, 43–47.

Magny, Joël. "Preston 'dynamite' Sturges." *Cahiers du cinéma*, no. 426 (December 1989), pp. 54–57.

Mariani, John F. "Interview with Frank Capra." *Focus on Film*, no. 27 (1977), pp. 46–47.

Marquet, Jean-Paul. "Sur deux films de Preston Sturges." *Positif*, vol. 2, no. 8 (1953), pp. 35–37.

McCloy, Sean. "Focus. Preston Sturges." *Film West: Ireland's Film Quarterly*, no. 25 (Summer 1996), pp. 24–26.

Nel, King, and G.W. Stoner. "Preston Sturges." *Sight and Sound*, vol. 28, no. 3–4 (Summer-Autumn 1959), pp. 185–86.

Parrish, Robert. "Johnny One Note. Souvenirs sur Preston Sturges." *Positif*, no. 200–202 (December-January 1977-78), pp. 116–19.

Rebello, Stephen. "King of Comedy, The Rise of Preston Sturges." *American Film*, vol. 7, no. 7 (May 1982), pp. 42–44.

Rubenstein, Elliot. "The End of Screwball Comedy: *The Lady Eve* and *The Palm Beach Story*." *Post Script*, vol. 1, no. 3 (Spring-Summer 1982), pp. 33–47.

Rubenstein, Elliot. "Hollywood Travels: Sturges and Sullivan." *Sight and Sound*, vol. 47, no. 1 (Winter 1977-78), pp. 50–52.

_____. "The Home Fires: Aspects of Sturges's Wartime Comedy." *Quarterly Review of Film Studies*, vol. 7, no. 2 (Spring 1982), pp. 131–41.

Sarris, Andrew. "The American Cinema." *Film Culture*, no. 28 (Spring 1963), p. 21.

_____. "The Golden Years: Preston Sturges." In Richard Corliss (ed.), *The Hollywood Screenwriters* (New York: Avon Books, 1972), pp. 93–106.

_____. "Preston Sturges." In Andrew Sarris, *Hollywood Voices: Interviews with Hollywood Directors* (Indianapolis: Bobbs-Merrill, 1971).

_____. "Preston Sturges." In Andrew Sarris, *Interviews with Film Directors* (New York: Avon Books, 1967), pp. 511–19.

_____. "Preston Sturges." In Stuart Byron and Elizabeth Weis (eds.), *Movie Comedy* (New York: Penguin, 1977), pp. 25–61.

_____. "Preston Sturges in the Thirties." *Film Comment*, vol. 6, no. 4 (Winter 1970-71), pp. 80–85.

Scott, Steven D. "'Like a Box of Chocolates': *Forrest Gump* and Postmodernism." *Literature Film Quarterly*, vol. 29, no. 1 (January 2001), pp. 23–31.

Shokoff, James. "A Kockenlocker by Any Other Word: The Democratic Comedy of Preston Sturges." *Post Script*, vol. 8, no. 1 (Fall 1988), pp. 16–28.

Signorelli, Angelo. "Preston Sturges." *Cineforum*, vol. 30, no. 292 (March 1990), pp. 65–69.

Strohm, Claire. "Au bout de la nuit." *Cahiers du cinéma*, no. 426 (December 1989), pp. 60–61.

Thomas, Francois. "De mille facettes un choix restreint." *Positif*, no. 281–282 (July-August 1984), pp. 20–23.

Tobin, Yann. "Je n'ai rien compris, mais vous etiez tres jolie en le distant." *Positif*, no. 349 (March 1990), pp. 34–35.

_____. "New York–Miami et Lady Eve." *Positif*, no. 310 (1986), pp. 64–66.
Turim, Maureen. "Cinemas of Modernity and Postmodernity." In Ingeborg Hoesterey (ed.), *Zeitgeist in Babel: The Postmodernist Controversy* (Bloomington: Indiana University Press, 1991).
Verdone, Mario. "Appunti su Preston Sturges." *Bianco e Nero*, no. 126 (May 1968), pp. 77–80.

Documentaries

McCarthy, Todd (writer), and Kenneth Bowser (director). *Preston Sturges, The Rise and Fall of an American Dreamer* (PBS, 1999).

Index

Numbers in **bold italics** indicate pages with photographs.

197